On Tangled Paths.

ON TANGLED

PATHS

George MacDonald

edited by
Dan Hamilton

VICTOR BOOKS™
A DIVISION OF SCRIPTURE PRESS PUBLICATIONS INC.
USA CANADA ENGLAND

Victor Books by George MacDonald

A Quiet Neighborhood
The Seaboard Parish
The Vicar's Daughter
The Shopkeeper's Daughter
The Prodigal Apprentice
The Last Castle
On Tangled Paths
Heather and Snow

Winner Books by George MacDonald

The Boyhood of Ranald Bannerman
The Genius of Willie MacMichael
The Wanderings of Clare Skymer

On Tangled Paths was first published in England in 1882, under the title of *Weighed and Wanting*.

Library of Congress Catalog Card Number: 86-63103
ISBN: 0-89693-791-7

VICTOR BOOKS
A division of SP Publications, Inc.
Wheaton, Illinois 60187

Contents.

5

6

Editor's Foreword

On Tangled Paths is the seventh George MacDonald novel from Victor Books, and was originally published in 1882 as *Weighed and Wanting*.

This was MacDonald's nineteenth major novel written for adults, and for its theme he turned once again to his favorite parable, the Prodigal Son, for the tale of a young man who leaves home and turns to evil ways. To this plot he added the dilemma of a young woman who desires to obey God, to find His will, and to use her life and talents for Him in a great work, but does not know where to begin. And with those he mixed the problems of a family facing approaching death.

Thus MacDonald was able to present three of his favorite messages:

First, that we should turn to God because He loves us and wants us safely back in His arms.

Second, that the way we may discover the entire will of God is to obey the commands He has already given us. Only we who take the first step of duty in obedience to the revealed will of God can come to know His larger will. God's ordinances as revealed in Scripture were given us that we might first obey them—not that we might first speculate, theorize, or analyze them, and obey only later, if at all.

Third, that death under God is simply more life.

Some writers ignore death, and write only novels with conventionally happy endings. But MacDonald never denied the reality, pervasiveness, and the inevitability of physical death; to do so would have been to deny the pressing facts of his own life. In nearly all of his novels there is an on-stage death scene, where family and friends gather as the lingering illness exacts its final tribute. Dickens would have milked each of those scenes for every last drop of pathos, but MacDonald used these opportunities to show that death, in God's hands, is only the beginning of a higher life. In *this* life we are redeemed, but in *that* life we shall be renewed.

On Tangled Paths has been edited for maximum understanding and enjoyment. My aim has been to make these excellent stories readable, affordable, and available to a new generation of readers who have no ready access to the dense, scarce, and dear original versions. Toward this goal, I have made no more changes to the original manuscript than were necessary—especially as this book, finished late in MacDonald's career, was reasonably well written. I have eliminated repetitive or irrelevant material, tightened dragging passages, bridged sudden jumps in the narrative, removed occasional inconsistencies in detail, and updated or clarified any words or phrases obscured by the changing English language. What is left is a stronger and purer story—the story that MacDonald told his country in his time, and would certainly wish to tell our country in our time.

Dan Hamilton
Indianapolis, Indiana
December 1986

Introduction.

George MacDonald (1824-1905), a Scottish preacher, poet, novelist, fantasist, expositor, and public figure, is most known today for his children's books—*At the Back of the North Wind, The Princess and the Goblin, The Princess and Curdie,* and his fantasies *Lilith* and *Phantastes.*

But his fame is based on far more than his fantasies. His lifetime output of more than fifty popular books placed him in the same literary realm as Charles Dickens, Wilkie Collins, William Thackeray, and Thomas Carlyle. He numbered among his friends and acquaintances Lewis Carroll, Mark Twain, Lady Byron, and John Ruskin.

Among his later admirers were G.K. Chesterton, W.H. Auden, and C.S. Lewis. MacDonald's fantasy *Phantastes* was a turning point in Lewis' conversion; Lewis acknowledged MacDonald as his spiritual master, and declared that he had never written a book without quoting from MacDonald.

Chapter 1.

BURCLIFF

It was a gray, windy noon in the beginning of autumn. The sky and the sea were almost the same ugly color. The horizon was a thick bar, blurred with waves that broke into white crests as they rushed at the shore. The wind troubled the trees and beat down the chimney smoke from the houses. Not one of the hundreds of fishing boats belonging to the coast was seen.

It was sad weather, and depressing to many of the thousands who had come to Burcliff to enjoy a holiday, for the days grew longer and longer with dreariness. The day wrapped them in a blanket of fog, and now and then squeezed down upon them the wettest of all rains. It seemed a huge bite snatched by that vague enemy out of the cake of happiness that by every right and reason belonged to them. Were they not born to be happy—and how could a human being fulfill his destiny in such circumstances?

There are men and women who can be happy in such circumstances and worse, but they are rare, and well worth knowing. There are many who, having secured the corner of a couch within the radius of a good fire, forget the world around them by help of the magic lantern of a novel that interests them. The noises of the waves on the sands, a storm in the chimney, and the rain on the windows but serve to deepen the calm of their spirits. But take the novel away, give the fire a black heart, let the smells born in a lodging-house kitchen invade the sitting room, and there will not be many mortals who can then be patient with a patience pleasant to other people.

11

Mrs. Raymount, half the head and more than half the heart of a family in a lodging in Burcliff, was one of these exceptional mortals. She was busy embroidering, but if you had taken her piece of work away and given her nothing to do instead, she would yet have looked and been as peaceful as she now looked.

The father met the current misfortune with tolerably good humor, but he was so busy writing a paper for one of the monthly reviews that he would have kept to the house had the day been fine. Therefore, he had no credit, and his temper must pass as not proven.

Cornelius, a longish lad, stood in the bow window and leaned his head on the shutter, in a mood of smoldering rebellion against the order of things. A creature of irreconcilable moods, he was constantly mistaking impulse for will, and had not yet begun to use his will to blend the conflicting elements of his nature into one. But in his own self-estimate he claimed the virtues present in his good moods, letting the bad ones slide, and taking no account of what was in them. He substituted forgetfulness for repudiation, a return of good humor for repentance, and at best a joke for an apology.

Mark, a pale, handsome boy of ten, and Josephine, a rosy girl of seven, sat on the opposite side of the fire, amusing themselves with a puzzle. The gusts of wind and great splashes of rain on the grass only made them feel cozier and more satisfied.

"Beastly weather!" remarked Cornelius, as he wriggled and sprung up and turned toward the room.

"I'm sorry you don't like it, Corney," smiled his elder sister Hester, who sat beside her mother trimming a pretty bonnet.

"Oh, it's all very well for girls!" returned Cornelius. "You don't do anything worth doing—and you've got so many things you like doing, and so much time to do them in, that it's all one to you whether you go out or stay at home. But when a fellow has a miserable three weeks and then back to a rot of work, then it is rather hard to have such a hole made in it! Day after day, as sure as the sun rises—if he does rise—of weather as abominable as rain and wind can make it!"

"My dear boy!" said his mother, without looking up.

"Oh, yes, mother, I know! You're so good you would have had Job himself take it coolly. It's only a breach in the laws of nature I'm grumbling at. I don't mean anything to offend you."

"Perhaps you mean more than you think," she answered with a deep-drawn breath that was nearly a sigh. "I should be far more miserable than any weather could make me, not to be able to join in the song of the three holy children."

"I've heard you say that before, mother," he said, in a tone that roused his sister's anger. Much that the mother let pass was resented by the daughter for the mother's sake. "But the three children hadn't much weather of any sort where they sang their song. Precious tired one gets of it before the choir's through with it!"

"They would have been glad enough of some of this weather you call beastly," said Hester, this time without any smile, for sometimes her brother was more than she could bear.

"Oh, I dare say! But then they knew when they got out, they wouldn't have to go back to a beastly bank, with notes and gold flying about all day like bats!"

His mother's face grew very sad as she bent over her work, and Cornelius saw her trouble. "Mother, don't be vexed with a fellow," he said more gently. "I wasn't made good like you."

"I think you were right about the holy children," she said quietly.

"What!" exclaimed Cornelius. "Mother, I never once before heard you say I was right about any mortal thing! I don't understand it, though."

"I think you were right when you implied it was the furnace that made them sing about the world outside of it. One can fancy the idea of the frost and the snow and the ice being particularly pleasant to them. And I am afraid, Cornelius, my dear son, you need the furnace to teach you that the will of God, even in weather, is a thing for rejoicing in, not for abusing. But I dread the fire for your sake, my boy!"

"I should have thought this weather and the bank behind it furnace enough, mother!" he answered, trying to laugh off her words.

"It does not seem to be," she said, with some displeasure. "But then," she added with a sigh, "you have not the same companion that the three holy children had. He has been knocking at your chamber door for some time. When He comes to the furnace door, perhaps you will open that to Him."

Cornelius made no answer. He felt his mother's seriousness

awkward, and said to himself she was unkind. Why couldn't she make some allowance for a fellow? He meant no harm! As much as he disliked going into the bank, he yet considered himself a man of the world in consequence, and so was still less patient with his mother's infrequent admonitions. He was like the child so sure he can run alone that he snatches his hand from his mother's and sets off through the dirt and the puddles. He could not perceive the kind of thing his mother cared about—not from moral lack alone, but from dullness and want of imagination as well.

With all her peace of soul, his mother's heart was very anxious about her son, but she said no more to him just now. She knew that the shower bath is not the readiest mode of making a child friendly with cold water.

Just then the sun broke out. The wind had at last blown a hole in the clouds, and through that at once, as is his wont, and the wont of a greater light than the sun, he shone.

"Come! There's something almost like sunshine!" said Cornelius. "Before it goes in again, as it's sure to do in five minutes, get on your bonnet, Hester, and let's attempt a walk."

Before Hester could answer, rain spattered the window.

"There! I told you so! That's always my luck! To set my heart on a thing is all one with being disappointed of it."

"But if the thing was not worth setting your heart on?" said Hester, speaking with forced gentleness.

"What does that signify? The thing is that your heart is set on it. What you think nothing, other people may yet be bold enough to take for something."

"Well, at least, if I had to be disappointed, I should like it to be in something that would be worth having."

"Would you now?" returned Cornelius spitefully. "I hope you may have what you want. For my part I don't desire to be better than my neighbor."

"Do you want to be as good as your neighbor, Corney?" said his mother, looking up through a film of tears. She waited a moment in vain for an answer, and then resumed, "But there is a more important question than that—whether you are content with being as good as yourself, or want to be better."

"To tell you the truth, mother, I don't trouble my head about such things. Philosophers agree that self-consciousness is the

14

bane of the age, and I mean to avoid it. If you had let me go into the army, I might have had some leisure for what you call thought, but that horrible bank takes everything out of a fellow. The only thing it leaves is a burning desire to forget it at any cost till the time comes when you must endure it again. If I hadn't some amusement in between, I should cut my throat, or take to opium or brandy. I wonder how the governor would like to be in my place!"

Hester rose and left the room, indignant.

"If your father were in your place, Cornelius," said his mother with dignity, "he would perform his duties without grumbling, however irksome they might be."

"How do you know that, mother? He was never tried."

"I know it because I know him," she answered. "And if you think it hard that you have to follow a way of life not of your own choosing, you must remember that we could never get you to express a preference for one way over the other, and that your father had to strain every nerve to send you to college—to the temporary disadvantage of others in the family. I am sorry to remind you also that you did not make it any easier for him by your mode of living there."

"I didn't run up a single bill, and my father knows it!"

"He also knows that your cousin Robert did not spend above two-thirds of what you did, and made more of his time too. And you know that your father's main design in placing you in your uncle's bank was that you might gain such a knowledge of business as will be necessary to properly manage the money he will leave behind him. When you have gained that knowledge, there will be time to look further."

His father's money was a continuous annoyance to Cornelius, for it was no secret from the family how Mr. Raymount meant to dispose of it. He intended to leave it under trustees, and he wished Cornelius to be one until he married, when it was to be divided equally among the Raymount children. This arrangement was not agreeable to Cornelius, who could not see what advantage he had in being the eldest.

"Now, mother!" he broke out. "Do you think it fair that I should have to look after the whole family as if they were my own?" This was not his real cause of complaint, but he chose to use it as his present grievance.

"You will have the other trustees," said his mother. "It need not weigh on you very heavily. And when you marry you will be rid of the responsibility."

"What if I should marry before my father's death?"

"Indeed, I hope you will. Your father's arrangements are a provision against the unlikely. When you are married, I don't doubt he will make another to meet the new circumstances."

"Now," said Cornelius to himself, "I do believe if I was to marry money—as why shouldn't I?—my father would divide my share among the rest, and not give me a farthing!"

Full of the injury of the idea, he rose and left the room. His mother, poor woman, wept as he vanished. She dared not allow to herself that her firstborn was not a lovely thought to her, dared not ask where he could have gotten such a mean nature— so mean that he did not know he was mean.

He had expended his ill humor on the cooking, on the couches, on the beds, and twenty different things that displeased him. He attributed it to the weather, but he had brought it with him. Always fitful and wayward, he had never before behaved so unpleasantly. Certainly his world had not improved him for his home. Yet his companions thought him the best-natured fellow in the world. To them he never showed any peevishness, but kept it for those who loved him a thousand times better, and would cheerfully have parted with their own happiness for his. He possessed no will of his own, yet enjoyed the reputation of having a strong one; moved by liking or any foolish notion, he would become obstinate. The common philosophy always takes obstinacy for strength of will, even when it springs from utter inability to will against liking.

Mr. Raymount knew little of the real nature of his son. The youth was afraid of his father, though he spoke of him with so little respect. Before his father he dared not show his true nature, and he knew and dreaded the scorn which would follow the least disclosure of his displeasure about the intended division of his father's money. He knew also that his mother would not betray him to his father; nor would anyone who had ever heard Mr. Raymount give vent to his judgment of any conduct he despised, have wondered at the reticence of either wife or son.

16

Chapter 2.

FATHER, MOTHER, AND SON

There were contradictions in Mr. Gerald Raymount's character. At least one strain was not far removed from the savage, while on the other hand there were marks of ages of culture. At the university he had read well beyond his required studies, and thus had developed a useful acquaintance with and faculty in literature.

His father had been a country attorney, a gentle, quarrelsome man who only upon absolute necessity carried a case into court. Mr. Raymount had inherited from his father less than twenty thousand pounds, and had found that his income was not sufficient to maintain his growing family in accustomed ease. With not one expensive personal taste between them, neither had the faculty for saving money. The free-handed Mrs. Raymount would go without a new bonnet till an outcry arose in the family that its respectability was in danger; but she could not offer two shillings a day to a seamstress who thought herself worth half-a-crown. Neither would she take to herself the spiritual fare provided in church without making acknowledgment in carnal coin.

And their liberal habits were naturally punished. He indulged in them, and did not check them in his wife, but loved her the more that she indulged in them also. The deplorable result was that Mr. Raymount was condemned to labor—the worst evil in the judgment of some. He was compelled to rouse himself from his somewhat self-indulgent reading of books, and betake himself to his study-table—there to write, if possible, such items as might add to their diminishing income. But there are others who dare not count that labor an evil which helps to bring out the best elements of human nature, and who remember the words of the Lord: "My Father worketh hitherto, and I work."

Labor made Gerald Raymount a man. He was compelled to think more carefully than before, and so his mind and also his moral and spiritual nature took a fresh start. He slid more into writing out the necessities and experiences of his own heart and history, and so by degrees gained power of the only true kind—that of rousing the will, and not merely the passions or inspiration, of men. The poetry in which he had disported himself at college now came to the service of his prose, and the deeper poetic nature, which is the prophetic in every man, awoke in him.

Until they had been together a good many years, his wife did not know his worth; nor was he half the worth when she married him that he had now grown to be. She grew proud of him and his work, and looked upon him as a great man; but he was not a great man, only a growing man.

Helen Raymount was a little woman of fifty, clothed in a sweet dignity, with plentiful gray hair and great, clear, dark eyes. She was the daughter of a London barrister, from what is called a good family. She had known something of what is called life before she married, and from mere dissatisfaction had begun to withdraw from the show and self-assertion of social life, seeking within herself the door of that quiet chamber whose existence is unknown to most. She found there a measure of quiet, but not rest—not at first heeding the certain low knocking of One who would enter and share it with her. But now for a long time, He who thus knocked had been her companion in the chamber whose walls are infinite.

Together the Raymounts built their family—two daughters and two sons. But they made the mistake common to all but the wisest parents, and had put off to a period more or less too late the moment of teaching their children obedience. If this be not commenced at the earliest possible moment, then it will be the harder every hour it is postponed. To one who has learned of all things to desire deliverance from himself, a nursery in which the children are humored and scolded and punished, instead of being taught obedience, looks like a moral slaughterhouse. The dawn of reason will doubtless help obedience, but obedience is yet more necessary to the development of reason. To require of a child only what he can understand the reason of, is simply to help make of himself his own god—that is, a devil.

Cornelius was a youth of good abilities, and with a few good qualities. Kindhearted yet full of self, he admired certain easy and showy virtues. He was not incapable of unthinking generosity, felt pity for picturesque suffering, and was tempted to kindness by the prospect of a responsive devotion. Unable to bear the sight of suffering, he was yet careless of causing it where he would not see it. Supremely conceited, his regard for the habits and judgments of certain men would have been veneration if given to a great man, and would have elevated his own being. But the sole essentials of life as yet discovered by Cornelius were a good appearance, good manners, self-confidence, and seeming carelessness in spending.

In a word, he fashioned a fine gentleman-god in his foolish brain, and then fell down and worshiped him with what worship was possible between them. And the opinion of father and mother was not to be compared in authority with that of one Reginald Vavasor—so poor as to be one of his fellow clerks, yet heir apparent to an earldom.

Chapter 3.

THE MAGIC LANTERN

Cornelius took refuge with his anger in his own room. The top of his chest of drawers was covered with yellow novels, the sole kind of literature which he cared to read—if his mode of swallowing could be called reading. His father would have drawn more pleasure from the poorest one than Cornelius could from a dozen. He had not one left unread, and was too lazy or prudent to encounter the wind and rain between him and the nearest bookshop. None of his father's books—science, philosophy, history, poetry—held for him any interest. He was a dreary soul in a dreary setting.

If Cornelius had at any time begun to do something he knew he ought to do, he would not now have been the poor slave of circumstances, a youth at the beck and call of the weather. When men face a duty, not merely will that duty become at once less unpleasant, but life itself will immediately begin to gather interest. In duty the individual comes into real contact with life—can see what life is, and grow fit for it.

Cornelius threw himself on the bed and dozed away the hours until tea, his only resource against the unpleasantness of the day. The others were nowise particularly weighed down by the weather, and the less so that Cornelius was not haunting the window with his hands in his pockets.

After tea, he rose from his chair and sauntered once more to the window. "Hullo!" he cried. "I say, Hester, here's a lark! The sun's shining as if his grandmother had just taught him how! Come, let's have a walk. We'll go hear the band in the castle gardens. I don't think there's anything going on at the theater."

"I would rather walk," said Hester. "One seldom sees good acting in the provinces—there is at best one star. I prefer a jewel to a gem, and a decent play to a fine part."

"Hester," reproved Cornelius, "I believe you think it a fine thing to be hard to please! But to allow a spot to spoil your pleasure in a beauty is to be too fond of perfection."

"No, Corney, I would rather say that one point of excellence is not enough to make anything beautiful—a face, a play, or a character."

Hester had a rather severe mode of speaking to this brother. She was the only person in the house who could ever have done anything with him, and she lost her advantage by shouting from the moral distance instead of whispering close by him. But for that she did not love him enough, neither was she yet calm enough in herself to be able for it. And he was now too self-satisfied for any such redemption. He feared his father, and resented his mother's interference. He was cross with his sister, caring little if she was vexed with him, and regarding the opinion of any girl too little to imagine himself reflected in Hester's last remark.

She did put on her hat and cloak, and presently they were in the street. It was one of those misty, clearing evenings. There was a great lump of orange color half melted up in the watery clouds of the west, but all was dreary save the clear spaces above, strung with stars that began to peep out of the blue hope of heaven.

Hester's eyes kept wandering to the stars as they walked, but soon she set her foot down unevenly, gave her ankle a wrench, and uttered a little cry.

"There now, Hester!" said Cornelius, pulling her up like a stumbling horse. "That's what you get for your stargazing! You are always coming to grief by looking higher than your head!"

"Oh, please, stop for a minute, Corney," returned Hester, for he would have walked on as if nothing had happened. "My ankle hurts so!"

"I didn't know it was so bad as that. There! Take my arm."

"Now I can go on again," she said, after a few moments.

"What bright, particular star were you worshiping now?" he scoffed. "You are always worshiping some paragon or other—

until you get tired of her, and throw her away for another!"

Hester, hurt, made no answer, for there was some ground for the accusation. She was ready to think extravagantly of any new acquaintances that pleased her. Frank and true and generous, it was natural that she should read others by herself. Nor was it unnatural that contact should soon reveal the other's common nature, chill the first feeling of welcome, and send the newfound friend floating far away on the swift ebb of disappointment. Those whom she treated thus called her fitful and changeable, whereas it was in truth the unchangeableness of her ideal and her faithfulness to it that exposed her to blame. She was so true, so much in earnest, and although gentle, had so little softness that she was disliked by many of her acquaintances.

"That again comes of looking too high, and judging with precipitation," resumed Cornelius. He was always ready to criticize, but had no bent to self-criticism. He would be hand-in-glove at a moment's notice with any man who looked a gentleman and made himself agreeable. Nor would he avoid such company because of moral shadiness, so long as the man was not looked down upon by others.

Hester stopped again. "Corney, my ankle feels so weak! You must let me stand a bit."

"I'm very sorry," he rejoined disagreeably. "We must take the first fly we meet and go home again. It's just my luck! I thought we were going to have some fun!"

They stood silent. She looked nowhere, and he stared now in this direction, now in that.

"Hullo! What's this?" he cried, fixing his gaze on a large building opposite. " 'The Pilgrim's Progress! The Rake's Progress!' Ha! As edifying as amusing, no doubt, and contrasted with each other. Is it a lecture or a magic lantern? Let's go in and see! We may at least sit there till your ankle is better. Sixpence may get us a good laugh—a thing cheap at any price!"

"I don't mind," said Hester, and they crossed the road.

It was a large, dingy, dirty, water-stained hall to which the stone stair within led them. A dim but not very religious light pervaded the gloom, issuing chiefly from the crude and discordant colors of a luminous picture on a great screen at the far end of the hall. There an ill-proportioned figure representing Christian was shown extended on the ground, with his sword a yard beyond his reach, and Apollyon straddling the way and taking him in the stride. But that huge stride was the fiend's sole expression of vigor; although he held a flaming dart ready to strike the poor man dead, his dragon countenance was so feeble it seemed unlikely he would have the heart to drive it home.

An old man, like a broken-down clergyman, kept walking up and down the particolored gloom, flaunting to the thirty or so people present a pretense of a lecture. He smelled abominably of strong drink.

"Here you behold the terrible battle between Christian—or was it Faithful?—I used to know, but trouble has played hooky with my memory. It's all here, you know," he said as he tapped the bald tableland of his head, "but somehow it ain't handy as it used! In the morning it flourisheth and groweth up; in the evening it is cut down and withereth. Man that is in honor and abideth not is like the beast that perisheth—but there's Christian and Apollyon, right afore you, and better him than me. When I was a young one, and that wasn't yesterday, I used to think—but that was before I could read—that Apollyon was one and the same as Napoleon. And I wasn't just so far wrong, neither, as I shall readily prove to those of my distinguished audience who have been to college like myself, and learned to read Greek like their mother tongue.

"For what is the very name Apollyon, but a hidden prophecy concerning the great conqueror of Europe! Nothing can be plainer! Of course the first letter, N, stands for nothing—a mere veil to cover the prophecy till the time of revealing. Cast it away as the mere nothing it is. Then what have you left but *apoleon!* Throw away letter after letter, and what do you get but words— *Napoleon, apoleon, poleon, oleon, leon, eon, on!* Now these are all Greek words—and pray, what do they mean? I will give you a literal translation, and I challenge any Greek scholar who may be here present to set me right, that is, to show me wrong: 'Napoleon the destroyer of cities, being a destroying lion.' Now I should like to know a surer word of prophecy than that! I take that now for an incon—incontrovertible proof of the truth of the Bible. But I am wandering from my subject, which error, I pray you, ladies and gentlemen, to excuse, for I am no longer what I was in the prime of youth's rosy morn—come, I must get on! Change the slide, boy, I'm sick of it. I'm sick of it all. I want to get home and go to bed."

He maundered on in this way, uttering even worse nonsense, and mingling with it soiled and dusty commonplaces of religion.

Cornelius scarcely tried to choke his fits of laughter. Hester's mood was very different, and when at last they arose to go, Cornelius was astonished to see tears in her eyes. The misery of the whole thing was too dreadful to her! The lantern and slides themselves were old and outworn remnants. And the wretched old man seemed to have taken to this as a last effort—had resumed some half-forgotten trade or accomplishment, only to find that the skill he had counted upon had deserted him.

Worst of all to Hester was the fact that so few people were present, many of them children at half price. When the hall and the gas were paid for, what would the poor old scrag-end of humanity have over for his supper? Alas for the misery of the whole thing!

When they came out and breathed again the blue, clean, rain-washed air instead of the musty smells of the hall, Hester's eyes involuntarily rose to the vault whose only keystone is the Father's will, whose endless space alone is large enough to picture the heart of God. How was that old man to get up into the high regions and grow clean and wise? For all the look, he must belong there as well as she! And were there not thousands equally miserable in the world—people wrapped in no tenderness, to whom none ministered, left if not driven to fold themselves in their own selfishness? And was there nothing she, a favored one of the family, could do to comfort one such of her own flesh and blood? To rescue a heart from the misery of hopelessness? To make one feel that there was a heart of love and refuge at the center of things? The moment she began to flutter her weak wings in aspiration, she found the whole human family hanging upon her; she could not rise except by raising them with her.

Yet all this was not the beginning of Hester's enthusiasm for her kind. Three-and-twenty now, she was one of the strong ones that grow slowly, and she had for some years been cherishing an idea, which every sight and sound of misery tended to quicken and strengthen.

"There you are again," said Cornelius, "stargazing as usual! You'll be spraining your other ankle presently!"

"I had forgotten all about my ankle, Corney, dear," returned Hester, softened by her sorrowful sympathy, "but I will be careful."

"You had better. Well, I think we had the worth of our shilling! Did you ever see such a ridiculous old bloke!"

"The old man made me very sad," said Hester.

"Now you do strand me, Hester! How could you see anything pitiful in that disreputable old humbug? A ludicrous specimen of tumbledown humanity, a drunken old thief! Catch me leaving a sovereign where he could spy the shine of it!"

"And don't you count that pitiful, Cornelius? Can you see one of your own kind, with heart and head and hands like your own, so self-abandoned, so low, so hopeless, and feel no pity for him? He seemed to despise himself!"

"And why not? Don't you trouble your head about *him*. You should see him when he gets home—he'll have his hot supper and his hot tumbler, don't you fear! Swear he will, and fluently, if it's not ready!"

"Now that seems to me the most pitiful of all," returned Hester. She was on the point of adding, "That is just the kind of pity I feel for you," but checked herself, and said instead, "Is it not most pitiful to see a human being, made in the image of God, sunk so low?"

"It's his own doing, so what can he complain of?"

"If he could not help it, and was not to blame, that would be sad enough. But to be such, and to be to blame for it, seems to me misery upon misery. It is not whether he has anything to complain of, but whether he has anything to be pitied for. I don't know what I wouldn't do to make that old man clean and comfortable!"

Cornelius again burst into a great laugh. No man was anything to him merely because he was a man. "Don't trouble your head about such riffraff. He's waste, and there's misery enough in the world without looking out for it, and taking other people's upon our shoulders."

Hester held her peace, humiliated that her own brother's one mode of relieving the suffering in the world should be to avoid as much as possible adding to his own.

Chapter 4.

HESTER ALONE

When the family separated for the night and Hester reached her room, she sat down and fell to thinking. She had all her life endeavored, with varying success, with frequent failures, and occasional brief lapses of effort, to do the right thing. There she but followed in the footsteps of her mother, walking steadily in the true path of humanity.

But she was frequently irritated with herself because of failure, and she had found the impossibility of satisfying the hard master Self who, while he flatters some, requires of others more than they can give. All these things tended to make her less evenly sympathetic with those about her than her heart's theory demanded. Willing to lay down her life for them, a matchless nurse in sickness, and revealing in trouble a perfectly lovely tenderness, Hester was yet not the first one to whom the younger children would flee with hurt or sorrow. She was not yet all human, because she was not yet at home with the divine.

Thousands that are capable of great sacrifices are yet not capable of little ones which are all that are required of them. God seems to take pleasure in working by degrees, for the progress of the truth is as the permeation of leaven, or the growth of a seed: a multitude of small successive sacrifices may work more good in the world than many a large one. *Being* is the mother of all *doing*, and is the precious thing. Hester had not had time, neither had she prayed enough to *be* quite yet. She was a good way up the hill, and the Lord was coming down to meet her—but they had not quite met yet, so as to go up the rest of

26

the way together.

In religious politics, Hester was a high churchwoman, and looked down with repugnance upon the whole race of dissenters. She regarded her own conscience as her lord, but had no respect for that of another man where it differed from hers. So she was scarcely in the kingdom of heaven yet, any more than thousands who regard themselves as choice Christians. She did not love her dissenting neighbor, and felt good and condescending when she behaved kindly to one. Such exclusiveness is simply pride—the evil thing that Christ came to burn up with His lovely fire, and which yet so many of us who call ourselves by His name keep hugging to us—the pride that says, "I am better than you."

But tenderness had large roots in her heart. Whatever her failings, whatever ugly weeds grew in the neglected corners of her nature, the moment she came into contact with any of her kind in whatever condition of sadness or need, the pent-up love of God would burst its barriers and rush forth, sometimes almost overwhelming her in its torrent. She would then be ready to die to help the poor and miserable.

The tide of action had been rising in her heart. She must not waste her life—she must *do* something! But how could she help? She said to herself that she had no money—but this is the last and feeblest of means for the doing of good, and is always the first to suggest itself to one who has not perceived the mind of God in the matter. The first thing in regard to money is to prevent it from doing harm. Neither Christ nor His apostles did anything by means of money; even he who would join them in their labors had to abandon his fortune.

This evening, then, the thought of the vulgar, miserable old man, with his wretched magic lantern, kept haunting Hester. And naturally, starting from him, her thoughts wandered abroad over the universe of misery. For was not the world full of men and women who groaned, not merely under poverty and cruelty, weakness and sickness, but under dullness and stupidity, hugged in the paralyzing arms of the devilfish Commonplace, or held fast to the rocks by that crab Custom, while the tide of moral indifference was fast rising to choke them? Was there no prophet, no redemption, no mediator for these? Could she do nothing? Even the man who by honest means makes people laugh sends a fire-headed arrow into the ranks of the enemy of his race—and he who beguiles from another a genuine tear makes heavenly wind visit his heart with a cool odor of paradise!

She had one special gift, and under the faithful care of her mother she had been cultivating it all her life. Endowed with a passion for music—and what is a true passion but a heavenly hunger?—she indulged and strengthened it, but never sated it, by the study of both theoretical and practical music. The piano and the organ were each an effectual door opening into regions of delight. But she was crowned with a fine contralto voice, of exceptional scope and flexibility. And now this night came to Hester, if not for the first time, yet more clearly than ever before, the thought that she might make use of her gift for the service she desired—the comfort and uplifting of humanity.

And this night came back to her again the memory of a year-past sermon on the text, "Glorify God in your body, and in your spirit, which are God's." It was a dull sermon, yet when she went out of that dark church into the sunshine, and heard the birds singing as if they knew that their bodies and spirits were God's, a sense awoke in her that the grand voice in her belonged not to her but to God, and must be used to work His will in His world.

She began to feel that perhaps God had given her this voice and this marriage of delight and power in music and song for some reason like that for which He had made the birds the poets of the animal world—to drive dull care away. What if she too were to be a doorkeeper in the house of God, and open or keep open windows in heaven that the air of the high places might reach the low swampy ground? If while she sang, her soul mounted on the wings of her song till it fluttered against the latticed doors of heaven as a bird flutters against its cage, then surely her song was capable of carrying more than merely herself up into the regions of delight! And might not there go forth from her throat a trumpet-cry of truth among such as could hear and respond to the cry? Then she would enter into the joy of her Lord. But to serve God in any true sense, she must serve Him where He needs service—among His children lying in the heart of lack, in sin and pain and sorrow. And she saw that if she was to serve at all, it must be with her best.

Chapter 5.

THE SWEET LIGHT

The cry of the human heart in all ages and in every moment is, "Where is God and how shall I find Him?" Whether the man knows it or not, his heart in its depths is ever crying out for God. Where the man does not know it, it is because the unfaithful Self has usurped consciousness, and is trampling on the heart and smothering it up in the rubbish of ambitions, lusts, and cares. If ever the cry reaches that Self, it calls it childish folly, and tramples the harder. It does not know that a child crying to God is mightier than a warrior clad in steel.

If we had none but fine weather, the demon Self would always keep the divine Self down; but bad weather, misfortune, ill-luck or whatever name but punishment or the love of God men may call it, sides with the Christ self down below, and helps to make its voice heard. But if we had nothing but fine weather, the hope of those in whom the divine Self is slowly rising would grow too faint. Without hope, can any man repent?

To the people at Burcliff came at last a lovely morning, with sky and air like the face of a child who has repented so thoroughly that the sin has passed from him, and he is no longer ashamed. The wind and water danced in the joy of a new birth, while the sun looked merrily down on the glad commotion his presence caused.

"Ah," thought Mrs. Raymount, as she looked from her windows ere she began to dress for this new live day, "how would it be if the Light at the heart of the sun were shining thus on the worlds made in His image?"

29

She was thinking of her boy, whom perhaps only she was able to love heartily—there was so little in the lad himself to help anyone to love him! But in the absolute, mere existence is reason for love, and upon that God so loves that He will suffer and cause suffering for the perfection of that existence. The mother's heart, more than any other God has made, is like Him in power of loving—but alas that she is so seldom like Him in wisdom, so often thwarting the work of God, and rendering more severe His measures with her child by her attempts to shield him from His law, and save him from saving sorrow. How often from his very infancy does she get between him and the right consequences of his conduct, as if with her feeble loving hand she would stay the flywheel of the holy universe. It is the law that the man who does evil shall suffer; it is the only hope for him, and a hope for the neighbor he wrongs. When he forsakes his evil, one by one the messenger dogs of suffering will halt and drop away from his track—and he will find at last they have but hounded him unto the land of his nativity, into the home of his Father in heaven.

As soon as breakfast was over, the whole family set out for a walk. Streets, hills, and sands were swarming with human beings, all drawn out by the sun. "I sometimes wonder," said Mr. Raymount, "that so many people require so little to make them happy. The sun breaks through the clouds, and sets them all going like ants in an anthill!"

"Yes," returned his wife, "but then see how little is required to make them miserable! The sun hides his head for a day, and they grumble!"

Making the remark, the good woman never thought of Cornelius, the one of her family whose conduct illustrated it. At the moment she saw him cheerful, and her love looked upon him as good. But she had never done anything to help him conquer himself, and now it was too late. Yet the moment his bad humors were over, she looked on him as reformed, and when he uttered worldliness, she persuaded herself he was but jesting. She still had no adequate notion of the selfishness of the man-child she had given the world.

This matter of the black sheep in the white flock is most mysterious. Sometimes the sheep is not so black as the whiter ones think—and perhaps neither are they so much whiter as they think, for to be altogether respectable is not to be clean. And the black sheep may be all the better than some of the rest because he looks what he is, and does not dye his wool. Yet he still may be a great deal worse than some of his own family think him.

"Then," said Hester after a longish pause, "those that need more to make them happy are less easily made unhappy?"

To this question she received no reply. Her parents felt it not an easy one to answer, with points to consider. But to Cornelius it was a mere girl's speech, not worth heeding where the girl was his sister. He snubbed it, having not the least notion of what it meant or involved.

His father had as little notion that Cornelius was a black sheep. He was not what the world would have called a black sheep, but his father, could he have seen into him, would have counted him a very black sheep indeed—and none the whiter that certain shades were of paternal origin. It was only to the rest of his family that Cornelius showed his blackness, for he was afraid of his father. Being proud of his children, his father would have found it hard to believe anything bad of them: like his faults they were his own! His own conceit blinded him to their faults as well as to some of his own. The discovery of any serious fault in one of them would sorely wound his vanity and destroy his self-content.

While he never obtruded his opinions upon others, he never imagined them disregarded in his own family. It never entered his mind that any member of it might think differently from himself. But both his wife and Hester were able to think, and did think for themselves, as they were bound in truth to do, and they walked in different paths from those he had trodden.

He supposed his wife and Hester and Cornelius all read what he wrote, and his wife and daughter did read most of it. But what would he think when he came to know that his son not only read next to nothing of it, but read that little with contempt because his father wrote it? The bond between father and son was by no means as strong as the father thought it. Indeed, the selfishness of Cornelius made him almost look upon his father as his enemy, because of his intentions with regard to the division of his property.

Chapter 6.

THE AQUARIUM

"*Let's go and see the people* at the aquarium," said Cornelius, seeking something that could be enjoyed while they were yet on their holiday.

"Do you mean the fishes?" asked his father.

"No, I don't care about them—I said the people," answered Cornelius.

"The people of the aquarium must surely be fishes, eh, Saffy?" said the father to Josephine who was walking hand-in-hand with him. Her eyes were so blue that but for the biblical association he would have called her Sapphira, and between the two he contented himself with *Saffy*.

"Ah, but papa," said Hester, "Corney didn't say the people *of* the aquarium, but the people *at* the aquarium!"

"Two of you are too many for me!" returned the father playfully. "Well then, Saffy, let us go and see the people *of* and the people *at* the aquarium. Which do you want to see, Hester?"

"Oh, the fishes, of course, papa!"

"Why 'of course'?"

"Because they're so much more interesting than the people," said Hester, rebuked in herself as she said it, before she knew why.

"Fishes more interesting than people!" exclaimed her father.

"They're so like people, papa!"

"Oh, then surely the people must be the more interesting after all, if it is the likeness of the fishes to people that makes them interesting! Which of all the people you love do you see

32

most like a fish now?"

"O papa!"

"What! Is it only people you hate that you see like fishes?"

"I don't hate anybody, papa."

Cornelius broke in. "There's a way of not caring about people, though—looking down on them and seeing them like fishes, that's precious like hating them." He enjoyed a crowd, and putting his sister in the wrong still better: to that end he could easily say a sensible thing.

"If you mean me, Corney, I think you do me injustice," said Hester. "The worst I do is to look at them the wrong way through the telescope."

"But why do you never see anyone you love like a fish?" persisted her father.

"Because I could not love anybody that was like a fish."

"Certainly there is something not beautiful about them!" said Mr. Raymount. "Let us look into it a little. What is it about them that is ugly? Their colors are sometimes very beautiful—and their shapes too."

"Their heads and faces," said Hester, "are the only parts of them in which they can be like human beings, and those are ugly."

"I'm not sure that you are right, Hester," said the mother. "There must surely be something human in their bodies as well, for now and then I see their ways and motions so like those of men and women, that I feel for a moment almost as if I understand how they are feeling, and am just about to know what they are thinking."

"I suspect," said Mr. Raymount, "your mother's too much of a poet to be trusted alone in an aquarium."

They had now reached the middle of the descent to the mysteries of the place, when Cornelius uttered a cry of recognition and darted down to the next landing. With a degree of respect he seldom manifested, they saw him accost and shake hands with a gentleman leaning over the balustrade. He was several years older than Cornelius, not a few inches taller, and much better looking—one indeed who could hardly fail to attract notice even in a crowd. The rest reached the landing, and Mr. Raymount asked Corney to introduce his friend.

Cornelius had been now eighteen months in the bank, and

had never even mentioned the name of a fellow clerk. He was one of those youths who take the only possible way for emptiness to make itself of consequence—that of concealment and affected mystery. Not even now, but for his father's request, would he have presented his bank friend to the family.

The friendly manners and approach of Mr. Vavasor at once recommended him to the friendly reception of all, from Mr. Raymount to little Saffy, who had the rare charm of being shy without being rude. It was a kind of company bearing he had, but dashed with indifference, except where he desired to commend himself. He shook hands with little Saffy as respectfully as with her mother, but with neither altogether respectfully—and immediately the pale-faced Mark unconsciously disliked him. He was beyond question handsome, with a Grecian nose and aristocratic look, favored by the simplicity of his dress. He turned with them, and redescended the stairs.

"Why didn't you tell me you were coming, Mr. Vavasor? I could have met you," said Cornelius, with just a little stretch of the familiarity between them.

"I didn't know myself till the last minute," answered Vavasor. "It was a sudden resolve of my aunt's. Neither had I the remotest idea you were here."

"Have you been seeing the fishes?" asked Hester, at whose side their new acquaintance was walking now they had reached the subterranean level.

"I have just passed along their cages," he answered. "They are not well kept—the glass is dirty, and the water too. I fancied they looked unhappy, and came away. I can't bear to see creatures pining. It would be a good deed to poison them all."

"Wouldn't it be better to give them some fresh water?" said little Saffy. "That would make them glad."

To this wisdom there was no response.

When they came to the door of the concert room, Cornelius turned into it, leaving the rest to go and look at the fishes. Mr. Vavasor kept his pace by the side of Hester.

"We were just talking about comparing people and fishes," said Hester. "I can't make it clear to myself why I like seeing the fishes better than the people."

"I fancy it must be because you call them fishes and not fish," replied Vavasor. "If the fishes were a shoal of herrings or mackerel, I doubt if you would. If, on the other hand, the men and women in the concert room were as oddly distinguished one from another as these different fishes, you would prefer going with your brother."

"And yet I suspect," said Mrs. Raymount to Vavasor, "many of the people are as much distinguished from each other in character as the fishes are in form."

"Possibly," interjected her husband, "they are as different in their faces also, only we are too much of their kind to be able to read the differences so clearly."

"Surely you do not mean," said Vavasor, "that any two persons in the concert room can be as much unlike each other as that flounder shuddering along the sandy bottom, and that yard of eel sliding through the water like embodied wickedness?"

Hester was greatly struck with the poetic remark.

"I think you may find people as different," replied her father, "if you take into account the more delicate as well as the more striking differences—the deeper as well as the surface diversities. Now I wonder whether all these live grotesques may not have been made to the pattern of different developments of humanity."

"Look at that dogfish," said Vavasor, pointing to the largest in the tank. "What a brute! Don't you hate him, Miss Raymount?"

"I am not willing to hate any living thing," smiled Hester, "from selfish motives, perhaps. I feel as if it would be to my own loss, causing me some kind of irreparable hurt."

"But you would kill such a creature as that—would you not?"

"In some circumstances," she answered, "but killing and hating have nothing necessarily to do with each other. He that hates his brother is always a murderer, not always he that kills him."

"This is another sort of girl from any I've met yet!" said Vavasor to himself. "I wonder what she's really like!" He did not know that what she really was like was just what he, with all his fancied knowledge of women, was incapable of seeing—so different was she.

"But just look at the head, eyes, and mouth of the fiend!" he persisted.

Hester forced herself to regard the animal for two or three minutes. Then a slight shudder passed through her, and she turned away her eyes.

"I see you've caught his look! Is he not a horror?"

"He is. But that was not what made me turn away; if I looked a moment longer, I should hate him in spite of myself."

"And why shouldn't you hate him? You would be doing the wretch no wrong. Even if he knew it, it would only be what he deserved."

"That you cannot tell except you know all about his nature, and every point of his history from the beginning of the creation till now. I dare not judge even a dogfish. And whatever his deserts, I don't choose to hate him, because I don't choose to hate." She turned away, and Vavasor saw she wanted no more of the dogfish.

"Oh!" cried Saffy, with a face of terror. "Look, mama! It's staring at me!" The child hid her face in her mother's gown, yet turned immediately to look again.

Mr. Raymount looked also. Through the glass, high above his head, and not far from the surface, he saw a huge thornback, bending toward them and seeming to look down on them, as it flew slowly through the water, the two sides of its body fringed with fins, and its long tail floating behind. But the terrible thing was his death's-head look. His white belly was toward them, and his eyes were on the other side, but his nostrils looked exactly like the empty sockets of eyes, and below them was a hideous mouth. These made the face that Saffy thought was hovering over her and watching them.

"Like an infernal angel of death!" thought Mr. Raymount, but would not rouse the imagination of the little one by saying it. Hester gazed steadfastly at the floating specter.

"You seem in no danger from hating that one," said Vavasor.

"Yes. I have no inclination to hate him."

"Yet the ray is even uglier than the dogfish."

"Who hates for ugliness? Ugliness only moves my pity."

"What, then, makes you feel as if you might hate?"

"If you will look again at the dogfish, and tell me the expression of its mouth, I may be able to answer you," she returned.

"I will," said Vavasor. Betaking himself to a farther portion of the tank, he stood there watching a little shoal of the sharks. While he was gone Cornelius rejoined them.

"I wish I knew why God made such ugly creatures," said Saffy to Mark.

The boy gave a curious half-sad smile, without turning his eyes from the thornback, and said nothing.

"Do you know why God made any creatures, pet?" said Hester to Saffy.

"No, I don't. Why did He, Hessy?"

"I am almost afraid to guess. But if you don't know why He made any, why should you wonder that He made those?"

"Because they are so ugly. Do tell me why He made them," she added coaxingly.

"You had better ask mama."

"But, Hessy, I don't like to ask mama," said Saffy, who was all the time holding her mother's hand, and knew she was hearing her. "Mama mightn't know what to say."

Hester thought, "I am sometimes afraid to pray lest I should have no answer!"

The mother's face turned toward her little one. "And what if I shouldn't know what to say, darling?" she asked.

"I feel so awkward when Miss Merton asks me a question I can't answer," said the child.

"And are you afraid of making mama feel awkward? You pet!" said Hester.

Cornelius burst into a great laugh, and Saffy into silent tears, for she thought she had made a fool of herself. She did not deserve the mockery with which her barbarian brother invaded her little temple. She was such a true child that her mother was her neighbor, and present to her heart and spirit.

The mother led her aside to a seat, saying, "Come, darling, we must look into this, and try to understand it. The question is why you should be ashamed when you cannot answer the questions of one who knows so much more than you, and why I should not be ashamed when I cannot answer the questions of my own little girl who knows so much less than I do. Is that it?"

"I don't know," sobbed Saffy.

"You shouldn't laugh at her, Corney; it hurts her!" said Hester.

"The little fool! How could that hurt her? It's nothing but temper!" said Cornelius with vexation. He was not vexed that he had made her cry, but vexed that she cried.

"You should have a little more sympathy with childhood,

Cornelius," said his father. "You used to be angry enough when you were laughed at."

"I was a fool then myself!" answered Cornelius sulkily.

He said no more, and his father put the best interpretation upon his speech. "Do you remember, Hester," he said, "how you were always ready to cry when I told you I did not know something you had asked me?"

"Quite well, papa," replied Hester, "and I think I could explain it now. I think it was because it seemed to bring you down nearer to my level. My heaven of wisdom sank and grew less."

"I hope that is not what Saffy is feeling now; your mother must be telling her she doesn't know why God made the animals. But no! She is looking up in her face with hers radiant!"

And yet her mother had told her she did not know why God made the animals! She had at the same time, however, made her own confessed ignorance a step on which to set the child nearer to the knowledge of God; for she told her it did not matter that she did not know, so long as God knew. The child could see that her mother's ignorance did not trouble her; and also that she who confessed ignorance was yet in close communication with Him who knew all about everything and delighted in making His children understand.

And now Vavasor returned from his study of the dogfish. His nature was a poetic one, though much choked with the weeds of the conventional and commonplace, and he had seen and felt something of what Hester intended. But he was not alive enough to understand hate. He was able to hate and laugh, but could not feel the danger of hate as Hester, for hate is death, and it needs life to know death.

"He is cruel, and the very incarnation of selfishness," he said. "I should like to set my heel on him."

"If I were to allow myself to hate," returned Hester, "I should hate him too much to kill him. I should let him live on in his ugliness, and hold back my hate lest it should wither him in the cool water. To let him live would be the worst revenge. I must not look at him, for it makes me feel as wicked as he looks."

She glanced at Vavasor, whose eyes were fixed on her. She turned away, uncomfortable. Could it be that he was like the dogfish?

"I declare," said Cornelius, coming between them, "there's no

38

knowing you girls! Would you believe it, Mr. Vavasor—that young woman was crying her eyes out last night over the meanest humbug I ever set mine on! There ain't one of those fishes comes within sight of him for ugliness. And she would have it he was to be pitied—sorrowed over—loved, I suppose." The last words of his speech he whined out in a lackadaisical tone.

Hester flushed, but said nothing. She was not going to defend herself before a stranger. She would rather remain misrepresented, even be misunderstood. But Vavasor had no such opinion of the brother as to take any notion of the sister from his mirror. When she indignantly turned from Cornelius, Vavasor passed behind him to the other side of Hester, and there stood apparently absorbed in the contemplation of a huge crustacean.

"Why, can it be?" she said to herself, but audibly, after a moment of silence, during which she also had apparently been absorbed in the contemplation of some inhabitant of the watery cage. But she had in truth been thinking of nothing immediately before her eyes, though they had rested first upon a huge crayfish, balancing himself on stilts innumerable, then turned to one descending a rocky incline.

"Yes, the fellow bristles with *whys*," said Vavasor. "Every leg seems to ask, 'Why am I a leg?'"

"I should have thought it was asking rather, 'What am I? Am I a leg or a failure?'" rejoined Hester. "But I am not thinking of the crayfish. He is odd, but there is no harm in him. He looks, indeed, highly respectable. See with what a dignity he fans himself!"

"And for the same reason," remarked her father, "as the finest lady at the ball—he wants more air."

"Are you thinking of the dogfish still?" asked Vavasor. The handsome girl's strange absorption attracted him even more than her beauty, for he did not like to feel himself unpossessed of the entree to such a house. He was also a fair writer of society verses, and had already begun to think something might be made of the situation.

"I *was* thinking of him," Hester answered, "but only as a type of the great difficulty—why there should be evil or ugliness in the world. There must be an answer to it! Is it possible it should be one we would not like?"

"I don't believe there is any answer," said Vavasor. "The ugly things are ugly just because they are ugly. It is a child's answer, but not therefore unphilosophical. We must take things as we find them. We are ourselves just what we are, and cannot help it. We do this or that because it is in us. We are made so."

"You do not believe in free will, then, Mr. Vavasor?" said Hester coldly.

"I see no ground for believing in it. We are but bottled-up forces. Everyone does just what is in him, and acts as he is capable." He was not given to metaphysics and, indeed, had few or no opinions in that department of inquiry; but the odd girl interested him, and he was ready to meet her on any ground. He had uttered his own practical unbelief, however, with considerable accuracy.

Hester's eyes flashed angrily. "I say *no*. Everyone is capable of acting better than he does."

"Why does he not then?" asked Vavasor.

"Ah, why?" she responded.

"How can he be made for it if he does not do it?" insisted Vavasor.

"How indeed? That is the puzzle," she answered. "If he were not capable there would be none."

"I should do better, I am sure, if I could," said Vavasor. Had he known himself, he ought to have added, "without trouble."

"Then you think we are all just like the dogfish—except that destiny has made none of us quite so ugly," rejoined Hester.

"Or so selfish," added Vavasor.

"That I can't see," returned Hester. "If we are merely borne helpless hither and thither on the tide of impulse, we can be neither more nor less selfish than the dogfish. We are pure nothings, concerning which speculation is not worth the trouble. But the very word *selfish* implies a contrary judgment on the part of humanity itself."

"Then you believe we can make ourselves different from what we are made?"

"Yes—we are made with the power to change. We are meant to take a share in our own making. We are made with a power in us that can lay hold on the original Power that made us. We are not made to remain as we are. We are bound to grow."

"You are too much of a philosopher for me, Miss Raymount," said Vavasor with a smile. "But what if a man is too weak to change?"

"He must change," said Hester.

Vavasor began to feel the conversation getting quite too serious. "Ah, well!" he said. "But you don't think this is rather—ah—don't you know?—for an aquarium?"

Vavasor was not one of the *advanced* of the age; he did not deny there was a God. When a man has not the slightest intention that the answer shall influence his conduct, why should he inquire whether there be a God or not? Vavasor cared more about the top of his cane than the God whose being he did not take the trouble to deny. He believed a little less than Miss Vavasor, the maiden aunt with whom he lived; she believed less than her mother, and her mother had believed less than hers. For generations the so-called faith of the family had been dying down, simply because all that time it had sent out no fresh root of obedience. It had in truth been no faith at all, only assent.

Miss Vavasor went to church because it was the right thing to do; God was one of the heads of society, and His drawing rooms had to be attended. Certain fictions were more or less countenanced in them, such as equality, love of your neighbor, and forgiveness of your enemy, but then nobody really heeded them. Religion had worked its way up to a respectable position, and no longer required the support of the unwashed—that is, those outside the circle whose center is Mayfair. As to her personal religion, why, God had heard her prayers, and might again—He did show favor occasionally. That she should come out of it all as well as other people when this life of family and incomes and matchmaking was over, she saw no reason to doubt. God knew better than to make the existence of thoroughly respectable people quite unendurable! She was kindhearted, and treated her maid like an equal up to the moment of offense—then like a dog of the east up to the moment of atonement. She had the power of keeping her temper even in family differences, and hence was regarded as a very model of wisdom, prudence, and tact. The young of her acquaintance fled to her for help in need, and she gave them no hard words, but generally more counsel than comfort—always, however, the best she had, which was an essence of wise selfishness, with a strong dash of self-respect.

41

Chapter 7.

AMY AMBER

The troubles of humanity caught upon Hester's heart as if it had been a thornbush, and hung there. It was not greatly troubled, neither was its air murky, but its very repose was like a mother's sleep, which is no obstacle between the cries of her children and her sheltering soul—it was ready to wake at every moan of the human sea around her. Unlike most women, she had not needed marriage and motherhood to open the great gate of her heart to her kind. The experience of the magic lantern had been as a mirror in which she saw the misery of the low of her kind, including, alas, her brother Cornelius. He had never before so plainly revealed to her his heartlessness, and the painful consequence of the revelation was that now, with all her swelling love for human beings, she felt her heart shrink from him as if he were of another nature. She could never indeed have loved him as she did except that, being several years his elder, she had had a good deal to do with him as a baby and child. The infant motherhood of her heart had gathered about him, and not an eternity of difference could after that destroy the relation between them. But as he grew up, the boy had undermined and weakened her affection, though hardly her devotion; and now the youth had given it a rude shock. This decay of feeling did not merely cause her much pain, but gave rise in her to much useless endeavor; while every day she grew more anxious and careful to carry herself toward him as a sister ought.

The Raymounts could not afford one of the best lodgings in Burcliff, and were content with a floor in an old house in an unfashionable part of the port. It was kept by two old maids whose hearts had been flattened by the pressure not of poverty, but of *care*. Pure poverty never flattened any heart; it is the care which poverty is supposed to justify that does the mischief; it gets inside it and burrows, as well as lies on the top of it. Our Lord never mentions poverty as one of the obstructions to His kingdom, but cares and desires He does mention. The sisters Witherspin had never suffered from the lack of a single necessity, yet they frayed their mornings, wore out their afternoons, scorched their evenings, and consumed their nights in scraping together provision for an old age they were destined never to see. They were a small, meager pair, with hardly a smile between them. One waited and the other cooked.

It looked as if God had forgotten them—toiling for so little all day long, while the fact was they forgot God, and were thus miserable and oppressed because they would not have Him interfere as He would so gladly have done. Instead of seeking the kingdom of heaven, and trusting Him for old age while they did their work with their might, they exhausted their spiritual resources to find and secure their future. If they could only have left pitying themselves and let God love them, they would have gotten on well enough.

The poor things, of course, had their weight on the mind of Hester, for, had they tried, they could not have hidden the fact that they tried to save: every moment and every tone betrayed it. And yet, unlike so many lodging-house keepers, they were strictly honest. Had they not been, Hester would not have been able to give them so much pity as she did, for she scorned dishonesty. Her heart, which was full of compassion for the yielding, the weak, the erring, was not yet able to spend much on the actively vicious—the dishonest and lying and traitorous.

The morning after the visit to the aquarium, Woeful Miss Witherspin, as Mark called her, entered to remove the ruins of breakfast with a more sad and injured expression of countenance than usual. It was a glorious day, and she was like a live shadow in the sunshine. Most of the Raymounts were already in the open air, and Hester was the only one in the room. She perceived that something in particular must have exceeded the general wrongness of things in the poor little gnome's world.

"Is anything the matter, Miss Witherspin?" asked Hester.

"Indeed, miss, there never comes nothing to sister and me but it's matter, and now it's a sore matter. But it's the Lord's will and we can't help it—and what are we here for but to have patience? That's what I keep saying to my sister, but it don't seem to do her much good."

She ended with a great sigh, and Hester thought if the unseen sister required the comfort of the one before her, whose evangel just uttered was as gloomy as herself, how unhappy she must be.

"No doubt we are here to learn patience," said Hester, "but I can hardly think patience is what we are made for. Is there any fresh trouble?"

"Well, I don't know, miss, as trouble can anyhow be called fresh—leastways to us it's stale enough; we're sick of it! I declare to you, miss, I'm clean worn out with havin' patience! An' now there's my brother John's wife gone after her husband an' left her girl, Amy, brought up in her own way an' every other luxury, an' there she's come on our hands! It's a responsibility will be the death of me."

"Is there no provision for her?"

"Oh, yes, there's provision! Her mother kep' a shop for fancy goods at Keswick—after John's death, that is—an' scraped together a good bit o' money, they do say; but that's under trustees—not a penny to be touched till the girl comes of age!"

"But the trustees must make you a proper allowance for bringing her up! And anyhow you can refuse the charge."

"No, miss, we can't. It was always John's wish when he lay a-dyin', that if anything was to happen to Sarah, the child should come to us. It's the trouble of the young thing, the responsibility—havin' to keep your eyes upon her every blessed moment for fear she do the thing she ought not to—that's what weighs upon me. Oh, yes, they'll pay so much a quarter for her. It's not that. But to be always at the heels of a young, sly puss after mischief—it's more'n I'm equal to, I assure you, Miss Raymount."

"When did you see her last?" inquired Hester.

"Not once have I set eyes upon her since she was three years old!" answered Miss Witherspin, and her tone seemed to imply in the fact yet additional wrong.

"Then perhaps she may be wiser by this time," Hester suggested. "How old is she now?"

44

"Sixteen. It's awful to think of!"

"But how do you know she will be so troublesome? She mayn't want the looking after you dread. You haven't seen her for thirteen years!"

"I'm sure of it. I know the breed, miss! She's took after her mother, you may take your mortal oath! The sly way she got round our John, an' all to take him right away from his own family as bore and bred him!"

"Girls are not always like their mother," said Hester. "I'm not half so good as my mother."

"Bless you, miss! If she ain't half as bad as hers—the Lord have mercy upon us! How I'm to attend to my lodgers and look after her, it's more than I know how to think of it with patience."

"When is she coming?"

"She'll be here this same blessed day, miss!"

"Perhaps, your house being full, you may find her a help instead of a trouble. It won't be as if she had nothing to employ her!"

"There's no mortal creature i' the bone or the blood of her!" sighed Miss Witherspin, as she put the tablecloth on the top of the breakfast things.

That blessed day the girl, Amy Amber, did arrive—sprang into the house like a rather loud sunbeam—loud for a sunbeam, not for a young woman of sixteen. She was small and bright with large sparkling black eyes, and a miniature Greek face containing a neat nose and changeable mouth. Her hair was a deep brown, mistakable for black, and curly. She had as little shyness as forwardness, being at once fearless and modest, gentle and merry, noiseless and swift. The sudden apparition of her in a rosebud print, to wait upon the Raymounts the next morning at breakfast, startled them all with a sweet surprise. Every time she left the room the talk about her broke out afresh, and Hester's information concerning her was welcome.

A more striking contrast than that between her and her two aunts could hardly have been found in the whole island. She was like a star between two gray clouds of twilight. But she had not so much share in her own cheerfulness as her poor aunts had in their misery. She so lived because she was so made. She was a joy to others as well as to herself, but as yet she had no merit in her own peace or its rippling gladness. So strong was the life in her that, although she cried every night over the loss of her mother, she was fresh as a daisy in the morning, ready to give smile for smile and smile for frown. She was one of those lovely natures that need but to recognize the eternal to fly to it straight; but such natures are very hard to wake to a recognition of the unseen. They assent to everything good, but for a long time seem unaware of the need of a perfect Father. To have their minds opened to the truth, they must suffer like other mortals, less aimable. Suffering alone can develop in such any spiritual insight, or cause them to care that there should be a live God caring about them.

She was soon a favorite with the family. Mrs. Raymount often talked to her. And Amy was so drawn to Hester that she never lost an opportunity of waiting on her, and never once missed going to her room to see if she wanted anything. The only one of the family that professed not to "think much of her" was the contemptuous Cornelius. Yet now and then he might have been caught glowering at her, and would sometimes, seemingly in spite of himself, smile on her sudden appearance.

Chapter 8.

CORNELIUS AND VAVASOR

If one were to meet Cornelius first in company other than that of his own family, he would have taken him for an agreeable young man. He would have perceived little of the look of doggedness and opposition he wore at home—that would have been unconsciously masked in a smile of general complaisance, ready to burst into full blossom to anyone who should address him. The rubbish he would then talk to ladies had a certain grace about it. Hester was absolutely astonished once to overhear some of it, and it set her wondering which reflected the real Cornelius, the seamy side turned always to his own people, or the silken flowers and arabesques presented to strangers. Among them, he said little or nothing, but uttered it pleasantly. The slouch, the hand-in-pocket mood—those flying signals that self was home to nobody but himself—for the time vanished. By keeping in the protective shadow of fashion, he always managed to be well dressed. Ever since he took the same tailor as Vavasor, his coats had been irreproachable; his shirt studs were single pearls, and he was very particular about both the quantity and quality of the linen showing beyond his coat cuffs.

Among the gifts which Cornelius was too tender to exhibit at home was a certain very small one of song. His home circle did not know he possessed it—and the thought was pleasant to him, for all his life he had loved concealment. He never came out with anything at home as to where he had been or what he was going to do or had done. He gloried especially in the thought that he did this or that of which his family knew not his capabili-

47

ty. He felt large and powerful and wise in consequence!

He had now been some eighteen months in the bank, and from the first, Vavasor had been taken with the easy manners of the youth and the evident worship of himself. He had patronized and allowed the young cub to enter by degrees the charmed circle of his favor. Gathering a certain liking for him, he occasionally made him a companion for the evening, and sometimes took him home with him. There Cornelius at once laid himself out to please Vavasor's aunt—and flattery went far with her, because she had begun to suspect herself no longer young or beautiful. Her house was a dingy little hut in Mayfair, full of worthless pictures and fine, old-fashioned furniture. Any piece of this she would at one time gladly have exchanged for new fashion; but as soon as she found such things themselves the fashion, she professed an unchangeable preference for them over any modern things. Cornelius soon learned what he must admire and despise if he would be in tune with Miss Vavasor.

From Miss Vavasor's he had been invited to several other houses, and he soon looked from an ever growing height upon his own people, judging not one of them fit for the grand company to which his merits, unappreciated at home, had introduced him. With the help of a few private lessons, a certain natural grace, and some facility of imitation, he was soon able to dance excellently, and sing with more or less dullness a few fashionable songs.

All this was one of his most precious secrets; none of his family had even heard of Vavasor before the encounter at the aquarium. Cornelius was astonished and a little annoyed at the favorable impression made by his family upon Vavasor. Nor did he conceal his opinion of his own people, feeling himself superior to Vavasor in this one regard. For what was it but superiority, to be able to look down where Vavasor looked up?

"My mother's the best of the lot," Cornelius said, "but she's nobody except at home. Look at her and your aunt together! Pooh! Because she's my mother, that's no reason why I should think her royalty!"

Vavasor straightway read him a lecture—well-meant and shallow—on what was good form in a woman. According to him, both she and Hester possessed such qualities in eminent degrees. Cornelius continued his opposition, but modified it, and began to think more of both women.

"She's a very good girl, of her sort," he said. " But she's too awfully serious—you haven't an idea! One half hour of one of her moods is enough to destroy a poor beggar's peace of mind forever. And there's no saying when the fit may take her."

Vavasor laughed, but said to himself there was stuff in her. What a woman might be made of her! To him she seemed fit— with a little development—to grace the best society. It was not polish she needed, but experience and insight, thought Vavasor, conceiving the ambition of having a hand in her worldly education. Through him she should come to shine as she deserved in the only circle he thought worth one's while. Through his aunt he could gain entrance where he pleased; in relation to her and her people he seemed to himself a man of power and influence.

Hester took to Vavasor from the first. His bearing was dignified, yet his manner was so pleasing that he roused none of that inclination to oppose which poor foolish Corney always roused in her. He could talk well about music and pictures and novels and plays, and she not only let him talk freely, but put a favorable interpretation upon things he said, trying to see humor where another might have found heartlessness or cynicism.

Vavasor, in his own eyes the model of an honorable gentleman, had only the world's way of judging things. Had he been a man of fortune he would have given to charities with some freedom, but he would not have denied himself the smallest luxury for the highest betterment of a human soul. He would give a half-worn pair of gloves to a poor woman in the street, but not the price of the new pair he was on his way to buy.

It would have enlightened Hester to watch him where he stood behind the counter of the bank. There he was the least courteous of proverbially discourteous bank clerks, treating those of his same social position in precisely the same way as less distinguished callers. But he never forgot to take up his manners with his umbrella as he left, along with his airy, cheerful way of talking, which was more natural to him than his rudeness.

Hester suspected he was not profound, but that was no reason why she should not be pleasant to him. So by the time Vavasor had spent three evenings with the Raymounts, Hester and he were on a standing of external intimacy.

Chapter 9.

SONGS AND SINGERS

The evening before the return of Cornelius from Burcliff to London and the durance vile of the bank, Vavasor presented himself for the Raymount family tea. There was a tolerably good piano in their rented drawing room, and Hester generally took to it after tea. But this time Cornelius walked up to it, dropped down on the piano seat, and began running his hands over the keys as if he could play if he would. Amy was taking away the tea things, and the rest were scattered about the room. Mr. Raymount and Vavasor were talking on the hearthrug for a moment before the former withdrew to his study.

"What a rose-diamond you have to wait on you, Mr. Raymount!" said Vavasor. "If I were a painter, I would have her sit for me."

"And ruin the poor thing for any life-sitting!" remarked Mr. Raymount rather gruffly, for he found that the easier way of speaking the truth. He saw some truths clearly, but used them blunderingly.

"I don't see why that should follow," said Vavasor in a softly drawling tone, the very reverse of his host's. Its calmness gave the impression of wisdom behind it. "If the girl is handsome, why shouldn't she derive some advantage from it—and the rest of the world as well?"

"Because she at least would derive only ruin. She would immediately assume to herself the credit of what was offered only to her beauty. It takes a lifetime, Mr. Vavasor, to learn where to pay our taxes. If the penny with the image and super-

50

scription of Caesar has to be paid to Caesar, where has a face and figure like Amy's to be paid?"

Vavasor did not reply, concluding that his host was talking rubbish. Amy came in again, and the conversation dropped. Mr. Raymount went to his writing, Vavasor toward the piano, willing to please Cornelius now that he had proved brother to such a sister as Hester.

"Sing the song you gave us the other night at our house," he said carelessly.

Hester could hardly credit her hearing, and was still more astonished when Cornelius actually struck a few chords and began to sing. The song was a common drawing room song, with the one mercy that the words and music went together in a perfect concord of weak worthlessness. But it remained a song written by a would-be poet, and set by a would-be musician, and Cornelius sang it like a would-be singer. When the song died a natural death, if that be possible where there never had been any life, Vavasor said, "Thank you, Raymount." But Hester, who had been standing with her teeth clenched under the fiery rain of discords, wrong notes, and dislocated rhythm, rushed to the piano with glowing cheeks and tear-filled eyes, and pushed Cornelius off the stool.

"Corney!" she cried. "You disgrace yourself! Anyone who can sing at all should be ashamed to sing no better than that!" Then, feeling that she ought not to be carried away, or quench with a fierce lack of sympathy the smoking flax of any endowment, she threw her arms around his neck and kissed him. He received her embrace like the bear he was, and looked appealingly at Vavasor as if to say, "You see how the women use me! They trouble me, but I submit!"

"You never let me suspect you could sing any more than a frog!" Hester went on, speaking excitedly and rapidly. "Or a toad, I mean, because a frog does sing a bit, and you don't sing much better! Listen to me, and I will show you how the song ought to be sung. It's not worth a straw, and it's a shame to sing it; but if it be sung at all, it might as well be sung well!"

This convulsion was new to Hester—never before had she been beside herself in the presence of another. She seated herself at the piano and began. The effect of her singing upon the song was as if the few poor shivering plants in the garden of

51

March had every one blossomed at once. Hester lay hold of what little meaning and sweetness was in the song, drew it out, made the best of it, and made a wholly new song of it. But the moment she ended, she rose ashamed, went to the window, and looked out over the darkening sea.

Vavasor had not heard her sing before, and did not even know that she cared for music. Hester did not regard her faculty as an accomplishment but as a gift, and treated it as a treasure to be hidden for the Day of the Lord rather than a flag to be flaunted in a civic procession. She was jealously shy over it, as a thing it would profane to show to any but loving eyes. To utter herself in song to any but the right persons, except indeed it was for some further and higher end justifying the sacrifice, appeared to her a kind of immodesty. Vavasor was astonished and yet more delighted. He was in the presence of a power! But all he knew of power was in society relations. It was not a spirit of might he recognized for the opening of minds and the strengthening of hearts, but an influence of pleasing and self-aggrandizement. Feeling it upon himself, he thought of it operating upon others, and was filled with a respect rising almost to the height of reverence. He followed her swiftly to the window, and through the gathering evening shadows she saw his eyes shine as he addressed her.

"I hardly know what I am about, Miss Raymount," he said, "except that I hear my own voice daring to address the finest nonprofessional singer I have ever heard."

Hester, to her own disgust and annoyance, felt her head give itself a toss she had never intended. She neither liked attracting his admiration by such a song, nor the stress he laid on the word *nonprofessional.*

"Excuse me, Mr. Vavasor, but how do you know I am not a professional singer?" she said with some haughtiness.

"All London would have known if you were."

This reply soothed Hester's vanity.

Then Cornelius appeared at the window. "Come, Hetty," he said, "sing that again! I shall sing it so much better after! Come, I will play the accompaniment!"

"It's not worth singing. It would choke me—poor, vapid, vulgar thing!"

"Hullo, sis! It's hardly civil to use such words about any song a

52

fellow cares to sing!"

Hester's sole answer was a smile in which Vavasor read the contempt—but he liked her none the worse for it. Cornelius turned back to the piano in offense and sang the song again, but not one hair better. How shall one who has no soul put soul into a song?

Mrs. Raymount was sitting at the fireside with her embroidery. She called Hester and said to her quietly, "Don't provoke him, Hester. I am more than delighted to find he has begun to take an interest in music. It is a taste that will grow upon him. Coax him to let you teach him—and bear with him if he sings out of tune. It is nothing wicked!" she added with a mother's smile.

Hester was silent, her conscience rebuking her more than her heart. She went up to Cornelius and said, "Corney, dear, let me find you a song worth singing."

"A girl can't choose for a man. You're sure to fix on some sentimental stuff or other not fit to sing!"

"My goodness, Corney! What do you call the song you've just been singing? 'In the days when my heart was aching like the shell of an overturned lyre.'"

She laughed prettily at it, struck an attitude of the mock heroic, and added on the spur of the moment, " 'And the oven was burning, not baking, the tarts of my soul's desire!' " For at that moment fumes had come storming up from the kitchen, as if a door had suddenly been opened in yet lower regions. Cornelius was too offended and self-occupied to be amused, but both Mrs. Raymount and Vavasor laughed, the latter recognizing in Hester's extemporization a vein similar to his own.

But Hester already had a song to her mind—one that was fit for Cornelius. "Come now, Corney. Here is a song I should like you to be able to sing!"

She turned to the keys and sang a spirited ballad of a battle between two knights. Vavasor was utterly enchanted, but too world-eaten to recognize the soul she almost waked in him for any other than the old one. Hester sang the last lines and rose at once, her mouth set, and her eyes gleaming, Vavasor felt *almost* as if he would have fallen down to kiss the hem of her garment, but she walked from the room, vexed with the emotion she was unable to control, and did not again appear.

The best thing in Vavasor was his love of music. He had cultivated what little gift he had, but did not really believe in music—did not really believe in anything except himself. He professed to adore it, but his greatest pleasure lay in hearing his own verse well sung by a pretty girl who would steal a glance at the poet from under her eyelids as she sang.

On his way home he brooded over the delight of having his best songs sung by such a singer as Hester; and from that night fancied he had received a new revelation of what music was and could do, confessing to himself that a similar experience in the next fortnight would send him head over heels in love with Hester—which must not be!

He went as often to the Raymounts' lodging as he dared—all but every night. But he was careful not to bring any of his own slight, windy, leaf-blowing songs under Hester's notice. He did not think them such, but he judged it prudent to postpone the pleasure; she would require no small amount of training before she could quite enter into the spirit and special merit of them!

In the meantime he knew a good song sometimes when he saw it, and always when he heard her sing it, and never actually displeased her with any he did bring to her notice. He had himself a very tolerable voice, and was capable of managing it with taste and judgment. By a scale of very natural degrees, he found himself, to his satisfaction, a pupil to Hester. She in turn gave herself a good deal of trouble to improve the quality of his singing. The relation between them, had it lasted, might have soon led to something like genuine intimacy, or at least revealed to each one what kind of being the other was.

But the day of separation arrived first, and it was only on his way back to London that Vavasor discovered what hold she had taken of his thoughts and his heart—an organ of which he had not previously had any convincing proof.

All the time at Burcliff, though, he had not once brought his aunt and the Raymounts together.

Chapter 10

HESTER AND AMY

Hester did not miss Vavasor quite so much as he hoped she might. She had been interested in him mainly because she found him both receptive and capable of development in the matter of music—ready to understand and willing to be taught. To have such a man listen with respect to every word she said, never denying, defending, or justifying what she might point out as fault, but setting himself at once to the correction of the same, and with some measure of immediate success, could not fail to be flattering to her.

Vavasor did not move the deepest in Hester. How should he? With that deepest he had no developed relation. There were worlds of thought and feeling already in motion in Hester's universe, while the vaporous mass in him had hardly yet begun to stir.

When Vavasor was gone she turned with greater diligence to her musical studies. Amy Amber continued devoted to her, and when she was practicing would hover about her. Her singing especially seemed to enchant and fascinate the girl, but the shadow of unseen cloud was occasionally visible on Amy's forehead, and unmistakable pools were left in her eyes by the ebbtide of tears. She was no less willing or cheerful in her service, yet she moved about her work with less elasticity, and the smile did not come so quickly. Both Hester and her mother saw the change, and marked even an occasional frown. In the morning, when she was always the first up, she was generally cheerful, but as the day passed the clouds came. Happily, however, her diligence did not relax. Sound in health, and by nature as active as cheerful, she took a positive delight in her work. Doing was to her as natural as singing to the birds. In a household with truth at the heart of it she would have been invaluable, and happy as the day was long. As it was, she was growing daily less and less happy.

One night she appeared in Hester's room as usual before going to bed. The small, neat face had lost for the time a great part of its beauty, and was dark as a little thundercloud. Her black, shadowy brows were drawn together over her luminous black eyes; her red lips were large and pouting, and their likeness to a rosebud gone. Her cheeks were swollen, and its whole aspect revealed the spirit of wrath roused at last, and the fire alight in the furnace of the bosom. She tried to smile, but what came was the smile of a wound rather than a mouth.

"My poor Amy! What is the matter?" cried Hester, sorry, but hardly surprised.

The girl burst into a passionate fit of weeping. She threw herself in wild abandonment on the floor and sobbed; then, as if to keep herself from screaming aloud, she stuffed her handkerchief into her mouth, kicked with her little feet, and beat her little hands on the floor. She was like a child in a paroxysm of rage—only that with her its extravagance came of the effort to overcome it.

Then she ceased suddenly, and sitting up on the floor, her legs doubled under her in eastern fashion, looked straight at Hester, and said thoughtfully as if the question had just come, with force to make her forget the suffering she was in, "I should like to know how you would do in my place—that I should, miss!"

"I am afraid, if I were in your place, I should do nothing so well as you, Amy," said Hester. "But come, tell me what is the matter. What puts you in such a misery?"

"Oh, it's not one thing nor two things nor twenty things!" answered Amy, looking sullen with the feeling of heaped-up wrong. "What would my mother say to see me served so! *She* used to trust me everywhere and always! I don't understand how those two prying suspicious old maids can be my relatives!"

"Don't they behave well to you?" asked Hester.

"It's not that they watch every bit I put in my mouth—I don't complain of that, for they're poor—but not to be trusted one moment out of their sight except they know exactly where I am—to be always suspected, and followed and watched, and me working my hardest—that's what drives me wild, Miss Raymount. I'm afraid they'll make me hate them out and out! I bore it very well for a while, for at first it only amused me. But they only grew worse, and I got tired of it altogether; and when I got tired of it, I got cross, till now I can't bear it. I'm not used to being cross, and my own crossness is much harder to bear than theirs. If I could have kept the good temper people used to praise me for to my mother, I shouldn't mind, but it is hard to lose it this way! I don't know how to get on without it. If there don't come a change somehow soon, I shall run away—I shall indeed, Miss Raymount. There are many would be glad enough to have me for the work I can get through."

She jumped to her feet, gave a little laugh, merry-sad, and before Hester could answer her, said, "You're going away so soon, miss! Let me do your hair tonight. I want to brush it every night till you go. It will rest me, and bring back my good temper. It will come to me again through your hair, miss."

"No, no, Amy," said Hester, a little conscience-stricken, "you can't have any of mine. I have none to spare. You will rather brush some into me, Amy. But do what you like with my hair."

As Amy lovingly combed and brushed the long, wavy overflow of Hester's beauty, Hester tried to make her understand that she must not think of good temper and crossness merely as things that could be put into her and taken out of her. She tried to make her see that nothing really our own can ever be taken from us by any will or behavior of another; that Amy had had a large supply of good temper laid ready to her hand, but that it was not hers until she had made it her own by choosing and willing to be good-tempered when she was disinclined—holding it fast with the hand of determination when the hand of wrong would snatch it from her.

"Because I have a book on my shelves," Hester said, "it is not therefore mine; when I have read and understood it, then it is a little mine; when I love it and do what it tells me, then it is altogether mine. It is like that with a good temper. If you have it sometimes and other times not, then it is not yours; it lies in you like that book on my table—a thing priceless were it your own, but as it is, a thing you can't keep even against your poor weak old aunts."

As she said this, Hester felt like a hypocrite, remembering her own sins. Amy listened quietly, brushing steadily all the time, but scarcely a shadow of Hester's meaning crossed her mind. If she was in a good temper, she was in a good temper; if she was in a bad temper, why there she was, she and her temper! She had not a notion that she was in any manner or measure accountable in regard to the temper she might find herself in. Could she have been persuaded to attempt to overcome it, the moment she failed, as of course everyone will many times, Amy would have concluded the thing required an impossibility. Yet the successful effort she made to restrain the show of her anger was far from slight. But for this, there would, long ere now, have been rain and wind, thunder and lightning between her and her aunts. She was alive without the law, not knowing what mental conflict was; the moment she recognized that she was bound to conquer herself, she would die in conscious helplessness, until strength and hope were given her from the well of the one pure will.

Although she had not understood Hester, Amy went to bed a little comforted. When the Raymounts departed Burcliff for London two or three days after, they left Amy at the top of the cliff-stair, weeping bitterly.

Chapter 11.

AT HOME

When the Raymounts reached London, Hester went directly to see her music mistress, and arranged for renewed lessons.

Miss Dasomma was one of God's angels; for if He makes His angels winds, and His ministers a flaming fire, much more are those live fountains which carry His gifts to their thirsting fellows His angels. Of Italian descent, English birth, and German training, her enthusiasm for her art was mainly the outcome of her own genius. Hence it was natural that she should exercise a forming influence on every pupil, and without her Hester could never have become what she was. For not merely had she opened her eyes to a vision of Music in something of her essential glory, but had taught her the necessity of labor.

Without Miss Dasomma, Hester would not have learned that at the root of all ease lies slow and seemingly profitless labor; as at the root of all grace lies strength; that ease is the lovely result of forgotten toil, sunk into the spirit and making it strong and ready; that never worthy improvisation flowed from brain of poet or musician unused to perfect his work with honest labor.

The Raymounts had not been home more than a week when one Sunday afternoon, Mr. Vavasor called—which was not quite agreeable to Mrs. Raymount, who liked their Sundays kept quiet. He was shown to Mr. Raymount's study.

"I am sorry," he said, "to call on a Sunday, but I am not so enviably situated as you, Mr. Raymount—I have not my time at my command. When other people make their calls, I am a prisoner." He spoke as if his were an exceptional case, and the whole happy world reveled in morning calls.

Mr. Raymount was pleased with him afresh, for he spoke modestly, with implicit acknowledgment of the superior position of the elder man. They fell to talking of the prominent question of the day, and Mr. Raymount was yet more pleased when he found the young aristocrat ready to receive enlightenment upon it. But the fact was that Vavasor had a facility for following where he was led, always preferring to make himself agreeable where there was no restraining reason. He had a light, easy way of touching on things, thus making himself appear master of the situation over which he merely skimmed on insect wing. Mr. Raymount took him not merely for a man of thought but one capable of forming an opinion of his own.

In relation to the wider circle of the country, Mr. Vavasor was so entirely a nobody that the acquaintance of a writer even so partially known as Mr. Raymount was something to him. Since his return Vavasor had instituted inquiries concerning Mr. Raymount, and finding both him and his family in good repute, he had told his aunt as much concerning them as he judged prudent, hinting it would give him pleasure if she should see fit to call upon Mrs. Raymount. Miss Vavasor, being naturally jealous of the judgment of young men, pledged herself to nothing, and made inquiries for herself. Learning that there was rather a distinguished-looking girl in the family, and having her own ideas for the nephew whose interests she had—for the sake of the impending title—made her own, she delayed and put off and talked the thing over, and at last let it rest. Vavasor went the oftener to see the people she thus declined calling upon.

On this his first London visit, he stayed the evening, and was afresh installed as a friend of the family. Although it was Sunday, and her ideas also a little strict as to religious proprieties, Hester received him cordially where her mother received him but kindly. Falling into the old ways, he took his part in the hymns, anthems, and what other forms of sacred music followed the family tea, and so the evening passed without irksomeness.

The tone, expression, and power of Hester's voice astonished Vavasor afresh. He was convinced, and told her so, that even in the short time since he heard it last, it had improved in all directions. And when, after they had had enough of singing, she sat down and extemporized in a sacred strain, weaving holy airs into the unrolling web of her own thought, Vavasor was so moved as to feel more kindly disposed toward religion—by which he meant "going to church, and all that sort of thing." He did not call the next Sunday, but came on the Saturday; and the only one present who was not pleased to see him was Miss Dasomma, who happened also to spend the evening there.

Miss Dasomma had for many years been a power for good as well as for music. Much too generous and helpful to have saved money, she was now, in middle age, working as hard as she had ever worked in her youth. Not a little experienced in the ways of the world, and possessing a high ideal in the memories of a precious friendship, she did not find her atmosphere gladdened by the presence of Mr. Vavasor. With tact enough to take his cue from the family, he treated her with studious politeness; but Miss Dasomma did not like Mr. Vavasor. She had to think before she could tell why, for there is a spiritual instinct also, which often takes the lead of the understanding, and has to search and analyze itself for its explanation. But in the shadow of a curtain, while Hester was playing, she watched his countenance, trying to read in it what the owner of the face never meant to write.

Miss Dasomma concluded that Vavasor was a man of good instincts but without moral development, pleased with himself and not undesirous of pleasing others, consistent with his idea of dignity, and at present more than moderately desirous of pleasing Hester Raymount, therefore showing to the best possible advantage. "But," thought Miss Dasomma, "if this be his best, what may not his worst be?" That he had no small capacity for music was plain; but if, as she judged, the faculty was unassociated in him with truth of nature, that only rather rendered him the more dangerous. For, at Hester's feet in the rare atmosphere and faint twilight of music, how could he fail to impress her with an opinion of himself more favorable than just? To interfere without solid grounds would be to waste the power that might be of use; but she was confident that if Hester once saw him as she did, she could no more look on him with favor. At the same time she did not think he could be meaning more than the mere passing of his time agreeably; she knew well the character of his aunt, and the relation in which he stood to her. In any case, she could for the present only keep a gentle watch over her pupil.

Chapter 12.

ACROBATS IN THE ATTIC

The Raymounts lived in a somewhat peculiar house in an old square in dingy, convenient, healthy Bloomsbury. On two sides it was closely pressed by poor neighbors—artisans, small tradespeople, outdoor servants, poor actors and actresses lived in the narrow branching streets. Hence Hester had grown up with none of that uncomfortable feeling so many have when brought into such mere contact with the poor as walking through their streets. Such a feeling is often in part composed of fear, often in part of a false sense of natural superiority, born of being better dressed, better housed, and better educated. From childhood used to the sight of such, her sympathies were soon and thoroughly wakened on the side of suffering humanity.

Those who would do good to the poor must attempt it in the way in which best they could do good to people of their own standing. They must make their acquaintance first. They must know something of the kind of the person they would help, and to learn if help be possible from their hands. Only man can help man; money without man can do little or nothing, and most likely less than nothing. As our Lord redeemed the world by being a man, the true Son of the true Father, so the only way for a man to help men is to be a true man to this neighbor and that.

And the only way to learn the rules of anything practical is to begin to do the thing. The sole way to deal with the profoundest mystery that is yet not too profound to draw us, is to begin to do some duty revealed by the light from the golden fringe of its cloudy vastness. Let every simplest relation toward a human being, if it be the act of buying a reel of cotton or a knife, be recognized as a relation with that human soul. In its poor degree, let its outcome be in truth and friendliness. Allow nature her course, and next time let the relation go further. To follow such a path is the way to find both the persons to help and the real modes of helping them. In fact, to be true to a man in any way is to help him. He who goes out of common paths to look for opportunity leaves his own door and misses that of his neighbor. It is by following the path we are in that we shall first reach somewhere. He who would be a neighbor, where a neighbor may be wanted, must cultivate the acquaintance of his neighbors. So shall he fulfill the part left behind of the work of the Master, which He desires to finish through him.

Hester had no such theory toward the poor, neither confined her hope of helping to them only. There are as many in every other class needing help as among the poor, and the need, although it wears different dress, is essentially the same in all. To make the light go on in the heart of a rich man, if a more difficult task, is just as good a deed as to make it go on in the heart of a poor man. But with her strong desire to carry help where it was needed, with her genuine feeling of the blood relationship of all human beings, with her instinctive sense that one could never begin too soon to do that which had to be done, she was in the right position to begin—and from such a one opportunity will not be withheld.

She went one morning into a small shop in Steeven's Road, to buy a few sheets of music paper from her acquaintance, Mrs. Baldwin. In the course of their talk, the clerk mentioned that she was in some anxiety about a woman in the house who was far from well, and in whom she thought Hester's mother would be interested.

"Mama is always ready," said Hester, "to help where she can. Tell me about her."

"Well, you see, miss," replied Mrs. Baldwin, "we're not in the way of having to do with such people, for my husband's rather particular about who he lets the top rooms to, only let them we must to one or another, for times is hard an' children is many, an' it's all as we can do to pay our way an' nothing over—only thank God we've done it up to this present—an' they looked so decent that I hadn't the heart to send them away on such a night as it was, bein' sort o' drizzly an' as cold as charity, an' the poor woman seekin' a decent place to lay her head. They had three children with them, the smallest o' them pickaback on the biggest, an' it's strange, miss, how it goes to yer heart to see one human bein' lookin' arter another! But my husban' was shy o' children, for children, you know, miss, 'cep' they be yer own, ain't nice things about a house, an' them poor ragged things wouldn't be no credit nowheres, only they were pretty clean, as poor children go, an' there was nothing in the top rooms as they could do much harm to. The man said theirs weren't like other children, for they had been brought up to do the things as they were told, an' to remember that things that belonged to other people were to be handled as sich—an', said he, they were always too busy earnin' their bread an' too tired to have much spare powder to let off, so we took 'em in, an' they've turned out quiet an' well-behaved, an' if they ain't got jest the most respectable way o' earnin' their livelihood, that may be as much their misfortin as their fault, though. I never could rightly understand what made one thing respectable an' another not."

"What is their employment then?" asked Hester.

"Something or other in the circus way. They didn't seem to have no engagement when they come to the door, but they paid the first week down afore they entered. You see, miss, the poor woman—she reminded me of my Susie, as I lost a year ago—it made me hate the thought of sending her away. Miss, ain't it a mercy everybody ain't so like your own! We'd have to ruin ourselves for them—we couldn't help it!"

"It will come to that one day though," said Hester to herself, "and then we shan't be ruined either."

"So then," Mrs. Baldwin went on, "the very next day the doctor had to be sent for, an' there was a baby! The doctor he come from the hospital, as nice a gentleman as you'd wish to see, miss, an' waited on her as if she'd been the first duchess in the land. 'I'm sure,' said my good husban' to me, 'it's a lesson to all of us to see how he do look after her as'll never pay him a penny!' An' now the poor thing's not at all strong, an' ain't a-gettin' back of her stren'th though we do what we can with her, an' send her up what we can spare.

"I fancy it's more from anxiety as to what's to come to them, than that anything's gone wrong with her. They're not out o' money yet quite, I'm glad to say, though he don't seem to ha' got nothing to do yet. That sort o' trade, ye see, miss, the demand's not steady in it. It's not like skilled labor, though it's labor enough an' to spare—an' if it ain't just what they call skilled, it's what no one out o' the trade can make a mark at. Would you mind goin' up an' having a look at her, miss?"

Hester followed her up the stairs. The top rooms were two poor garret ones. In the largest, the ceiling sloped to the floor till there was but just height enough left for the small chest of drawers of painted deal to stand back to the wall. A similar washstand and a low bed completed the furniture. On the bed lay the woman, with a thin petticoat and threadbare cloak under her head. Hester saw a pale, patient, worn face, with eyes large, thoughtful, and troubled.

"Here's a kind lady come to see you, Mrs. Franks," said her landlady.

This speech annoyed Hester. She hated to be called kind, and perhaps spoke the more kindly to the poor woman that she was displeased with Mrs. Baldwin's patronizing.

"It's dreary for you to lie here alone, I'm afraid," she said, and stroked the thin hand on the coverlet. "May I sit a few minutes beside you? I was once in bed for a whole month, and found it very wearisome. I was at school then. I don't mind being ill when I have my mother."

The woman gazed up at her with eyes that looked like the dry wells of tears. "It's very kind of you, miss," she said. "It's a long stair to come up." She lay and gazed, and said nothing more. Her life was of a negative sort just at present. Her child lay asleep on her arm, a poor little washed-out rag of humanity.

Hester sat down and tried to talk, but found it hard. Religion she could not talk offhand without feeling like a hypocrite. For she found herself speaking so of the things she fed on in her heart as to make them look to herself the merest commonplaces in the world!

A dead silence came. "What can be the good of a common creature like me going to visit people?" she asked herself. "I have nothing to say—I feel nothing in me but a dull love that would bless her if I could!"

Just before the silence became unendurable, the baby woke and began to whimper. The mother drew him to her, and began to nurse him. Hester's heart was pierced to the quick at how ill-fitted was the mother for what she had to do. "Can God be love?" she said to herself. "If I could help her! It will go on like this for weeks and months, I suppose."

The baby did not complain against the slow fountain of his life, but made the best he could of it, while his mother every now and then peered down on him lovingly. The same God is at the heart of all mothers, and all sins against children are against the one Father of children.

Then Hester began to sing low and softly, taking a common hymn and putting into it as much sweetness and smoothing strength as she could. With a trembling voice she sang, and never before had she been so anxious for some measure of success. Not daring to look up, she sat like one rebuked, with the music flowing over her lips like the slow water from some stone fountain. She had her reward; when the hymn was done, and she ventured to raise her eyes, she saw both mother and babe fast asleep. Her heart ascended on a wave of thanks to the Giver of song. She rose softly, crept from the house, and hastened home to tell her mother what she had heard and seen.

The same afternoon a basket of nice things arrived at the shop for the poor lodger. The care of the Raymounts did not relax till she was fairly on her feet again; neither till then did a day pass on which Hester did not see her, and scarcely one on which she did not sing to her and her baby. Of the father she had seen next to nothing. On the few occasions when he happened to be at home, the moment she entered he crept out with a shy, humble salutation, as if ashamed of himself. He was a man of middle height, with a strong face and frame, dressed like a workman. His three boys followed him from the room, and seemed to imitate his salutation as they passed her—all but the youngest, who made her a profound bow accompanied by a wonderful smile. The eldest was about twelve, the youngest about seven. They were rather sickly looking, but had intelligent faces and inoffensive expressions.

Chapter 13.

A PRIVATE EXHIBITION

Hester had not been near the Frankses for two or three days. It was getting dusk now, but she would just run across the square and down the street, and look in upon them. Tomorrow was Sunday, and she felt as if she could not go to church without having seen the little flock committed in some measure to her charge. Not that she imagined anything exclusive in her relation to them, for she had already begun to see that we have to take care of those *parts* of each other which we can best help. From the ambition to lord it over individuals have arisen worse evils perhaps than from a wider love of empire. When a man desires personal influence or power over anyone, he is of the thieves and robbers who enter not in by the door. But the right and privilege of ministering belongs to anyone who has the grace to claim it and be a fellow-worker with God.

But when she knocked on and opened the door, she hesitated. The bed was pushed to the back of the room, and the floor was empty except for a cushion or two lying in the middle. The father and the three boys stood together near the fire, like gentlemen on the hearthrug expecting visitors. And a man was bending over the bed in the far corner. Could it be the doctor again? The father pulled off the cap he invariably wore, and came forward with bashful courtesy.

"I hope your wife is not worse," said Hester.

"No, miss, I hope not. She's took a bit bad. We can't always avoid it in our profession, miss."

"I don't understand you," she answered, feeling uneasy. Were there new horrors to be revealed?

"If you will do us the honor to take a seat, miss, we shall only be too happy to show you as much as you may please to look upon with favor."

Hester shuddered, but mastered herself. Mr. Franks saw her hesitate, and resumed. "Dr. Christopher—the gentleman there—he's been that kind to her an' me an' all on us in our trouble, an' never a crownpiece to offer him. So we thought we'd do our best for him, an' try an' give him a pleasant evenin', just to show as we was grateful. So we axed him to tea, an' he come, like the gentleman he be, an' so we shoved the bed aside an' was showin' him a trick or two on our craft, miss—me an' the boys here—stan' forward, Robert and the rest of you an' make your bows to the distinguished company as honors you with their presence to cast an eye on you an' see what you can show yourselves capable of."

Here Dr. Christopher turned and approached them, saying, "She'll be all right in a minute or two, Franks."

"You told her, doctor, the boy ain't got the smallest hurt? It 'ud break my heart nigh as soon as hers to see the Sarpint come to grief. She knows well enough, only, you see, we can't always help letting the looks of things get a hold of us in spite of the facts. But I think for the present it will be better to drop it."

Franks turned to Hester to explain. "One of the boys, miss— that's him—not much of him—the young Sarpint of the Prairie, we call him in the trade—he don't seem to ha' much amiss with him, do he now? He had a bit of a fall on them pads a few minutes ago, the more shame to the Sarpint, the rascal!" Here he pretended to hit the Sarpint, who never moved a coil in consequence, only smiled. "But he ain't the worse, never a hair—or a scale I should say. Bless you, we all knows how to fall as well's how to get up again! Only it's the most remarkable thing, though she's been married fourteen years come next Candlemas, she's not got used to seein' the children, her own flesh and blood, that's them boys, miss, a standin' on my head, or it might be one on my head an' the other two on my shoulders. She can't abide it, miss. By some strange delusion, she takes me for about the height of St. Paul's, which if you was to fall off the dome, you might break your neck an' a few bones besides, miss. But bless you, there ain't no danger, only, as the doctor says, she can't abide the look o' the thing. But as the doctor thinks it better to drop it, it's drop it we will till a more convenient time when mother's a bit stronger."

Hester was astonished at this unaccustomed outpouring, but the naturally reticent Franks was emboldened by the presence of the doctor. However, the moment his wife heard him give up thus their little private exhibition in honor of the doctor, she raised herself on her elbow.

"Now, you'll do no such thing, John Franks!" she said with effort. "It's ill it would become me, for my whims to prevent you from showin' sich a small attention to the gentleman as helped me through my trouble—God bless him, for it can't be no pleasure! So I'm not agoin' to put on no airs as if I was a fine lady. I've got to get used to't—only I'm slow at it!" she added with a sigh. "Up you go, Moxy!"

Franks looked at the doctor, who nodded his head as much as to say, "You had better do as she wishes," but Hester saw that the eyes of the young doctor were more watchful of the woman than of the performance.

Immediately Franks, with a stage bow, offered Hester a chair. She sat down, and for the first time in her life became a spectator of the feats of a family of acrobats.

All of them were astonishingly proficient, the obvious fruit of much training and persistence. She believed this proficiency bore strong witness to some kind of moral excellence in them, and that theirs might well be a nobler way of life than many in which money is made more rapidly, and which are regarded as more respectable. There were but two things in the performance she found painful: one, that the youngest seemed hardly equal to the physical effort required. He had not mastered all the tricks, and it was very plain this was the chief source of trial to the mother. He was a sweet-looking boy, with a pale interesting face, bent on learning his part, but finding it difficult. The other thing was that the moment they began to perform, the manner of the father toward his children changed—his appearance and the very quality of his voice—so that he seemed hardly the same man. Just as some men alter their tone and speak roughly when they address a horse, so Franks now assumed the tyrant and spoke in a voice between the bark of a dog and the growl of a brown bear. Though the roughness had in it nothing cruel, he ordered his boys about with fierce sternness, swore at them occasionally, and made Hester feel very uncomfortable.

"Come, come, Franks!" said Dr. Christopher, on one of these outbreaks.

The man stood silent for a moment, turned to Miss Raymount first, and next to his wife, and said, taking off his cap, "I humbly beg your pardon, ladies. I forgot what company I was in. But bless you, I mean nothing by it! It's only my way, ain't it now, mates—you as knows the old man, and don't mind?"

"Yes, father. 'Tain't nothin' more'n a way you've got, and we don't mind," responded the boys, the little one loudest.

"But," said Franks, with an imprecation, "if ever I hear one o' you a usin' of sich improper words, I'll break every bone in his carcass."

"Yes, father," answered the boys with one accord.

"It's all very well for fathers," he went on, "an' when you're fathers yourselves, an' able to thrash me—not as I think you'd want to, kids, I sha'nt ha' no call to meddle with you. So here goes!"

Casting a timid glance at Hester, in the assurance that he had set himself right with her, he resumed.

As to breaking the boys' bones, there hardly seemed any bones in them to break, so wonderful were their feats, and their pranks so strange. They were evidently anxious to please, and their glances were full of question as to their success in making their offering acceptable. Their bodies seemed mere rubber in response to their wills. A strangely mingled touch of pathos appeared in the occasional suffering it caused Moxy, the youngest, to do as his father required, but oftener in the incongruity between the lovely natural expression of the boy's face, and the oddity of it when it had to grin like a demon. Hester found its sweet innocence, and the veil of suffering cast over its best grin, almost discordantly pathetic. The gentle suffering face seemed far from its own sphere, that of a stray angel come to give her a lesson in the heavenly patience. His mother, whose yellow hair and clear gray eyes were just like his, covered her eyes with her hand every time he had to do anything by himself.

All at once the master of ceremonies drew himself up, wiped his forehead, and gave a deep sigh, as much as to say, "I have done my best, and if I have not pleased you, the more is my loss, for I have tried hard," and the performance was over.

The doctor rose, and in a manly voice more pleasing to Hester than his unappealing look, proceeded to point out to Franks one or two precautions which his knowledge of anatomy enabled him to suggest, and with special regard to little Moxy. At the same time he expressed himself greatly pleased with what his host had so kindly shown him, remarking that the power to do such things implied labor more continuous and severe than would have sufficed to the learning of two or three trades.

Franks, mistaking the drift of the remark, and supposing the doctor counted it a waste of labor, replied in a sad tone, "What's a fellow to do, sir, when he 'ain't got no dinner? He must take to the work that takes to him. There was no other trade handy for me. My father was a poor laborer, an' died early, o' hard work an' many mouths. My mother lived but a year after him an' I had to do for the kids whatever came first to hand. There was two on 'em dead 'atwixt me an' the next alive, so I was a long way ahead o' the rest, an' I couldn't ha' seen them goin' to the dogs for want o' bread while I was learnin' a trade. I always was a lively lad, and I used to amuse myself an' the rest by standin' on my head an' twistin' o' my body into all sorts of shapes. An' when the circus come round, I would make friends wi' the men, helpin' 'em to look after their horses, an' they would sometimes teach me tricks, an' they did say for a clodhopper I got on very well. But that, you see, sir, set my monkey up, an' I took an oath to myself I would do what none o' them could do afore I dies— an' some thinks, sir," he added modestly, "as how I've done it. But the p'int is, that, when they all come upon my hands, I was able to gather a few coppers for 'em. I set to an' dressed myself like a proper clown, an' painted my face beautiful, an' from that time till they was able to do some'at for their selves, I managed to keep the kids in life. An' if they're none o' them doin' jest so well as they might, there's none o' them been in pris'n yet, an' that's a comfort. An' when folk tells me I'm adoin' o' no good, an' my trade no use to nobody, I says to them, says I, 'Beggin' your pardon, but do you call it nothink to nigh fill four hungry little bellies at home afore I wur fifteen?' An' after that, they ain't in general said nothink—an' one gentleman he gave me half-a-crown."

"The best possible answer you could have given, Franks,"

rejoined Dr. Christopher. "But your objectors might have gone on to explain that most trades did something on both sides—not only fed the little ones at home, but did good to the persons for whom the work was done; that the man, for instance, who cobbled shoes, gave a pair of dry feet to some old man at the same time that he filled his own child's hungry little stomach."

Franks was silent for a moment, thinking. "I understand you, sir," he said. "But I knows trades as makes a deal o' money, an' them they makes it out on's the worse an' not the better. It's better to stand on a fellow's own head than to sell gin, an' it's as good as the fireworks trade."

"There's not a doubt of it," answered Dr. Christopher. "I don't for a moment agree with those who say your trade is of no use. I was only explaining to you what they meant, for it's always best to know what people mean, even where they are wrong."

"Surely, sir, and I thank you kindly. Everybody's not so fair." He broke into a quiet laugh, pleased to have the doctor take his part.

"I think," Dr. Christopher went on, "to amuse people innocently is often the only good you can do them. When done lovingly and honestly, it is a Christian service."

This rather shocked Hester—acrobatics a Christian service! With her grand dawning idea mingled yet some foolish notional remnants. She still felt as if going to church and there fixing your thoughts on the prayers and the lessons and the hymns and the sermon was the serving of God. She felt that honesty called her to speak, but not a word came to her lips, for not a thought had arisen in answer to his bold assertion. She was one of the few who know when they have nothing to say.

"Suppose," Christopher went on, "somebody is walking along the street, brooding over an injury, and thinking how to serve the man that had done it to him. Life passes him on both sides and he takes no notice of anything. But he spies a man showing tricks in the middle of a small crowd, and he stops, and stares, and forgets for a moment or two that there is one brother-man he hates and would kill if he could."

Here Hester found words, and said, almost inaudibly, "He would only go away when he had had enough, and hate him all the same!"

"I know very well it would not make a good man of him,"

answered Christopher, "but it must be something to stop the bad mood in a man for a moment, just as it is something to a life to check a fever. For the moment at least, the man is open to influences from another source than his hate. If the devil may catch a man unaware when he is in an evil or unthinking mood, why should not the good Power take His opportunity when the evil spirit is asleep through the harping of a David or the feats of a Franks? I sometimes find, as I come from a theater where I have been occupied with the interests of a stirring play, that, with a sudden rush of intelligence, I understand the things best worth understanding better than before."

The illustration would have pleased Hester much had he said, "coming out of a concert," for she was not able to think of God being in a theater. Perhaps that had some relation to her inability to tell Saffy why God made the animals; she could have found her a reason why He made the dogs, but not why He made the monkeys. We are surrounded with things difficult to understand, and most people do not look at them lest they should find out they have to understand them. But she had herself begun to have a true notion of serving man, at least; therefore there was no fear of her not coming to see by and by what serving God meant. She did serve Him, and therefore she could not fail of finding out the words that belonged to the act. No one who does not serve Him ever can find out what serving Him means.

Some people are constantly rubbing at their skylights, but if they do not keep their other windows clean also, there will not be much light in the house. God is all about us, and prefers to shine in upon us sideways. We could not endure the power of His vertical glory. No mortal man can see God and live, and he who loves not his brother whom he has seen shall not love his God whom he has not seen. He will come to us in the morning through the eyes of a child, when we have been gazing all night at the stars in vain.

Hester rose, a little frightened at the very peculiar man and his talk. She had tried to see him in the dull light as he watched the acrobatics, which apparently he enjoyed more than to her seemed reasonable.

She saw a rather thickset man about thirty, in a rough shooting jacket of a brownish gray with many pockets, a striped shirt, and a tiny black necktie. He had a big head, with a pale complexion, rather thick and long straggling hair, a large forehead, and large gray eyes. The remaining features were well-formed but rather fat, like the rest of his not very elegant person. She thought he had quite a careless, if not slightly rakish look; but a man would have seen in him something manly and far from unattractive. He had a rather gruff but not unmusical voice, with what some might have thought a thread of pathos in it. He was hardly above middle height, and wore his hat on the back of his head, which would have given anyone a foolish look. Hester, not attracted by the man at all, declined his offer to see her home.

The next time she went to see the Frankses, they were gone. They had told Mrs. Baldwin that they were sorry to leave, but they must look for cheaper lodging—a better they could not hope to find.

Hester was disappointed not to have seen them once more, and make them a little present as she had intended. Her memory of them was naturally the more interesting that on Mrs. Franks she had first made experiment in the hope of her calling, and in virtue of her social gift had given sleep and rest to her and her babe. And if it is a fine thing to thrill with delight the audience of a concert, surely it was not a little thing to hand God's gift of sleep to a poor woman weary with the lot of women!

74

Chapter 14.

VAVASOR AND HESTER

Vavasor's continued visits were more frequent, and he stayed longer. Mrs. Raymount and Miss Dasomma noted with some anxiety that he began to appear at their church—a dull enough place, without any possible attraction for a man like Vavasor; they could only believe he went for the sake of seeing Hester. Then he began to join them as they came out, and then to walk home with them. And next he was asked in to stay to lunch.

Mrs. Raymount did not think it possible Hester could fall in love with such a man as Vavasor, but she was pleased with the idea of a possible marriage of such distinction for her daughter. They knew nothing against the young man, and in Addison Square he was on his good behavior and concerned with looking his best—which always means looking better than one's best. He not merely felt comfortable and kindly disposed, which he was, but good in himself and considerate of others, which he was not. Hester seemed to be gaining an elevating influence and power over him, and had begun to bring out and cherish what was best in a disposition far from unamiable, although nearly ruined by evil influences on all sides. Both glad and proud to see her daughter thus potent, Mrs. Raymount wondered if she should interfere. It was plain he was improving. Not once did they ever hear him jest on anything belonging to church! As to anything belonging to religion, he scarcely knew enough in that province to have any material for jesting. If Vavasor was falling in love with Hester, the danger was for him—lest she, who to her mother appeared colder than any lady she knew, should not respond with like affection.

Miss Dasomma knew better than Mrs. Raymount the kind of soil in which this human plant had been reared, and saw more danger ahead. She feared the young man was but amusing himself, was flirting with her—which had the more danger for Hester that there was not in her mind the idea corresponding to the phrase. He declined asking himself where the enjoyment of the hour was leading, and he found it more easy to set aside the question because of the difference between his social position and that of the lady.

Vavasor had never turned his mind in the direction of good, and it was far more from circumstance than refusal that he was not yet the more hurtful member of society which his lack of principles was surely working to make him.

Hester was, of course, greatly interested in him. She had been but little in society, had not in the least studied men, and could not help being pleased with the increasing power she plainly had over him. Even the unobservant Corney remarked on the gentleness of his friend's behavior in their house. Vavasor followed every word of Hester's about his singing, and showed himself anxious to win her approval by the pains he took and the amount of practice he went through to approach her idea of song. He had not only ceased to bring forward his heathenish notions as to human helplessness and fate, but seemed on the way to allow there might be some reality in Hester's opposing beliefs of individual mission and duty. For Hester thought first only of doing him good, and not until she imagined some success did her danger begin.

In all these things Vavasor never once consciously laid himself out to deceive her, or make her think him better than he thought himself. He had but the most rudimentary notion of truth in the inward parts, and could deceive the better that he did not know he was deceiving. He had as little notion of the nature of the person he was dealing with, or the reality to her of the things of which she spoke. Belief was to him at most the mere difference between decided and undecided opinion. She spoke the language of a world whose existence he was incapable at present of recognizing, for he had never obeyed one of its demands. He hardly knew such a thing as reform was required of, possible to, or desirable in him. Nothing mattered to him except "good form."

He was certainly falling more and more into what most people call love. When intoxicated with the idea of her, when thinking what a sensation she would make in his grand little circle, he felt it impossible to live without her; some way must be found! It could not be his fate to see another man triumph in her!

He called his world a circle rightly enough—it was no globe, nothing but surface. Whether or not she would accept him he never asked himself; almost awed in her presence, he never doubted she would. Had he had anything worthy the name of property coming with the title, he would have proposed to her at once, he said to himself. But who, with only the most beautiful wife in the world, would encounter a naked earldom! The thing would be as unjust to Hester as to himself. How just, how love-careful he was not to ask her!

But perhaps she might have expectations! That could hardly be—no one with anything would slave as her father did, morning, noon, and night. True, his own governor was her uncle, so there was money in the family—but people never left their money to their poor relations! To marry her would be to live on his salary in a small house in Camden Town, ride home in the omnibus every night like one of a tin of sardines, wear half-crown gloves, cotton socks, and ten-and-six-penny hats. Would the sweetness of the hand that darned his socks make his over-filled shoe comfortable? And when the awful family began to come on, she would begin to lose her appeal! A woman like her, living in ease and able to dress well, might keep her best points till she was fifty! If there was such providence as Hester referred to, it certainly did not make the best things the easiest to get. In all probability Hester would fall to the lot of some quill-driver like her father—a man that made a livelihood by drumming his notions into the ears of people that did not care a brass farthing about them! Thus would Vavasor's love fits work themselves off, declining from cold noon to a drizzly twilight.

It was not soon that he risked an attempt to please her with a song of his own. There was just enough unconscious truth in him to make him a little afraid of Hester, and he would not for less than a fortune have risked encountering her scorn. For he rightly believed that she was capable of scorn, and that of no ordinarily withering quality. Hester had not yet gathered the sweet gentleness that comes of long breathing the air of the high countries. While there is left in us the possibility of scorn, we know not quite the spirit we are of—still less if we imagine we may keep this or that little shadow of fault. But he had come to understand Hester's taste so far as to know certain qualities she would not like in a song. He could even be sure she would like this one or that, and although of many he could not be certain, having never reached the grounds of her judgment, he had not yet offended her with any he brought her.

And so by degrees he generated the resolve to venture something himself in the hope of pleasing her—he flattered himself he knew her *style*. He was very fond of the word, and thought that all writers, to be of any account, must fashion their style after that of this or the other master. How the master got it, or whether it might not be well to go back to the seed and propagate no more by cutting, it never occurred to him to ask. He already at odd moments cultivated his style by reading aloud the speeches of parliamentary orators, but the thought never came to him that there was no such thing *per se* as *speaking well,* that there was no cause of its existence unless *thinking well* were the grandfather, and *something to say* the father of it—something so well worth saying that it gave natural utterance to its own shape. Had he even perceived this truth, he would immediately have desired some fine thing to say, in order that he might say it well! He could not have been persuaded that, if one has nothing worth saying, the best possible style for him is just the most halting utterance that ever issued from empty skull. To make a good speech was the grand thing for Vavasor! What side it was on, the right or the wrong, was a point unthinkable with him. Even whether the speaker believed what he said was of no consequence—except that, if he did not, his speech would be the more admirable, as the greater accomplishment, and himself the more admirable as the cleverer fellow.

Knowing that Hester was fond of a good ballad, he thought at first to try his hand on one. But he found that, like everything else, a ballad was easy enough if you could do it, and more than difficult enough if you could not. After several attempts he wisely yielded the ambition—his gift did not lie in that direction! He had, however, long been writing drawing room verses, and so produced a love song of that kind. He would present it as one he had written long ago; as such it would say the more for him while it would not commit him.

So one evening as he stood by her piano, he said to Hester, "By the bye, Miss Raymount, last night, as I was turning over some songs I wrote many years ago, I came upon one I thought I should like you just to look at. The music is worth nothing, but the words are not so bad."

"Do let me see them!" said Hester, hiding none of the interest she felt, though fearing a little she might not have to praise them so much as she would like.

He took the song from his pocket, and smoothed it out before her on the piano. Vavasor went halfway toward Mrs. Raymount, then turned, and now stood watching Hester. So long was her head bent over his paper that he grew uncomfortably anxious. At length she placed it on the stand before her and began to try its music. Then Vavasor went to her hurriedly, for he felt convinced that if she was not quite pleased with the verses, it would fare worse with the music.

Hester, however, would not yield the paper, but began to read it again. Why she did not quite like his verses she did not yet know, and was anxious not to be unfair. They were clever, they had his own air of unassumed ease, and she could not but feel they had some claim to literary art. Had she had a suspicion of the lie he had told her, and that they were the work of yesterday, it would at once have put leagues between them, and made the verses hateful to her. As she read and thought, the time Vavasor stood there waiting appeared to both of them three times as long as it really was.

"You have discovered," he said at last, "that the song is an imitation of Sir John Suckling!"

"I don't know anything of him," answered Hester.

He had never thought of the man while writing it, and knew nothing was more unlikely than that she should know anything of him.

"But tell me," she continued, "where is the good of imitating even the best of writers? Our own original, however poor, must be the thing for us! To imitate is to repudiate our own being."

"That I admit," answered Vavasor, who never did anything original except when he followed his instincts. "But for a mere trial of skill an imitation is admissible—don't you think?"

"Oh, surely," replied Hester. "Only it seems to me a waste of time—especially with such a gift as you have of your own!"

"At all events," said Vavasor, hiding his gratification with false humility, "there was no great presumption in a try at Suckling!"

"Then the more waste," returned Hester. "I would sooner imitate Bach or even Handel than Verdi."

Vavasor could stand a good deal of censure if mingled with some praise—which he called appreciation. His mental condition was much like that of one living in a vacuum, in which the sole objects must be such as he was creator enough to project from himself. He had no feeling that he was in the heart of a crowded universe, between whose great verities moved countless small and smaller truths. Little notion had he that to learn these, after the measure of their importance, was his business, with eternity to do it in!

When he was gone, leaving his manuscript behind him, Hester set to it again, and trying to make the music over, was by it so far enlightened that she despaired of finding anything in it, and felt a good deal disappointed. The difficulty Hester found in his song came of her trying to see more than was there; her eyes made holes in it, and saw the less.

But she still had no suspicion of how empty he was, for it was scarcely possible for her to imagine a person indifferent to the truth of things, or without interest in his own character and its growth. Being all of a piece herself, she had no conception of a nature all in pieces, with no unity but that of selfishness. Her nature did now and then receive a jar and shock from his, but she succeeded in accounting for such as arising from his lack of development—which her influence over him would favor.

Women are being constantly misled by the fancy and hopes of being the saviors of men! It is natural to goodness and innocence, but nonetheless is the error a disastrous one. It may well be that a woman does more to redeem a man by declining than by encouraging his attentions. One who obeys God will scarcely imagine herself free to lay her person in the arms and her happiness in the bosom of a man whose being is a denial of Him. God cares nothing about keeping a man respectable, yet will give His very self to make of him a true man. But that needs God; a woman is not enough for it. This cannot be God's way of saving bad men.

Chapter 15

A SMALL FAILURE

Vavasor at length found he must not continue to visit Hester so often, while he was not ready to go further. He began, therefore, to limit his appearances in Addison Square. But in so doing he became more aware of her influence, and found that he had come to feel differently about certain things—that her opinion was a power on his consciousness.

He had nowise begun to change his way; he had only been innoculated, and was therefore a little infected with her goodness. In his ignorance he took the alteration for one of great moral significance, and was wonderfully pleased with himself. His natural kindness toward the poor and suffering—such at least as were not offensive—was quickened. He took no additional jot of trouble about them, only gave a more frequent penny to such as begged of him, and had more than a pennyworth of relief in return. It was a good thing, but it did not indicate any advanced stage of goodness. He prided himself on one occasion that he had walked home to give his last shilling to a poor woman, whereas in truth he walked home because he found he had given her his last.

Hester was annoyed to find herself disappointed when he did not appear, and yet more diligently exercised her growing vocation. She began to widen her sphere a little by going about elsewhere with a friend belonging to a sisterhood. But in her own quarter she always went alone, and seldom entered a poor house without singing in several of its rooms before she came away—often having to sing some old song before her audience would listen to anything new, and finding the old song generally counted the best in her visit—except by the children, to whom she would frequently tell a fairy tale, singing the little rhymes she made come into it.

About this time the experiment was made in several places of gathering small assemblies of the poor in the neighborhood of their own dwellings, that the ladies in charge of the houses in which they lived might, with the help of friends, give them a concert. At one of these concerts Hester was invited to assist, and went gladly, prepared to do her best. It had, however, been arranged that any of the audience who would like to sing, should be allowed to make their contributions also to the enjoyment of the evening; it soon became evident that the company cared for no singing but that of their own acquaintance. They were so bent on singing, and so supported and called for by each other, that it seemed at length the better way to abandon the platform to them. There was nothing very objectionable in the character of any of the songs sung, but the singing was for the most part atrocious, and the resulting influence hardly what the projectors of the entertainment had had in view.

It might be well that they should enjoy themselves so; it might be well that they should have provided for them something better than they could produce; but, to judge from the experiment, it seemed useless to attempt the combination of the two. The affair set Hester thinking, and before morning she was ready with a scheme.

Chapter 16

THE CONCERT ROOM

The Raymounts' house had, beside the ordinary accommodation of a good-sized London house with three drawing rooms on the first floor, a quite unusual provision for the receiving of guests. At the top of the first landing, rather more than halfway up the stair, there was a door through the original wall of the house to a long gallery, which led to a large and lofty room—apparently, from the little orchestra halfway up one of the walls, intended for dancing. Since they had owned the house it had been used only as a playroom for the children. Mr. Raymount always intended to furnish it, but had not yet done so.

Beneath the concert room was another of the same area, but very low, being but the height of the first landing of the stairs. It was difficult to discover any use that could be made of it, and it continued even more neglected than the other. Below this again were cellars of alarming extent and obscurity, reached by a long, vaulted passage. They would have held coal and wood and wine, everything natural to a cellar, enough for one generation at least. The history of the house was unknown. There was a nailed-up door in the low-ceilinged room which was said to lead into the next house; but as the widow who lived there took every opportunity of making herself disagreeable, they had not ventured an investigation. The great room was now haunting Hester's brain and heart; if only her father would allow her to give in it a concert to her lowly friends and acquaintances!

Questions concerning the condition of the poor in our large towns had, from the distance of speculation and the press, been of late occupying a good deal of Mr. Raymount's attention, and he believed that he was enlightening the world on those most important perhaps of all the social questions of our day, their wrongs and their rights. He little suspected that his daughter was doing more for the poor, almost without knowing it, than he with all his conscious wisdom. She could not, however, have made her request at a more auspicious moment, for he was just then feeling specially benign toward them, an article having come forth that very day in which he had, as he believed, uttered himself with power on their behalf. Besides, though far from unprejudiced, he had a horror of prejudice, and the moment he suspected a prejudice, hunted it almost as uncompromisingly in himself as in another. Most people surmising a fault in themselves rouse every individual bristle of their nature to defend and retain the thing that degrades them! He therefore speedily overcame his first reluctance, and agreed to his daughter's strange proposal.

For nearly a fortnight there were busy doings in the house. Mr. Raymount committed the dingy place to cleaners, painters, and paperhangers, under whose hands it gradually put on a gracious look fit to welcome the human race. The place looked lighter and larger, and to Saffy and Mark their playroom seemed transformed into a temple; they were almost afraid to enter it. Every noise in it sounded twice as loud as before, and every muddy shoe made a print.

The day for the concert was at length fixed a week off, and Hester began to invite her poorer friends and neighbors to spend that evening at her father's house, when her mother would give them tea, and she would sing to them. The married women were to bring their husbands if they would come, and each young woman might bring a friend. Most of the men, as a matter of course, turned up their noses at the invitation, but were nevertheless from curiosity inclined to go. Some declared it impossible that any house in the square should hold the number invited. Some spoke doubtfully; they might be able to go, but they were not sure, and seemed to regard consent as a favor, if not condescension. Of these, however, two or three were hampered by the uncertainty as to the redemption of their best clothes from the pawnbroker.

The hall and gallery were brilliantly lighted, and the room

itself looked charming. Tea was ready before the company began to arrive, and was handed round by the ladies and gentlemen. The meal went off well, with a good buzz of conversation. Several of the guests, mindful like other dams of their cubs at home, slipped large pieces of cake into their pockets for their behalf; but this must not be judged without a just regard to their ways of thinking.

When the huge urns and the remnants of food were at length removed, and the windows had been opened for a minute to change the air, a curtain rose suddenly at the end of the room, and revealed a stage decorated with green branches and artificial flowers. In the center of it was a piano; on the piano music, and at the piano Hester. When the assembly caught sight of her turning over the leaves of her music, a great silence fell. The moment she began to play, all began to talk. With the first tone of her voice, every other ceased. She had chosen a ballad with a sudden and powerful dramatic opening, and a little anxious, a little irritated also with their talking while she played, began in a style that would have compelled attention from a herd of cattle. But the ballad was a little too long for them, and by the time it was half sung they had begun to talk again, and exchange opinions concerning it. All agreed Miss Raymount had a splendid voice, but several of those who were there by secondhand invitation could find a woman to beat her easily! Their criticisms were not unfriendly but condescending and patronizing. Most of them regarded their presence as a favor granted her. Had they not come that she might show off to them, and receive their approval?

Chapter 17

AN UNINVITED GUEST

Vavasor had not heard of the gathering, for Hester had not
mentioned it to him. Yet when she lifted her eyes at the close of
her ballad, not a little depressed at having failed to secure the
interest of her audience, it was with a great gush of pleasure that
she saw him near the door. She concluded that he had heard of
her purpose, and had come to help her. Even at that distance
she could see that he was looking very uncomfortable—annoyed, she did not doubt, by the behavior of her guests. A rush
of new strength and courage went from heart to brain. She rose,
advanced to the front of the little stage, called out in a clear
voice that rang across the buzz and stilled it, "Mr. Vavasor, will
you come and help me?"

Vavasor was not a little disgusted at what he beheld. He had
called without a notion of what was going on, had seen the row
of lights along the gallery as he was making for the drawing
room, and had changed his direction and followed it, knowing
nothing of the room to which it led. Blinded by the glare and a
little bewildered by the unexpectedness of the sight, he did not
at first discern the kind of company he had entered. But presently his eyes adjusted and confirmed the fact that he was in the
midst of a notable number of the unwashed. He had often
talked with Hester about the poor, as they were now a fashionable subject. But in the poor themselves he could hardly be said
to have the most rudimentary interest; and that a lady should
degrade herself by sending her voice into such ears, and coming
into actual contact with such persons and their attendant dis-

gusts, exposing both voice and person to their abominable remarks, was to him a thing simply incomprehensible. The admission of such people to a respectable house, and the entertainment of them as at a music hall could have its origin only in some wild semipolitical scheme of the old fellow, who had more crotchets in his head than brain could well hold! It was a proceeding as disgraceful as extraordinary! Puh! Could the tenth part of the air be oxygen? To think of the woman he worshiped being in such hell!

The woman he could honor little by any worship he gave her, was far more secure from evil eyes and evil thoughts in that company than she would have been in any drawing room of his world. Her angel would rather see her where she was.

But the glorious tones ceased, the ballad was at an end, and the next moment, to his dismay, the voice which he had delighted to imagine thrilling listeners in a great Belgravian drawing room came to him in prose across the fumes of that Bloomsbury music hall, clear and brave and quiet, asking him, the future Earl of Gartley, to come and help! Was she in trouble? Had her father forced her into the false position in which she found herself? And did she seek refuge with *him* the moment he made his appearance? Certainly such was not the tone of her appeal! With perfect command of his outer being he was instantly on his way to her, shouldering a path in the gentlest manner through the malodorous air.

"This comes," he said to himself as he went, "of her foolish parents receiving so little company that for the free exercise of her great talent she is driven to such as this! For song must have audience, however unfit! Genius is always eccentric! If I could but be her protection against that political father, that puritan mother, and that idiotic brother of hers, and put an end to this sort of thing before it comes to be talked about!" He grew bitter, as with smiling face but shrinking soul he made his way through that crowd of fellow-creatures whose contact was defilement. He would have lost them all rather than a song of Hester's.

He sprang on the stage, and made her a low bow.

"Come and sing a duet with me," she said, and indicated one on the piano before her which they had several times sung together.

He smiled what he meant to look his sweetest smile, and

almost immediately their duet began. They sang well, and the assembly was a little more of an audience now, perhaps because there were two singers instead of one. But it was plain that, had there been another verse, most would have been talking again.

Hester next requested Vavasor to sing a certain ballad which she knew was a great favorite with him. Inwardly protesting, he obeyed. His singing was a little wooden, as was everything Vavasor did; being such himself, how could he help his work being wooden? They were all talking before he had ended.

After a brief pause, Hester invited a gentleman prepared for the occasion to sing them something patriotic. He responded with Campbell's magnificent song, "Ye Mariners of England!" which was received with hearty cheers.

He was followed by another who, well-acquainted with the predilections of his audience, gave them a specially sentimental song about a grandfather's chair, which was not only heard in silence but followed by a tremendous cheering. Possibly it was a luxury to some who had no longer any grandfather to kick, to cry over his chair; but, like the most part of their brethren, the poor greatly enjoy having their feelings gently troubled.

Thus the music of the occasion was gradually sinking to the intellectual level of the company—with a consequence unforeseen, therefore not provided against.

Chapter 18.

CATASTROPHE

The tail of the music kite had descended near enough to the earth to be a temptation to some of the walkers afoot, and they must catch at it! The moment the guest's song was ended, almost before its deathnote had left the lips of the singer, one of his friends was on his feet. Without a word of apology, without the shadow of a request for permission, he called out in a loud voice, knocking with his chair on the floor.

"Ladies and gen'lemen, Mr. William Blaney will now favor the company with a song."

Thereupon immediately a pale, pockmarked man of diminutive height, with high retreating forehead and long thin hair, rose and at once proceeded to make his way to the stage. Hester and Vavasor looked at each other, and one whisper passed between them, after which they waited the result in silence. The countenance approaching, kindled by conscious power and anticipated triumph, showed a white glow through its unblushing paleness.

Scrambling with knee and hand upon the stage, the poor feeble fellow plunged into his song, executed in cracked and strained falsetto. The result, aided by the pathetic and dubious moral nature of the song, must have been excruciating to every good ear and every sensitive nature. Long before the relief of its close arrived, Hester had made up her mind that it was her part to protect her guests from such. It was compensation no doubt to some present to watch the grotesque contortions of the singer squeezing out of him the precious pathos of his song, in which

89

he screwed his eyes together and opened his mouth in a long ellipse in the middle of one cheek, but that was not the kind of entertainment she had purposed. She sat ready, against the moment when he should end, to let loose the most thunderous music in her mental repertoire, annoyed that she had but her small piano on the stage. Vanity, however, is as suspicious of vanity as hate is of hate, and Mr. Blaney, stopping abruptly in the middle of the long last note, screeched aloud, ere she could strike the first chord, "I will now favor the company with a song of my own composure."

But before he had got his mouth into its singing place in his left cheek, Hester rose and began to speak; when she knew what had to be done, she never hesitated. Mr. Blaney started, and his mouth, after a moment of elliptic suspense, slowly closed and returned, as he listened, to a more symmetrical position in his face.

"I am sorry to have to interfere," said Hester, "but my friends are in my house, and I am accountable for their entertainment. Mr. Blaney must excuse me if I insist on keeping the management of the evening in my own hands."

The vanity of the would-be singer was sorely hurt, as he was too selfish for the briefest comparison of himself with others. "The friends as knows me and what I can do," returned Mr. Blaney with calmness, "will back me up. I have no right to be treated as if I didn't know what I was about. I can warrant the song homemade, and of the best quality. So here goes!"

Vavasor made a stride toward him, but then Mr. Raymount spoke from somewhere near the door. "Come out of that," he shouted, and made his way through the company as fast as he could.

Vavasor drew back and stood like a sentinel on guard. Hester resumed her seat at the piano. Blaney, fancying he had gained his point and, that if he began before Mr. Raymount reached him, he would be allowed to end in peace, again got his mouth into position and began to howl. But his host jumped on the stage from behind, reached him at his third note, took him by the back of the neck, shoved him down, and walked him through the crowd and out of the room before him like a naughty boy. Propelling him thus to the door of the house, he pushed him out, closed it behind him, and reentered the concert room to be greeted by a great clapping of hands, as if he had performed a deed of valor. But, notwithstanding the miserable vanity and impudence of the man, it had gone to Hester's heart to see his puny form in the mighty clutch of her father.

The moment silence was restored, up rose a burly, honest-looking bricklayer, and said, "I beg your pardon, miss, but will you allow me to make one remark?"

"Certainly, Mr. Jones," answered Hester.

"It seems to me, miss," said Jones, "as it's only fair play on my part as brought Blaney here, as I'm sorry to find behave himself improper, to say for him that I know he never would ha' done it if he hadn't had a drop as we come along to this 'ere tea party. That was the cause, miss, an' I hope as it'll be taken into account, an' considered a lucidation of his conduct. It takes but very little, I'm sorry to say, miss, to upset his behavior—not more'n a pint at the outside. But it don't last, bless you! There's not a morsel of harm in him, poor fellow. Not as the guv'nor do anything more'n his duty in puttin' of him out! But when he've got a drop in his nob, it's always for singin' he is—an' that's the worst of *him*. Thank you kindly, miss."

"Thank *you*, Mr. Jones," returned Hester. "We'll think no more of it."

Loud applause followed, and Jones sat down, well satisfied.

The order of the evening was resumed, but the harmony of the assembly remained disturbed. All hope of quiet was gone, for they now had something to talk about! Everyone knew that Blaney felt himself of importance; had he not a superior right of opinion upon his behavior? Nor was he without a few sympathizers—was he not the same flesh and blood, they said? After the swells had had it all their own way so long, why shouldn't poor Blaney have his turn? But those who knew Hester, especially the women, were indignant with him.

Hester sang again and again, but no song would go quite to her mind. Vavasor also sang as often as Hester asked him, but inwardly he was disgusted with the whole affair—as was natural, for could any fish have found itself more out of the water than he? Everything annoyed him, most of all that the lady of his thoughts should have addressed herself to such an assembly. Why did she not leave it to him or her father! If it was not degrading enough to appear before such a low crowd, surely to

91

sing to them was! Justifiable as was her desire for appreciation, how could a woman of refinement seek it from such a repulsive assemblage? But Vavasor would have been better able to understand Hester, and would have met the distastes of the evening with far less discomposure, if he had never been in worse company. One main test of our dealings in the world is whether the men and women we associate with are the better or the worse for it. Vavasor had often been where at least he was the worse, and no one the better for his presence. For days a cloud hung over the fair image of Hester in his mind.

He called on the first possible opportunity to inquire how she was after her exertions, but avoided further allusion to the events of the evening. She thanked him for the help he had given her, but was so far from satisfied with her experiment, that she too let the subject rest.

Mr. Raymount was so disgusted that he said nothing of the kind should ever again take place in his house; he had not bought it to make a music hall of it!

Chapter 19.

YRNDALE

It was now the month of March. The middle day of it had been dreary all over England, dreariest of all, perhaps, in London. Great blasts had gone careering under a sky whose miles-thick vault of clouds they never touched. Now and then a few drops would fall on the stones as if the day's fierce misery were about to yield to sadness; but it did not yield, and up rose again a great blundering gust, and repentance was lost in rage. The sun went down on its wrath, and the night was tempestuous.

But the next morning rose bright and glad, looking as if it would make up for its father's wildness by a gentler treatment of the world. The wind was still high, but the hate seemed to have gone out of it and given place to a laborious jollity. It swept huge clouds over the sky, granting never a pause, never a respite of motion; but the sky was blue and the clouds were white, and the dungeon-vault of the world was broken up and carried away.

Everything in the room where the Raymounts were one by one assembling was discolored and dark. The reds had grown brown, and the blues a dirt slate. But the fire was burning in glory, and in the middle of the table on the white cloth stood a piece of red pottery full of crocuses, the earnest of the spring.

Mr. Raymount was very silent, seemed almost a little gloomy, and the face of his wife was a shade less peaceful in consequence. There was nothing the matter, only he had not yet learned to radiate. Mr. Raymount had some light, but he let it shine mostly in reviews, not much in the house. He did not lift up the light of his countenance on any.

The children were rosy, fresh from their baths, and ready to eat like breakfast-loving English. Cornelius was half his breakfast ahead of the rest, for he had daily to endure the hardship of being at the bank by nine o'clock, and made the best of it by claiming immunity from the rules of the breakfast table. Never did he lose a moment in helping anybody. Even little Saffy he allowed to stretch out a very long arm after the butter—unless it happened to cross his plate, when he would sharply rebuke her breach of manners. It would have been all the same if he had not been going until noon, but now he had hurry and business to rampart his laziness and selfishness. Mark would sooner have gone without salt to his egg than ask Corney to pass it.

This morning the pale boy sat staring at the crocuses.

"Why don't you eat, Mark, dear?" said his mother.

"I'm not hungry, mama," he answered.

The mother looked at him a little anxiously. He was not a very vigorous boy, but, unlike his father, his light was almost always shining, and making the faces about him shine.

After a few minutes, he said, his eyes fixed on the crocuses, "I can't think how they come!"

"They grow!" said Saffy.

Said her father, willing to set them thinking, "Didn't you see Hester make the paper flowers for her party?"

"Yes," replied Saffy, "but it would take such a time to make all the flowers in the world that way!"

"So it would—but if a great many angels took it in hand, I suppose they could do it."

"That can't be how," said Saffy, laughing, "for you know they come up out of the earth, and there ain't room to cut them out there!"

"I think they must be cut out and put together before they're made!" said Mark, very slowly and thoughtfully.

The supposition was greeted with a great burst of laughter from Cornelius. In the midst of a refined family he was the vulgar one, and behaved as the blind and stupid generally behave to those who see what they cannot see. Mockery is the share they choose in the motions of the life eternal!

"Stop, Cornelius!" said his father. "I suspect we have a young philosopher where you see only a silly little brother. He has got a glimpse of something he does not yet know how to say."

94

"In that case, don't you think, sir," said Cornelius, "he had better hold his tongue till he does know how to say it?" It was not often he dared speak so to his father, but he was growing less and less afraid of him, though not through increase of love.

His father looked at him a moment before he replied, and his mother looked anxiously at her husband. "It *would* be better," he answered quietly, "were he not among *friends.*"

His emphasis was lost on Cornelius. "They take everything for clever the little idiot says!" he remarked to himself. "Nobody made anything of *me* when *I* was his age!"

The letters were brought in, and among them was a black-bordered one for Mr. Raymount. He looked at the postmark. "This must be the announcement of cousin Strafford's death!" he said. "I knew she was not expected to live. She was a strange old soul!"

"Didn't you used to be close to her, papa?" asked Hester.

"Yes, at one time. But we differed so entirely it was impossible it should last. She would take up the oddest notions as to what I thought and meant and wanted to do, and then she would fall out upon me as advocating things I hated quite as much as she did. But people seldom know what they mean themselves, and can hardly be expected to know what other people mean. Only, the amount of mental and moral force wasted on hating and talking down the nonexistent is a pity."

"I can't understand why people should quarrel so about their opinions," said Mrs. Raymount.

"A great part of it comes of indignation at not being understood, and another great part from despair at being understood—and that while all the time the person thus indignant and despairing takes not the smallest pains to understand the neighbor whose misunderstanding of himself makes him so sore."

"What is to be done, then?" asked Hester.

"Nothing," answered her father with something of a cynical smile, born of this same frustrated anxiety to impress his opinions on others.

He took up his letter, slowly broke the large black seal, and began to read it. His wife saw his countenance change a little, then flush a little, then grow a little fixed, and quite inscrutable. He folded the letter, laid it by the side of his plate, and began to eat again.

"Well, dear?" said his wife.

"It is not quite what I thought," he answered, with a curious smile, and ate his toast in a brooding silence. Never in the habit of *making* secrets, like his son, he disliked showing his feelings, and from his wife even was inclined to veil them.

The hopeless and hardly indulged ambition of Mr. Raymount's life was to possess a small portion of the earth's surface—if only an acre or two. He came of his relatives possessing such property, but none of it had come near him except that belonging to the cousin mentioned. He was her nearest relation, but had never had much hope of inheriting from her, and after a final quarrel put an end to their quarreling, had had none. For many years there had not been the slightest communication between the cousins. But in the course of those years all the other relatives of the old lady had died, and he was now, after all, heir to the property, a small estate in a lovely spot among the roots of the Cumberland hills. It was attended by not a few thousand pounds in government securities. But while Mr. Raymount was not a money-lover in any notable sense, his delight in having land of his own was almost beyond utterance. His new sense of room and freedom made him so glad he could hardly get his toast down.

Mrs. Raymount was tolerably familiar with her husband's moods, but she had never seen him look just so, and was puzzled. He had never before had such a pleasant surprise, and sat absorbed in a foretaste of bliss. But presently he arose and went to his study, and his wife followed him. The moment she entered, he turned and took her in his arms.

"Here's news, wifie!" he said. "Yrndale is ours after all! Thank God! It is a lovely place. Nothing could have happened to give me more pleasure."

"You always had a fancy for playing the squire."

"A great fancy for a little room, rather—not much for the duties of a squire. I know little of them, but happily we shall not be dependent on the result of my management. There is money as well, I am glad to say—enough to keep the place up, anyhow."

"I have no doubt you will be a model farmer and landlord."

"You must take the business part, at least until Corney is fit to look after it."

96

But her main thought was what influence the change would have on Hester's prospects. In her heart she abjured the notion of property having anything to do with marriage—yet this was almost her first thought! Inside us we play more fantastic tricks than any we play in the face of the world.

"Are the children to be told?" she asked.

"It would be a shame not to let them share in our gladness, and yet one hates to think of their talking about it."

"I am not afraid of the children," returned his wife. "I have but to tell them not to."

When she returned to the dining room Cornelius was gone, but the rest were still at the table. She told them that God had given them a beautiful house in the country, with hills and woods and a swift-flowing river. Saffy clapped her hands, cried, "*O mama!*" and could hardly sit on her chair. Mark was perfectly still, but his face shone as if it had been heaven he was going to. No color, only light came to the surface of it, and broke in the loveliest smile. When Mark smiled, his whole body and being smiled. He turned and kissed Saffy, but still said nothing.

Hester's face flushed a celestial rosy red. Her first thought was of the lovely things of the country and the joy of them. She looked back on the desert of a London winter, and forth from a blustering spring into a land of promise. Her next thought was that she would be able to do less for her poor than ever— Yrndale was so far from London! If only her parents would let her stay behind! But it might be God's will to remove her because she was doing more harm than good! She had never been allowed to succeed in anything, and now her endeavor would be at an end! Her pleasure was speedily damped, the celestial red yielded to earthly pale, and tears came in her eyes.

"You don't like the thought of leaving London, Hester!" said her mother with concern. She thought it was because of Vavasor.

"I am very glad for you and papa," answered Hester. "I was thinking what my poor people would do without me."

"I have sometimes found the things I dreaded most served me best, and furthered what I thought they would ruin."

"Thank you, dear mother, you can always comfort me," rejoined Hester. "For myself I could not imagine anything more pleasant. If only it were near London! Or," she added, smiling through her tears, "if one hadn't a troublesome heart and con-science playing into each other's hands!" She was still thinking of her poor, but her mother was in doubt.

"I suppose, father," said Cornelius when he was told, "there will be no occasion for me to go to the bank anymore?"

"There will be more occasion than ever," answered his father. "Will there not be the more to look after when I am gone? What do you imagine you could employ yourself with down there? When you leave the bank it will be to learn farming and estate management—after which you will be welcome to Yrndale."

Cornelius made no reply. He looked upon the estate as his nearly as much as his father's, and his father's words deeply offended him. The father had not spoken so kindly as he might, but had he known his son, he would often have spoken severely; such feelings of Cornelius in no case deserved consideration, as they were so selfish. What right had his father to keep from him a share in the good fortunes of the family? He left the study almost hating his father.

Too sore for silence, and filled with what seemed to him righteous indignation, he took the first opportunity of pouring everything out to Vavasor. His friend responded very sensibly, trying, without exactly saying it, and without success, to make him see what a fool he was. He congratulated him all the more warmly on his good fortune—of which he too vaguely hoped for a portion. Hester would likely come in for a personal share, and if he could exist without his aunt's money, he would marry Hester, and risk his aunt's displeasure. At the same time she would doubtless now look with more favor on his preference. There could be nothing insuperably offensive to her pride in his marrying the daughter of a country squire. She would get over it fast enough! In the meantime he would, as Cornelius begged him, be careful to make no allusion to the matter.

Mr. Raymount went to look at his property, and returned more delighted with house, land, and landscape than he had expected. As soon as the warm weather came they would mi-grate, and so immediately began their preparations. The house was to be left in charge of the housekeeper, Sarah, who would also wait on Cornelius.

Chapter 20.

THE JOURNEY

It was a lovely morning when they left London, and late in the afternoon when they reached the station at which they must leave the railway for the road. Before that the weather had changed, or they had changed their weather, for the sky was one mass of cloud, and rain was falling persistently. Through the rain and the mists the hills, neither lofty nor lovely, looked lost and dreary.

Saffy had been sound asleep this part of the journey, but Mark had been standing at the window of the railway carriage, gazing out on an awful world. What would he do, he thought, if he were lost there? Would he be able to sit still all night without being frightened, waiting for God to come and take him? As they rushed along, the panorama flitted through his mind and heart, and there like a glacier scored its passage. Hills and woods and valleys and plains and rivers and seas, entering by the gates of sight into the live mirror of the human, are transformed to another nature, a living wonder, a joy, a pain, a breathless marvel as they pass. Nothing can receive another thing, not even a glass can take into its depth a face, without altering it. In the mirror of man, things become thoughts, feelings become life, and send their streams down the cheeks or their sunshine over the countenance. Before Mark reached the end of that journey, there was gathered in the bottom of his heart a great mass of fuel, there stored for the future consumption of thinking, and for reproduction in forms of power.

They got into their own carriage at the station. The drive was a long and tedious and dark one, for the roads were rough and muddy and often steep, and they could see little in the rainy dusk as they followed the course of a swollen river through the valley.

Long before they reached their new home, Saffy and Mark were sound asleep, and the father and mother sat in unbroken silence, hand in hand. Hester was sunk in her own thoughts. Save what she learned among the thousand musics of the river along which they had been driving for the past hour, Hester knew nothing of the country for which she had left the swarming city. Ah, that city—so full of fellow creatures, so many of them her friends, and struggling in the toils of so many foes!

As young as Hester was, she no longer shrank from the thought of that invisible, intangible solvent in which the generations of man vanish from the eyes of their fellows. She said to herself what a blessed thing was death for countless human myriads—doubtless for the whole race! It looked sad enough for an end, but then it was not the end. Except for the thought of the change to some other mode of life, the idea of this world would have been unendurable to her. But even now she felt as if the gulf of death separated her from those to whom it had been her painful delight to minister! The weeping wind and the moaning rush of the river deepened her mood.

They turned and went through a gate, then passed through trees that made yet darker pieces of the night. By and by appeared the faint lights of the house, and presently the carriage stopped. Both children continued dead asleep, and were carried off to bed. The father and mother knew the house of old time, and revived for each other old memories. But to Hester all was strange, and what with the long journey, the weariness, and the sadness, she entered the old hall as if walking in a dream.

It had a quiet, dignified look, and everything in the house looked somber and solemn, as if it had not forgotten its old mistress, who had been so many years in it, and was such a little while gone out of it. They had supper in a long, low room with dark furniture. Caught in the fringes of the rain gusts, heavy roses now and then softly patted against the windows. The dusky room, the perfect stillness within, the low mingled sounds of swaying trees and pattering rain without, the sense of the great darkness folding in its bosom the beauty so near and the

moaning city miles and miles away—all grew together into one
mood which possessed Hester's mind.

Who by words can fix the mood that comes and goes unbid-
den, like a ghost whose acquaintance is lost with his vanishing,
whom we know not when we do not see? A single happy phrase,
the sound of a wind, the odor of the mere earth may send us
into some lonely, dusky realm of being. But how shall we take
our brother with us, or send him there when we would? Even
the poet cannot work just what he means on the mind of his
fellow. We cannot meet save in God.

But the nearest mediator of feeling, the most potent, most
delicate, and least articulate, yet perhaps the most like the
breath moving upon the soft face of the waters of chaos, is
music. It swelled like a soft irrepressible tide in Hester's heart,
and she rose and walked around the shadowy room searching
for a piano. But there was no such creature there among the
aged furniture; she returned again to the table, and the mood
vanished in weariness.

Fatigued, they did not linger long in the room. The housekeeper, the ancient authority of the place, in every motion and
tone expressing herself wronged by their intrusion, conducted
them to their rooms. Every spot they passed was plainly far
more hers than theirs! But she had allotted their rooms well,
and they approved her judgment.

Weary as she was, Hester was charmed with her room. It was
old-fashioned to her heart's content, and full of shadowy histor-
ies, to which she now was to add hers.

Chapter 21.

MOTHER AND DAUGHTER

When she awoke it was to a blaze of sunlight, caught in the net of her closed curtains. The night had passed and carried the tears of the day with it. Ah, how much is done in the night when we sleep and know nothing! Things never stop. The sun was shining as if he too had wept and repented. All the earth beneath him was like the face of a child who has ceased to weep and begun to smile, but has not yet wiped away his tears.

Raindrops everywhere—millions and millions of them! Every one with a sun in it! For Hester had sprung from her bed, and opened the eyes of her room. How different was the sight from what she saw when she looked out in Addison Square! If heaven be as different from this earth, and as much better, we shall be happy children. On each side she saw green, undulating lawn, with trees and meadows beyond; but just in front the grassy slope grew steep and fell into the swift river which, swollen almost to unwieldiness, went rolling and sliding brown and heavy toward the far-off sea. When its swelling and tumult were over it would sing, but now it tumbled along with a roaring muffled in sullenness. Beyond the river, the bank rose in a wooded hill. She could see walks winding through the wood and, a little way up the valley, the rails of a rustic bridge that led to them. It was a paradise! For the roar of London along Oxford Street, there was the sound of the river; for the cries of rough human voices, the soprano of birds and the soft, mellow bass of the cattle in the meadows. The only harsh sound in this new world was the cry of the peacock, but that had somehow the

102

color of his tail in it and was not unpleasant. The sky was a shining blue without a cloud to be seen. Quietly it looked down, as if saying to the world over which it stood vaulted, "Yes, you are welcome to it all!"

She thanked God for the country, but soon was praying to Him for the town. The neighborly offer of the country to console her for the loss of the town she received with alarm, realizing that God cared more for one miserable, selfish, wife-and-donkey-beating costermonger of unsavory Shoreditch, than for all the hills and dales of Cumberland, and even all the starry things of His heavens.

She would care only as God cared, and from all this beauty gather strength to give to sorrow. She dressed quickly, and went to her mother's room. Her father was already out-of-doors, but her mother was having breakfast in bed. They greeted each other with such smiles as made words almost unnecessary.

"What a *lovely* place it is, mama! You did not say half enough about it," exclaimed Hester.

"Wasn't it better to let you discover for yourself, my child?" answered her mother. "You were so sorry to leave London, that I would not praise Yrndale for fear of prejudicing you against it."

"Mother," said Hester, with something in her throat, "I did not want to change. I was content and had my work to do! I never was one to turn easily to new things. And perhaps I need hardly tell you that the conviction has been growing upon me for years and years that my calling is among my fellow creatures in London."

She had never yet, even to her mother, spoken plainly concerning the things most occupying her heart and mind. Every one of the family, except Saffy, found it difficult to communicate—and perhaps to Saffy it might become so as she grew. Hester trembled as if confessing a fault. What if to her mother the mere idea of having a calling should seem a presumption!

"Two things must go, I think, to make up a call," said her mother, greatly to Hester's relief. "You must not imagine, my child, that because you have never opened your mind to me, I have not known what you were thinking, or have left you to think alone about it. Mother and daughter are too near not to hear each other without words."

"O mother!" cried Hester, overjoyed to find she thought of them thus so near to each other. "I am so glad! Please tell me the two things you mean."

"Both impulse and possibility are wanted in a call," replied Mrs. Raymount. "The first you know well; but have you sufficiently considered the second? One whose impulse or desire was continually thwarted could scarcely go on believing herself called. The half that lies in an open door is wanting. If a call comes to a man in prison, it will be by an angel who can let him out. Neither does inclination always determine fitness. When your father was an editor, he was astonished at the bad verse he received from someone who had a genuine delight in good verse."

"I can't believe, mama," returned Hester, "that God gives any special gift, particularly when accompanied by a special desire to use it, and that for a special purpose, without intending it should be used. That would be to mock His creature in the very act of making her."

"There are some who never find a use for their special gifts."

"Yes, but perhaps they have not sufficiently cultivated their gifts, or they have not done their best to bring them into use. Or may they not have wanted to use them for ends of their own and not of God's? I feel as if I must stand up against every difficulty lest God should be disappointed in me. Surely any frustration of the needs to which their very being points must be the person's own fault. May it not be because they have not yielded to the calling voice that they are all their lives prey to unsatisfied longings? They may have gone picking and choosing, instead of obeying."

"There must be truth in what you say, Hester, but I am pretty sure it does not reach every case. At what point would you pronounce a calling frustrated? You think yours is to help your poor friends, but you are not with them now. Is your calling frustrated? Surely there may be delay without frustration! Or is it for you to say when you are ready? Willingness is not everything. Might not one fancy her hour come when it was not come? May not part of the preparation for work be the mental discipline of imagined postponements?"

Hester gave a great sigh. Postponement indefinite is terrible to the young and eager. "That is a dreary thought, mother."

"Is it, my child?" returned her mother. "Painful the will of God may be—that I well know, as who that cares anything about it does not! But *dreary*, no! Have patience, my love. Your heart's deepest desire must be the will of God, for He cannot have made you so that your heart should run counter to His will; let Him but have His own way with you, and your desire He will give you. To that goes His path. He delights in His children; so soon as they can be indulged without ruin, He will heap upon them their desires, for they are His too."

Hester was astonished at the grasp and power of her mother. The child may for many years have but little idea of the thought and life within the form and face he knows and loves better than any. But at last the predestined moment arrives, the two minds meet, and the child understands the parent. Hester threw herself on her knees, and buried her face in her mother's lap. The same moment she began to discover that she had been proud, imagining herself more awake to duty than the rest around her. She began to understand that if God has called, He will also open the door. She kissed her mother, and went to her own room.

Chapter 22.

GLADNESS

Scarcely had she reached it when the voices of the children came shouting along some corridor, on their way to find their breakfast. She must go and minister, postponing meditation on the large and distant for action in the small and present. But the exuberance, the foaming overflow of life and gladness in Saffy, and the quieter, deeper joy of Mark were an immediate reward. They could hardly be prevented from bolting their breakfast like puppies, in their eagerness to rush into the new creation around them. But Hester thought of the river flowing turbid and swift at the foot of the lawn; she must not let them go loose! When she told them they must not go without her, their faces fell, and even Mark began a gentle expostulation.

A conscientious elder sister has to bear a good many hard thoughts from the younger ones on whom, without a parent's authority and reverence, she has to exercise a parent's restraint. Well for her if she comes out of the trial without having gathered some needless severity, some seeming hardness, some tendency to peevishness! These weak evils are so apt to gather around a sense at once of the need and of the lack of power.

"No, Mark," she said, "I cannot let you go alone. You are like two kittens, and might be in mischief or danger before you knew. But I won't keep you waiting."

Beauties met them at every turn, and I doubt if some of the children in heaven are always happier than Saffy and Mark were that day. Hester had thoughts which kept her from being so happy as they, but she was more blessed. Glorious as is the child's delight, the child-heart in the grown woman is capable of tenfold the bliss. Saffy pounced on a flower like a wild beast on its prey; Mark stood and gazed at one; and Hester would gaze till the tears came in her eyes.

Mark was in many things an exception—a curious mixture of child and youth. He had never been strong, and had always been thoughtful. When very small he used to have a sacred rite of his own, neither play nor church. He would set two chairs in the recess of a window, "one for Mark and one for God," then draw the curtains around and sit in silence for a space.

When a little child sets a chair for God, does God take the chair or does He not? God is the God of little children, and is at home with them.

Before their ramble was over, what with the sweet twilight gladness of Mark, the merry noonday brightness of Saffy, and the loveliness all around, Hester's heart was quiet and hopeful. She had some things to trouble her, but none of them had touched the quick of her being. And this day her thoughts kept rising to Him whose thought was the meaning of all she saw, the center and citadel of its loveliness.

If once the suspicion wakes that God never *meant* the things that go to and fro in us as we gaze upon the world, that moment is the universe worthless as a doll to a childless mother. If God be not, then the steam engine is better than the flower, for it has the soul of man in it, and the flower has no soul at all. Nothing can mean if it is not meant. It is God that means everything as we read it, however poor or mingled with mistake our reading may be. And the soothing of His presence in what we call nature was beginning to work on Hester, helping her toward that quietness of spirit without which the will of God can scarcely be perceived.

Chapter 23.

DOWN THE HILL

When Franks and his family left Mrs. Baldwin's garret to go to another yet poorer lodging, it was with heavy hearts that they crept silently away, to go down yet another step of the world's stair.

God has more to do with the fortunes of the poor than with those of the rich. In the fortunes of the poor there are many more changes, and they are of greater import as coming closer to the heart of their condition. To careless eyes these fortunes appear on an almost dead level of toil and privation, but they have more variations of weather, more checkers of sunshine and shade, more storms and calms, than lives passed on airier slopes.

The Frankses were on the downward side of the hill Difficulty, and down they must go, unable to help themselves. They had found a cheaper lodging, but entered it with misgiving, as their gains had been moderate and their expenses great. And Franks was beginning to feel his strength and elasticity not quite what they had been, and the approach of old age helped to relax the springs of his hopefulness. His wife had not gotten over her last confinement, and the baby was sickly as well. And there was not much popular receptivity for acrobatics in the street—coppers came in slowly, the outlay was heavy, and the outlook was gray without the gold.

But his wife's words were always cheerful though their tone was mournful—the tone came of temperament, the words themselves of love and its courage. The daughter of a gamekeeper, the neighbors had regarded her as throwing herself away when she married Franks; but she had obtained an honest and brave husband, and never repented giving herself to him.

For a few weeks they did pretty well in their new lodging. They managed to pay their way and had food enough, though not quite so good as husband and wife wished each for the other, and both for their children. The boys had not yet in London exhausted their own wonder. Their lives were a continuous romance, and being happy they could eat anything and thrive on it.

The father, according to his lights, was a careful and conscientious parent, and his boys were strongly attached to him; they never thought of shirking their work, and endured a good deal of hardness and fatigue without grumbling. Their eyes were open to see that their father took a full share in all he required of them and did his best for them. They were greatly proud of their father, believing him not only the first man in his profession, but the best man ever in the world—and to believe so of one's parent is one of the strongest aids to righteousness.

They were now reduced to one room, and the boys slept on the floor. This was no hardship, and to the mother at least it was a pleasure to have all her chickens in the nest with her.

One evening after the boys were in bed, the parents sat talking.

"Well, I dunnow!" said Franks, after a long silence. "There's that Dr. Christopher, as was such a friend! You don't disremember what he used to say about the Almighty—how a man could no more get out o' the sight o' His eyes than a child could get out o' sight o' his mother's eyes as was a watchin' of him?"

"Yes, John, and a great comfort it was to me to hear him say so, an' many's been the time since, when I had no other but you an' the children."

"What troubles me is this," he resumed, "if that there mother was to see her child doin' no better'n you an' me, an' day by day gettin' further on the wrong way, I should say she wan't much of a mother to let us go on that way."

"She might ha' got her reasons for it, John," returned his wife, in some fear lest the hope she cherished was going to give way in her husband. "P'r'aps she might see that he could go further and fare none the worse. When the children want their dinner very bad, I ha' heerd you say to them, 'Now kids, ha' patience. What

109

if ye do be hungry, you ain't a dyin' o' hunger. You'll wear a bit longer yet!' Ain't I heerd you say that, John?"

"I ain't a goin' for to deny it—but this is a drivin' of it jest a *leetle* too far! Here we be come up to Lon'on a thinkin' to better ourselves—not wantin' no great things, but jest thinkin' as how it wur time to lay by a shillin' or two to keep us out o' the workus, when't come onto rain, an' let us die i' the open like, where a poor body can breathe! An' here fust one shillin' goes, an' then another, till we ain't got one, as I may almost say, left! An' there ain't no luck! Instead o' gettin' more we get less, an' the hard work wearin' out me an' the boys an'—"

A cry from the bed interrupted him. "I ain't wore out, father!" said Moxy. "I'm good for another go!"

"I ain't neither, gov'nor. I got a lot more work in me!"

"No, nor me!" said the third.

"Hold your tongues, you young rascals, an' go to sleep," growled the father, pretending to be angry with them. "You've no call to be awake when your father an' mother want to be by theirselves—a listenin' to what they've got to say to one another!"

"We wasn't a listenin', father—we was only hearin' 'cause we wasn't asleep."

"Well, boys, there's things as fathers an' mothers can understan' and talk about, as no boy's fit to see the end on, an' so you better go to sleep, or I'll break every bone in your bodies!"

"Yes, father, yes!" they answered together, nowise terrified. They had heard this threat every day of their lives, and not yet known it carried out.

But now the father changed his tone, without the least hypocrisy; knowing that his children were awake, he preferred looking at the other side of the argument. After a few moments' silence he began again.

"Yes, as you was sayin', wife, an' you're always in the right, if the right be anyhows to be got at, there's no sayin' when the Almighty He may come to see as we have had enough on it, an' turn an' let us have a taste o' luck again! Luck's sweet, an' it may be as He likes to give His childer a taste o' sweets now an' again, jest as you an' me, when we can afford it, an' that's not often, likes to give ourn a bull's-eye or a bit of toffy. I don't doubt *He* likes to see us enjoyin' of ourselves jest as well as we like to see

110

our little uns enjoyin' o' *theirselves*! It stands to reason, wife, don't it?"

"So it do seem to me, John!"

"Well," said Franks, "I dessay He do the best He can, an' give us as much luck as is good for us. We can't allus do as well as we would like for our little uns, but we *always* does the best we can. It may take time even with all the influence *He* has, to get the better o' things! We'll suppose yet a while, anyhow, as how He's lookin' arter us."

The Frankses went on slowly down the hill, and finding it harder to keep their footing. The baby grew worse, and they sought help at the hospital, but saw no Dr. Christopher, and the baby did not improve. At length Franks almost ceased to hope, and grew more and more silent, until at last he appeared morose. What we too often count righteous care, but our Lord calls the care of the world, consumes the life of the heart as surely as the love of money. At the root they are the same. Yet evil thing as anxiety is, it were a more evil thing to be delivered from it by anything but the faith of the Son of God—faith in His Father and our Father.

Franks was not very able to encounter the problems of life; but on the other hand he was one to whom wonders might safely be shown, for he would use them not speculatively but practically. Almost nothing sees miracles except misery, perhaps because to misery alone, save it be to the great unselfish joy, is it safe to show miracles. Those who must see ere they will believe, may have to be brought to the verge of the grave that a condition fit for seeing may be effected in them. "Blessed are they who have not seen and yet have believed."

Chapter 24.

OUT OF THE FRYING PAN

Amy Amber was unable any longer to endure a life bounded by the espionage, distrust, and ill-tempered rebuke of the two wretched dragons whose misery was their best friend, saving them from foreboded want by killing them while yet they had something to live upon. At last she did as she had threatened, and one morning her aunts could not find her in or out of the house. She had fled to a friend in London, a girl whom she had known before they both came to England. Her friend shared her lodging with Amy and helped her in seeking a situation. Her appearance and manners being altogether in her favor, she soon obtained her desire—a place behind a counter in one of the largest shops. There she was kept hard at work, and the hours of the business were long, but the labor was by no means too much for the fine health and spirits which now blossomed in her.

Her aunts raised an outcry of horror and dismay first, then of reprobation, accusing her of many things, among them those faults of which they were in reality guilty toward her. As to gratitude and affection, the debt was great on their part, and very small indeed on hers. They wrote to her trustees to acquaint them with the shocking fact of her flight, but dwelt far more upon the badness of her behavior to them from the first, the rapidity with which she had deteriorated, and the ghastliness of their convictions as to the depth of the degradation she had preferred to the shelter of their moth-eaten wings.

The younger of the two trustees was a man of business, who at once took proper measures for discovering her. It was not, however, before the lapse of several months that he succeeded. By that time her employers were so well satisfied with her that, after an interview with them, followed by one with the girl herself, he was convinced that she was much better where she was than with her aunts, whose dispositions were not unknown to him. So he left her in peace.

Knowing nothing of London, interested in all she saw, and much occupied with her new way of life, Amy did not at once go to find Miss Raymount. She often recalled her kindness, often dreamed of the beautiful lady who had let her brush her hair, and always intended to seek her as soon as she could feel at leisure. But the time wore away, and still she had not gone.

She continued a well-behaved girl, went regularly to church on Sundays, had many friends but few intimates, and lived with the girl who had been her friend before her mother's death. Her new way of life was dangerous, no doubt, from its lack of home ties, and of the restraining if not always elevating influences of older people. No kite can soar without the pull of the string, but danger is less often ruin than some people think. He who can walk without falling will learn to walk the better that his road is not always the smoothest.

Such were the respective conditions of Amy Amber and the Franks family when the Raymounts left London. The shades were gathering around the family, and the girl had passed from the shadow into the shine. Hester knew nothing of the state of either, and it was not at all for them she was troubled in the midst of the peace and rest of her new life when she felt like a shepherd compelled to leave his sheep in the wilderness. Were not her poor friends the more sorely tried that she was dwelling at ease? Could it be right? Yet for the present she could see no way of reaching them. All she could do for them was to cultivate her gifts, in the hope of one day returning to them the more valuable for the separation.

One good thing that came of the change was that she and her father were drawn closer together. When Mr. Raymount's hours of writing were over, he missed the more busy life into which he had been able to turn at will, and needed a companion. His wife not being able to go with him, he naturally turned to his daughter, and they took their walks abroad together. In these Hester learned much. Her father was not chiefly occupied with the best things, but he was of both a learning and a teaching nature. There are few that in any true sense can be said to be alive; of Mr. Raymount it might be said that he was coming alive, and it was no small consolation to Hester to get thus nearer to him. Like the rest of his children she had been a little afraid of him, and fear, though it may dig deeper the foundations of love, chokes its passages. Before a month was over, she was astonished to find how much of companions as well as friends they had become to each other.

Most fathers know little of their sons and less of their daughters. Being familiar with every feature of their faces, every movement of their bodies, and the character of their every habitual pose, they take it for granted they know them! There are few parents who might not make discoveries in their children which would surprise them. Some such discoveries Mr. Raymount began to make in Hester.

She kept up a steady correspondence with Miss Dasomma, and that also was a great help to her. She had a note now and then from Mr. Vavasor, and that was no help. A little present of music was generally its pretext. He dared not trust himself to write to her about anything else—not from the fear of saying more than was prudent, but because he was afraid of encountering her disapproval. In music he thought he did understand her, but was in truth far from understanding her. For to understand a person in any one thing, we must at least be capable of understanding him in everything. Even the bits of news he ventured to send her all concerned the musical world, except when he referred now and then to Cornelius, and he never omitted to mention his having been to his aunt's. Hester was always glad when she saw his writing, and always disappointed with the letter; she could hardly have said why, for she never expected it to go beyond the surface of things. He was not yet sufficiently at home with her, she thought, to lay open the stores of his heart and mind.

Vavasor found himself in her absence haunted with her face, her form, her voice, her song, her music, and sometimes with the peace and power of her presence, with the uplifting she exercised upon him. It is possible for a man to fall in love with a woman he is centuries from being able to understand—but how the form of such a woman must be dwarfed in the camera of such a man's mind! It is the falsehood of the silliest poetry to say he deifies the image of his beloved. He is but a telescope turned wrong end upon her. If such a man could see such a woman after her true proportions and not as the puppet he imagines her, thinking his own small great things of her, he would not be able to love her at all. To see how he sees her—to get a glimpse of the shrunken creature he has to make of her, so that he can get her through his proud door into the narrow cellar of his poor, pinched heart, would be enough to secure any such woman from the possibility of falling in love with such a man. Hester knew that in some directions he was much undeveloped, but she thought she could help him; and had he thoroughly believed in and loved her, which he was not capable of doing, she could have helped him. But a vision of the kind of creature he was capable of loving—therefore the kind of creature he imagined her in loving her—would have been sickening to her.

At length, in one of his brief communications, he mentioned that his yearly resurrection was at hand—his butterfly month as he called it—when he ceased for the time to be a caterpillar, and became a creature of the upper world, reveling in the light and air of summer. He must go northward, he said; he wanted not a little bracing for the heats of the autumnal city. The memories of Burcliff drew him, but he would too sadly be met by its realities. He had an invitation to the opposite coast which he thought he would accept. He did not know exactly where Paradise lay, but if he found it within accessible distance, he hoped her parents would allow him to call some morning and be happy for an hour or two.

Hester answered that her father and mother would be glad to see him, and if he were inclined to spend a day or two, there was a beautiful country to show him. If his holiday happened again to coincide with Corney's, perhaps they would come down together. If he cared for sketching, there was no end of picturesque spots as well as fine landscapes. Of music or singing she said not a word.

By return post came a grateful acceptance. About a week after, they heard from Cornelius that his holiday was not to make its appearance before vile November. He did not inform them that he sought an exchange with a clerk whose holiday fell in that undesirable month.

Chapter 25.

INTO THE FIRE

One lovely evening in June, Amy Amber thought she would make an effort to find Miss Raymount. She had learned the address from a directory, and was now sufficiently acquainted with London to reach Addison Square. Having dressed herself in the daintiest, brightest little bonnet, and gloves that clung closer to the small short hand than they had clung to the bodies of the rodents from which they came, she set out.

In every motion and feeling, Amy Amber was a little lady. She had not much experience, and could not fail to show ignorance of some of the small ways and customs of the next higher social stratum. But such knowledge is not essential to ladyhood, though half ladies think themselves whole ladies because they have it. To become ladies indeed they have to learn what those things and the knowledge of them are really worth. Amy was incapable of being disagreeable, and from the thing in itself ill-bred she recoiled instinctively. Without knowing it, she held the main secret of all good manners—she was simple. Many imitate simplicity, but Amy possessed it. She never put anything on, never wished to appear anything, never tried to look pleasant.

She got into an omnibus, and all the way distinguished herself by readiness to make room. Amy's hospitable nature welcomed a fellow creature even into an omnibus. She found Addison Square and the house. It looked dingy and dull, for many of the shutters were closed, and there was an air of departure about it. She knocked and asked if Miss Raymount was at home.

Now Sarah had not been to Burcliff, and did not know Amy.

116

"They are all out of town, miss, except Mr. Cornelius."

At that moment Cornelius stepped on the landing of the stair, on his way out. The moment he heard her voice, he hurried down, his face glowing in pleasure. But as he drew near, she seemed so changed that he could hardly believe his eyes. Her face beamed at the sight of him, and she stepped within the door.

"Amy! Who would have thought of seeing you here? When did you come to town?" he asked as he shook hands with her.

"I have been in London a long time," she answered.

Corney thought she looked as if she had. "How deuced pretty she is!" he said to himself. "Quite a lady!"

"Come upstairs," he said, "and tell me all about it."

He turned and led the way, and Amy followed him. Sarah stared after them, wondering who the lady could be. Mr. Cornelius was so at home with her! "A cousin from Australia," she concluded, as the Raymounts did have cousins there.

They went into the drawing room, where Cornelius opened the shutters of a window, congratulating himself on his good luck. Not often did anything so pleasant enter the old place! He made her sit beside him on the sofa in the half dark, and in a few minutes had all her story. Moved by her sweet bright face and pretty manners, and pleased with the respect she showed him, he began to think her the nicest girl he had ever known.

But after a half-hour conversation, she rose.

"What!" said Corney. "You're not going already!"

"Yes, sir," replied Amy. "But I am so sorry not to see Miss Raymount! She was very kind to me."

"You mustn't go yet," said Corney. "Come—you used to like music. I will sing to you, and you shall tell me if I have improved."

He went to the piano, and Amy sat down again. He sang with his usual inferiority—which was not so inferior that he failed of pleasing Amy. Then he showed her a book of photographs, portraits of the more famous actresses of the day. He kept her until Sarah grew fidgety, and was on the point of stalking up from the kitchen, when she heard them coming down.

Cornelius took his hat and stick to walk with her. Amy was pleased to have his company, and he went with her all the way to her lodging in Kensington. Before they parted, she had begun to fill what little there was of Corney's imagination.

Chapter 26.

AWAITING A PURPOSE

The hot dreamy days rose and sank in Yrndale. Hester would wake in the morning oppressed with the feeling that there was something she ought to have begun long ago, and must positively set about this new day. She had no great work to do—only the common family duties of the day. In the heat of the day, she would seek a shady spot with some favorite book for her companion. Under the shadow of some rock, the tent-roof of some beech, or the solemn gloom of some pine grove, the brooding spirit of the summer would day after day find her and fill her with a sense of repose. Then nothing seemed required of her but to live; mere existence was conscious well-being. But the feeling never lasted long, as the dread awoke that she was forsaking the way, that she was too willing to be idle, to rest in inaction. Then would faith rouse itself and say, "But God will take care of you in this thing too. You have not to watch lest He should forget, but to be ready when He gives you the lightest call. You have to keep listening."

As regularly as she went to bed at night and left it in the morning, she went from the teatable in the afternoon to the piano she had discovered in the house. And more often than she knew, Mark would be somewhere in the dusk listening to her play, a lurking cherub feeding on her music and sometimes ascending on its upward torrent to a solitude where only God could find him.

At such times the thought of Vavasor would come to Hester, but it was chiefly as one who would be a welcome helper in her work. Then mostly would she think what it would be to have a man for a friend, one who would strengthen her heart and make her bold to do what was needful and right; and if then the thoughts of the maiden would fall to the natural architecture of maidens, and build one or two of the airy castles into which no man has looked or ever can look, and if through them flitted the form of Vavasor, who will wonder! It is not the building of such castles that is to be blamed, but the building of such as Inspector Conscience is not allowed to enter. The ideal of a man, with whom to walk on her way through the world, is as right for a woman to cherish as it was for God to make them male and female; and to the wise virgin it will ever be a solemn thought, dwelt upon in loveliness, and never mockingly, even if playfully, handled.

But there is a poor ambition to be married, which is the thought most present with too many young women. They feel as if their worth remains unacknowledged, as if there is no place of their own in society until they find a man to take them under his wing. It says ill for the relation of father and mother if the young women of a family recoil from the thought of being married, but it says ill for the relation of parents and children if they are longing to be married.

One evening toward the end of July, Hester was sitting under a fir tree on the gathered leaves of numberless years, with pine odors filling the twilight around her. The wind awoke, and began to sing the strange, thin ghost song of the pine grove. The sweet melancholy of the hour moved her spirit. When alone with nature, she seldom longed for her piano—she *had* the music and did not need another kind. As she sat in music-haunted reverie, she heard a slight rustle on the dry carpet around her feet, and saw in the gloom the form of a man. She was startled, though he spoke instantly to her.

It was Vavasor. She was still, and could not answer for a moment.

"I am sorry I frightened you!" he said.

"It is nothing," she returned. "But why can't one help being silly?"

"Nothing is more startling than to find someone near when you thought you were alone."

"Except," said Hester, "finding yourself alone when you

thought someone near. But how did you find me?"

"They told me at the house you were somewhere in this direction. So I came to look for you, and something led me right. All the time I seem on my way to lose myself instead of finding you."

"It might be both," returned Hester, "for I don't know my way certainly in the dusk."

"I cannot have lost myself if I have found you."

"It is time we were moving," said Hester. "Who knows when we may reach the house?"

"Let us risk it a few minutes longer," said Vavasor. "This is delicious—my first burst from the dungeonland of London for a whole year! This is paradise! I could fancy I was dreaming of fairyland! But it is such an age since you left London that you must be getting used to it, and will scarcely understand my delight!"

"It is only the false fairyland that children grow tired of."

As they talked, Vavasor seated himself beside her. She asked about his journey and about Cornelius, and then rose to her feet before Vavasor. The way seemed to reveal itself to her as they went, and they were soon at home.

Vavasor spent the next fortnight at Yrndale. In those days Nature had the best chance with him she had yet had. Society may have sought to substitute herself for both God and Nature, and may have had a horrible amount of success—yet any man is potentially a true man, however far he may be from actual manhood. Who knows what may be awakened in him? During that fortnight, Vavasor developed not merely elements of which he had no previous consciousness, but also elements in whose existence he could not be said to have really believed.

And one morning he got up in time for the purpose of seeing the sun rise. It is not surprising that he formed the resolution the night before; something Hester had said was enough to account for that. But that a man like him should, in the sleepiness of the morning, come to keep the resolve he had made in the wakefulness of the previous night, was a great stride forward. And he really enjoyed the clear, invigorating, clean air that filled his lungs like a new gift of life and strength. He had poetry enough to feel something of the indwelling greatness that belonged to the vision itself and knew a power present to his soul—but he set it all down to poetic feeling, which he never imagined to have anything to do with fact. It was the drawing of the eternal Nature in him toward the naturing Eternal whom he was made to understand, but of whom he knew so little.

That same evening, after almost a surfeit of music, they went out to wander about the house in the twilight.

"In such an evening," said Vavasor, "I could almost doubt whether there was indeed such a constantly recurring phenomenon in nature as I saw this morning."

"What did you see?" wondered Hester.

"I saw the sun rise."

"Did you really? I'm so glad! That is a sight rarely seen in London."

"One goes to bed so late and so tired!" he replied simply.

"True! And even if one be up in time, where could you see it from?"

"I *have* seen it rise coming home from a dance—but then somehow one doesn't seem to have anything to do with it. But this morning I felt as if I had never seen the sun before. He seemed to mean his shining, where in London he always looks indifferent—just as if he had to do it and couldn't help it, like everybody else in the horrible place. Who was it that said, 'God made the country, and man made the town'?"

"I think it was Cowper," answered Hester, "but it can't be quite true. I suspect man has more to do with the unmaking than the making of either. We have reason to be glad he has not come near enough to us here to destroy either our river or our atmosphere. I have been thinking about it lately; it is the rubbish that makes all the difficulty—the refuse of the mills and the pits and ironworks and the potteries that does all the mischief."

"So it is! And worst of all is the human rubbish, especially that which gathers in our great cities and gives so much labor in vain to clergyman and philanthropist!"

"What do you mean by the human rubbish, Mr. Vavasor?"

He saw he must be careful, and would fence a little. "Don't you think," he said slowly, measuring his words, "that in the body politic there is something analogous to the waste in matter?"

"Certainly," she answered. "Only we might differ as to the persons who were to be classed in it. We should be careful of our judgment as to when that state has been reached. None but God can read in a man what he really is. It can't be a safe thing to call human beings, our own kith and kin born into the same world with us, and under the same laws of existence, *rubbish*."

"I see what you mean," he said to Hester. But to himself he said, "Good heavens!"

"You see," Hester went on as they walked among the dusky trees, "rubbish with life in it is an awkward thing to deal with. Rubbish proper is that out of which the life is gone, and so rendered useless that it cannot even help the growth of life in other things. But suppose this rubbish, say that which lies about the mouth of a coal pit, could by some process be made to produce the most lovely flowers, or if neglected, would bring out horrible poison weeds to infect the air, or horrid creeping things, then the word *rubbish* would mean either too much or too little. You see, Mr. Vavasor, I have been thinking a great deal about all this kind of thing. It is my business in a way."

"But would you not allow that the time comes when nothing can be done with them?"

"I will not allow it of any that I have to do with, at least before I can say with confidence I have done all I can. After that another may be able to do more. And who shall say when God can do no more—God who is laboriously working to get His children home."

"I confess," said Vavasor, "the condition of our poor in our large towns is the great question of the day."

"Which everyone is waking up to *talk* about," said Hester.

Vavasor began to think that if ever the day came when he might approach Hester as a suitor for her hand, he must be very careful over her philanthropic craze. But if ever he should in earnest set about winning her, he had full confidence in the artillery he could bring to the siege; he had not yet made any real effort to gain her affections. Neither had he a doubt that, having succeeded, he could do with her much as he pleased. His wife, once introduced to such society as would then be her right, would speedily be cured of any such extravagance or foolish enthusiasm.

Under the influence of the lovely place, of the lovely weather, and of his admiration for Hester, he was now—to use the phrase with which he confessed the fact to himself—"over head and

122

ears in love with her." Notwithstanding the difficulties in his way, it was a pleasant experience to him; like most who have gone through the same, he was at this time nearer knowing what bliss may be than he had ever been before.

And it began to grow plain to him that now his aunt could no longer look unfavorably upon the idea of such an alliance. It was a very different thing to see Hester in the midst of such grounds and in such a house, with all the old-fashioned comforts and luxuries of an ancient and prosperous family around her, instead of in the dingy region of Bloomsbury, where everything was respectable in a very inferior and snuffy kind of way. If he could get his aunt to see Hester in the midst of these surroundings!

By degrees, emboldened mainly by the influences of the soft dusky twilights, he came to speak with more warmth and nearer approach as his heart was tuned above its ordinary pitch.

"How strangely this loveliness seems to sink into the soul," he said one evening, when the bats were coming and going like wild thoughts. "For the moment you seem to be the soul of that which is around you, yet oppressed with the weight of its vastness, and unable to account for what is going on in it."

"I think I understand you," returned Hester. "It is strange to feel at once so large and so small, but I presume that is how all true feeling seems to itself."

"You are right," responded Vavasor, "for when one loves, how it exalts his whole being; yet in the presence of the woman he worships, how small he feels, and how unworthy!"

For the first time in her life Hester felt a vague pang of jealousy, though she did not know what it was. She was silent, and Vavasor judged he might venture a little further. But with all his experience in the manufacture of compliments and in high-flown poetry, he was now at a loss—he had no fine theories of love to talk from! With him, love *at its best* was the something that preceded marriage—after which it must take its chance. But as he considered God's loveliest idea, exposed to the mightiest enchantment of life, little imagining it an essential heavenly decree for the redemption of the souls of men, he saw for broken moments and with half-dazed glimpses into the eternal, and spoke as if in a gracious dream.

"If one might sit forever thus!" he whispered. "Forever and

ever, needing nothing, desiring nothing! Lost in perfect, absolute bliss! The very soul of me is music, and needs not the softest sound of earth to keep it alive."

At that moment a sigh of the night wind bore to their ears the whispered moan of the stream away in the hollow, as it broke its being into voice over the pebbly troubles of its course.

"Still!" said Vavasor. "Do not speak to me—I cannot attend even to your watery murmur. A sweeter music, born of the motions of my own spirit, fills my whole hearing. That God in the mercy of a God would make this moment eternal!" He ceased, and was silent.

Hester could not help being thrilled by the rhythm and moved by the poetic phrases, yet she was not altogether pleased. "I do not quite understand you," she said. "I can scarcely imagine the time should ever come when I should wish it should last forever."

"Have you had so little happiness?" he asked sympathetically.

"Indeed, I have had a great deal," she replied. "But I do not think much of happiness. Perhaps that is a sign that I have not had much of what is not happiness. But no amount of happiness that I have known yet would make me wish the time to stand still. I want to be always growing, and while one is growing, Time cannot stand still even if he would—you drag him on with you! I want to be always becoming more and more capable of happiness."

"Ah!" returned Vavasor. "You are as usual out of sight beyond me. You must take pity on me and carry me with you, else you will leave me miles behind, and I shall never look on you again—and what eternity would be to me without your face to look at, God only knows. There will be no punishment necessary for me but to know there is an impassable gulf between us."

"But why should it be so!" answered Hester tenderly. "Our fate is in our own hands. It is ours to determine the direction in which we shall go. I don't want to preach to you, dear Mr. Vavasor, but so much surely one friend may say to another! Why should not everyone be reasonable enough to seek the one best thing, and then there would be no parting—whereas all the love and friendship in the world would not suffice to keep people together, if they were inwardly parted by such a difference as you imply."

Vavasor's heart was touched in two ways by this simple speech. He could not help thinking for a moment what a blessed thing it must be to feel good and have no weight upon you, as this lovely girl plainly did, and live in perfect fearlessness of whatever might happen to you. Religion would be better than endurable in the company of such an embodiment of it! And clearly she was not disinclined to be on terms of closer intimacy with him. So why should he not accept the implied offer of help? That would and could bind him to nothing.

From that night he placed himself more than ever in the position of her pupil, hoping for the natural effect of the intimacy. To keep up and deepen the relation, he went on merely imagining himself in this difficulty or that. He was no conscious hypocrite in the matter; his intellect alone was concerned where he talked as if his being was. No answer could have had the smallest effect on the man, for Vavasor only decided what he would say next. Hester kept trying to meet him as simply and directly as she could, although to meet these supposed difficulties she was compelled to transform them into something that she understood—still something very different from anything in Vavasor's thoughts.

So long as she would talk to him, he cared not a straw whether she understood what he said; and with all her misconception, she understood it better than he did himself.

Chapter 27.

MAJOR H.G. MARVEL

One afternoon Vavasor was in his room writing a letter to his aunt. Mr. Raymount was in his study, Mrs. Raymount in her own room, and the children out-of-doors. A gentleman was shown in as Hester sat alone in the drawing room at her piano.

The name on the card was *Major H.G. Marvel.* She vaguely thought she had heard of it, but in the suddenness of the meeting was unable to recall a single idea concerning the owner of it. She saw before her a man whose decidedly podgy figure bore a military air, and was not without a certain grace of confidence. There was self-assertion of the inviting sort, and his person beamed with friendship. Above the middle height, the impression of his stature was reduced by a too great development of valor in the front of his person, which must always have met the enemy considerably in advance of the rest of him. His head was round and smooth and shining like ivory. His face was pleasant to look at, with irregular features, a retreating and narrow forehead over keen gray eyes that sparkled with intelligence and fun, prominent cheekbones, a large mouth ready to show a set of white, regular teeth, and a double chin.

"Cousin Hester!" he said, advancing and holding out his hand.

Mechanically she gave him hers. The voice that addressed her was at once a little husky and very cheery; the hand that took hers was small and soft and kind and firm. A merry, friendly smile lighted up his eyes and face as he spoke. Hester could not help liking him at first sight, yet she felt a little shy of him. She

126

thought she had heard her mother speak of a cousin somewhere abroad.

"You don't remember me," he said, "seeing you were not in this world until a year or two after I left the country; and, to tell the truth, had I been asked, I should have objected to your appearance on any terms."

As this speech did not seem to carry much enlightenment with it, he went on to explain. "The fact is, my dear young lady, that I left the country because your mother and I were too much of one mind."

"Of one mind?" said Hester, bewildered.

"Ah, you don't understand!" said the Major, who was all the time standing before her with the most polite though confident bearing. "I liked your mother better than myself, and so did she, and without any jealousy of one another, it was not an arrangement for my happiness. I had the choice between two things—stopping at home and breaking my heart by seeing her the wife of another man, and going away and getting over it the best I could. So you see I must by nature be your sworn enemy; only it's of no use, for I've fallen for you at first sight. So now, if you will ask me to sit down, I will swear to let bygones be bygones, and be your true knight and devoted servant as long as I live. You do remind me of your mother, only you're twice as handsome."

"Do pray sit down, Mr. Marley—"

"Marvel, if you please," interrupted the major, "and I'm sure it's a great marvel if not a great man I am, after what I've come through! But don't you marvel at me too much, for I'm a very good sort of fellow when you know me."

"I will let my mother know you are here," said Hester, turning to the door.

"I shouldn't wonder if she thought me troublesome in those days. But I bear no malice now, and I hope she doesn't either. Tell her I say so. It's more than five-and-twenty years ago, though to me it don't seem more than so many weeks. Tell her Old Harry is come to see her—very much improved since she turned him about his business."

Hester, much amused, ran to find her mother. "There's the strangest gentleman downstairs, mama, calling himself Old Harry. I never saw such an odd man!"

Her mother laughed—a pleased little laugh. "Go to him, Hester dear, and say I shall be down directly."

"Is he really a cousin, mama?"

"To be sure—my second cousin! He was very fond of me once."

"Oh, he has told me all about that already. He says you sent him about his business."

"It is true enough that I wouldn't marry him, but he doesn't know what I went through for always taking his part. I always stood up for him, though I never could bear him near me. He was such a rough, good-natured bear, always saying the thing he ought not to, and making everybody, ladies especially, uncomfortable! He never meant any harm, but never saw where fun should stop. You wouldn't believe the vulgar things Harry would say out of pure fun. But I daresay he's much improved by this time."

"He told me to tell you he was. But if he is much improved—well, what he must have been! I like him though, mama—I suppose because you liked him a little. So take care you are not too hard upon him; I'm going to take him up now."

"I make over to you my interest in him, and have no doubt he will be pleased enough with the change, for a man can't enjoy finding an old woman where he had all the time been imagining a young one. But I must warn you, Hester, as he seems to have made a conquest of you already, that he has in the meantime been married to a Hindu woman."

"That's nothing to his discredit with you, mama, I hope."

"She has been dead now for some ten years. I believe he had a large fortune with her, which he has since increased considerably. He is really a good-hearted fellow, and was kind to every one of his own relations as long as there was one left to be kind to."

"Well, I shall go back to him, mama, and tell him you are coming as soon as you have got your wig and your newest lace cap on, and your cheeks rouged and pearl-powdered, to look as like the lady that would have none of him as you can."

Her mother laughed merrily, and pretended to box her daughter's ears. It was not often any mood like this rose between them—yet who may so well break out in childlike merriment as those whose life has in it no moth-eaten mammon pits, who have

128

no fear, no greed, and live with a will, rising like the sun to fill the day with the work given them to do!

"Look what I have brought you, cousin," said Major Marvel, the moment Hester reentered the room, holding out to her a small necklace. "You needn't mind taking them from an old fellow like me, for it don't mean that I want to marry you offhand before I know what sort of temper you've got."

Hester drew near, and looked at the necklace. "How strangely beautiful it is! All red, pear-shaped, dull, scratched-looking stones, hanging from a savage-looking gold chain! What are they, Mr. Marvel?"

"You have described it like a book!" he said. "It is a barbarous native necklace, but they are fine rubies—only rough—neither cut nor polished."

"It is beautiful," repeated Hester. "Did you really mean it for me?"

"Of course, I did!"

"I will ask mama if I may keep it."

"Where's the good of that? I hope you don't think I stole it? But here comes the mother! Helen, I'm so glad to see you once more!"

Hester slipped away with the necklace in her hand, and left her mother to welcome her old admirer before she would trouble her about the offered gift.

They met like trusting friends whom years had done nothing to separate, and while they were yet talking of bygone times, Mr. Raymount entered, received him cordially, and insisted on his remaining with them as long as he could; although rivals, they were old friends, and there never had been any ground for bitterness between them. The major agreed, and Mr. Raymount sent to the station for his luggage.

Chapter 28.

THE MAJOR AND VAVASOR

During dinner the major took the greater part of the conversation upon himself, and evidently expected to be listened to. But that was nearly all he wanted—let him talk and hear you laugh when he was funny, and he was satisfied. He was fond of telling tales of adventure, some wonderful, some absurd, some having nothing in them but his own presence—but he was just as willing to tell a story with the joke turned against himself. Like many of his day, he was full of the amusements and sports with which so much otherwise idle time is passed by Englishmen in the East, who seem to think nothing connected with the habits of their countrymen there could fail to interest those at home.

Every now and then he would say, "Oh, that reminds me!" and then tell something that happened when someone of the regiment was out tiger shooting, or pig sticking, or whatever the sport might be—"and if Mr. Raymount will take a glass of wine with me, I will tell him the whole story." He was constantly drinking, after the old fashion, with this or that one of the company.

As the major, for all the rebuffs he had met with, had not yet learned to entertain the smallest doubt as to his personal acceptability, so he was on his part most broad in his receptivity. But there were persons whom from the first glimpse he disliked, and then his dislike was little short of loathing. And if his suspicion or dislike was roused, he was just as likely as any other man to arrive at a correct judgment of a man he did not love.

When he and Vavasor were introduced to each other, he

glanced at him, drew his eyebrows together, made his military bow, and included him among the listeners to his tales. Vavasor was annoyed at his presence, and could not help thinking what his aunt would say to such a relative. So while Vavasor retained the blandest expression, and was ready to drink a glass of wine with the newcomer, he privately set the major down not only as a boaster and an ill-bred man, in which there was some truth, but also as a liar and a vulgar-minded man as well, in which there was little or no truth.

The major had been relating a thrilling adventure with a man-eating tiger. He saw the wide, listening eyes of little Mark and Saffy, and saw Hester, who was still child enough to prefer an adventure to a lovetale, fixed as if her hair would stand on end. But he also surprised a certain expression on Vavasor's face, who was annoyed to see Hester's absorption—she seemed to have eyes for no one but the man who shot tigers as Vavasor would have shot grouse.

The major swallowed something that was neither food nor good for food, and said, though not quite so carelessly as he intended, "I see by your eyes, Mr. Passover, you think I'm drawing the long bow, eh?"

"No, 'pon my word!" said Vavasor earnestly. "I was only admiring the coolness of the man who would creep into the mouth of the jungle after a man-eating tiger. And isn't a man-eating tiger something tremendous? When he once takes to that kind of diet, they say he likes nothing else half so well! A man must be a very Münchhausen to venture in."

"I don't know the gentleman," said the major, and none of the listeners recognized the name of the king of liars. "But you are quite mistaken in the character of the man-eating tiger. It is true that he does not care for other food after once getting a passion for the more delicate; but it does not follow that the indulgence increases either his courage or his fierceness. The fact is it ruins his moral nature and undermines his natural courage. He is a sneak, and the ruffian knows he is a rebel against the law of his Maker, and a traitor to his natural master. The man-eater is the devil of his kind. The others leave you alone except you attack them, but he attacks you and then runs when you go out after him. You can never get any sport out of him. *He* will never fly at your elephant, or climb a tree, or take to the water after you. If there's a creature on earth I hate, it's a coward!"

Said Vavasor to himself, "The man's a coward!"

Hester asked, "But *why* should you hate a coward so?" With the vision of a man-eating tiger in front of her, she felt she must herself come under that category. "How can a poor creature made without courage help being one?"

"Such as you mean I wouldn't call cowards," returned the major. "Nobody thinks worse of the hare, or even the fox, for going away before the hounds. Men whose business it is to fight go away before the enemy when they have no chance, and when it could do no good to stand and be cut down. To let yourself be killed when you ought not is to give up fighting. There is a time to run and a time to stand—but the man will run like a man and the coward like a coward."

Said Vavasor to himself, "You'll know when to run, at least!"

"What can harmless creatures do but run?" resumed the major. "But when the wretch that has done all the hurt it could will not show fight for it, but turns tail the moment danger appears, I call him a contemptible coward. Man or beast, I would set my foot on him. That's what made me go into the hole to look for the brute."

"But he might have killed you, though he was a coward," said Hester, "when you left him no room to run."

"Of course he might, my dear! Where else would be the fun of it? Without that the thing would be no better than this shooting of pigeons and pheasants by men who would drop their guns if a cock were to fly in their faces. You *had* to kill him, you know. He's first cousin to the woman-eating tiger that abounds in English society; if the woman be poor, he devours her at once; if she be rich he marries her, and eats her up slowly at his ease in his den."

"As with his black wife!" thought Mr. Raymount, who had been little more than listening.

But Mr. Raymount did not really know anything about that part of his friend's history. The black wife had been the daughter of an English merchant by a Hindu wife, a young creature when he first made her acquaintance, unaware of her own power, and kept almost in slavery by the relatives of her deceased father, who had left her all his property. Major Marvel had made her acquaintance, and became interested in her through a devilish attempt to lay the death of her father at her door. The shine of her gold had blinded her relatives into imagining, if not believing, her guilty. The major had taken her part, had been of the greatest service, and she was acquitted entirely. But although nobody believed her in the smallest degree guilty, *society* looked askance upon her.

Then the major had said to himself, "Here am I a useless old fellow, living for nobody but myself! It would make one life at least happier if I took the poor thing home with me. She's rather too old, and I'm too young to adopt her, but I daresay she would marry me." He did not then know that she had more than a very moderate income, and it turned out to be a very large fortune, indeed, when he inquired into things. The major rejoiced over his fortune, but would still have been an honorable husband had she had nothing.

When she left him the widowed father of a little girl, he mourned her sincerely. When the child followed her mother, he was for some time a sad man indeed. Then, as if her money was all he had left of her, and he must lead what was left of his life in its company, he went heartily into speculation with it, and at least doubled his fortune. He had now returned to England to find almost every one of his old friends dead, or so changed as to make them all but dead to him.

And it was with a kind of heart despair that he sought the cousin he had loved. And scarcely had he more than seen the daughter of his old love than he saw at once that she was a grand and gracious sort of creature. At the same time he unconsciously claimed a property in her—to have loved the mother seemed to give him a right in the daughter. But all this was only in the region of feeling, not at all in that of thinking.

In proportion as the major was taken with Hester, he profoundly disliked the fine gentleman visitor that seemed to be dangling after her. He might be a woman-eater, and after her money—if she had any. Such suspects must be watched and followed and their haunts marked.

"But," said Hester, fearing the conversation might take a dangerous turn, "when you know that a beast may have you down and begin eating you any moment, what is it that keeps you up? What have you to fall back upon? Is it principle, or faith, or what is it?"

"Ho, ho!" said the major, laughing. "A metaphysician in the very bosom of my family! I had not reckoned upon that! No, you don't think about it at all. It's partly your elephant and partly your rifle, and partly perhaps that as an Englishman you are sent to that quarter of the world to kill their big vermin for them! But no, you don't think of that at the time. You've got to kill him—that's it."

"If the animal should kill you, is that all right?" asked Hester.

"By no means, I give you my word of honor," laughed the major.

"Well, now," answered Hester, "unless I had made up my mind that if I was killed it was all right, I couldn't meet the tiger."

"You do not know what it is to have confidence in your eye and your rifle. It is a power in you—a power to destroy the thing that opposes you!"

Hester fell to thinking, and the talk went on without her. She never heard the end of the story, but was roused by the laughter that followed it.

"It was no tiger at all!" said the major. "There was a roar of laughter when the brute—a great lumbering, floundering hyena—rushed into the daylight and bit together the barrel of my rifle as a schoolboy does a quill pen."

"And what became of the man-eater?" asked Mark, disappointed.

"Stopped in the hole until it was safe to come out."

"Just imagine that horrible growl behind you as it came out of a whole mine of teeth inside!" said Hester.

"By George! For a young lady," said the major, "you have an imagination! Too much of that won't go to make you a good hunter of tigers!"

"Then you owe your coolness to want of imagination?" suggested Hester.

"Perhaps so," returned the major, with a merry twinkle in his eye. "Perhaps we hunters are but stupid fellows—too stupid to be reasonably frightened!"

"I don't mean that exactly. I think that perhaps you do not know so well as you might where your courage comes from. For my part, I would rather be courageous to help the good than to destroy the bad."

"Ah, but we're not all good enough ourselves for that," said the major, with a serious expression. The habitual twinkle of fun had for the moment vanished from his clear eyes. "Some of us are only fit to destroy what is worse than ourselves."

"To be sure we can't *make* anything," replied Hester thoughtfully, "but we can help God to make. To destroy evil things is good, but the worst things can only be destroyed by being good, and that is so hard!"

"It *is* hard," said the major. "So hard that most people never try it!" he added with a sigh, and a gulp of his wine.

Mrs. Raymount rose, and withdrew with Hester and the children. The major rattled on after they left, and Vavasor sat silent, with an expression that seemed to say, "I am amused, but I don't eat all that is put on my plate."

Chapter 29.

BRAVE DEEDS

During the whole of his visit, the major kept as near Hester as he could, much to Vavasor's annoyance. Vavasor thought the major a most objectionable and low fellow, full of brag and vulgarity, and the major thought Vavasor a supercilious idiot. Vavasor, without ceasing for a moment to be conventionally polite, and all deference toward Hester and her parents, allowed Major Marvel to see unmistakably that his society was not welcome. Entirely ignorant each of the other's pursuits, and nearly incapable of sympathy upon any point, each would have gladly shown the other to be the fool he counted him.

After breakfast the next day, all but Mr. Raymount went out for a walk together. It seemed destined to be a morning of small adventures. As they passed the gate of the Home Farm, out rushed a half-grown pig right between the legs of the major, throwing him backward into a place he would certainly not have chosen for the purpose. A look of gratification rose in Vavasor's face, but he was much too well-bred to allow it to remain. The fallen hero returned cleverly and cheerfully to his feet, and showed either a sweetness or a command of temper which gave him a great lift in Hester's estimation.

"Confound the brute!" he laughed. "He can't know how many of his wild relatives I've stuck, else I should set it down to revenge. What a mess he has made of me! I shall have to throw myself in the river for purification."

Saffy laughed right merrily over his fall and the fun he made of it, but Mark looked concerned. He ran and pulled some grass and proceeded to rub the major down.

"Better let the mud dry," said the major. "It will come off much better then. Come along—you shan't have your walk spoiled by my heedlessness."

"The pig didn't mean it, sir," said Mark. "He only wanted to get out."

But there seemed to be more creatures about the place that wanted to get out—a spirit of liberty was abroad. Mark and Saffy rushed away like wild rabbits every now and then, making a round and returning, children once more. It was one of those cooler warm mornings that rouse all the life in heart, brain, and nerves, making every breath and movement a conscious pleasure.

They had not gone much farther when, just as they approached the paling of a paddock, a horse came blundering over the fence, and would soon have been ranging the world. The ladies and children drew back, and Vavasor also stepped a little aside, making way for the animal to follow his own will. But the major went up to him, took him by nose and ear, led him back to the gap, made him jump in again, and replaced the bar he had knocked away.

"Thank you! How brave of you, Major Marvel!" said Mrs. Raymount.

The major laughed with his usual merriment. "If it had been the horse of the Rajah of Rumtool, I should have been brave indeed—only there would have been nothing of me left to thank! A man would have needed courage to take him by the head! But a quiet, good-tempered carriage horse—none but a cockney would be frightened at him!"

With that he began, to the awful delight of the children, to tell them the most amazing and horrible tales about the Rajah's horse. They may or may not have been true—but the major only told what he had heard and believed, or had himself seen.

Vavasor, annoyed at the natural nervousness he had himself displayed, turned his annoyance on the major, who by such an insignificant display of coolness had gained so great an advantage over him in the eyes of the ladies.

They were now following the course of the river, and had gradually descended from the higher ground to the banks, which spread out into a small meadow on each side. Saffy pulled stalks of feathery grasses, while Mark walked quietly along the brink of the stream, stopping every now and then to look into it. The bank was overhung with long grass, and here and there a bush of rushes, and in parts was a little undermined. On the opposite side lower down was a meal mill, and nearly opposite was the head of the millrace, whose weir dammed back the river and made it deeper here than in any other part—seven feet at least, and that close to the shore.

The ladies and gentlemen were walking along the meadow, some distance behind the children, when Saffy ran back toward them screaming, and no Mark to be seen. All started running to meet her, but Mrs. Raymount sank on the grass. Vavasor reached Saffy first, but she answered his anxious questions by shrieking with every particle of available breath. When the major came up, he heard enough to know that he must use his wits and lose no time with Saffy. He kept close to the bank, looking for some sign of the spot where Mark had fallen in, until he heard Hester crying behind him, "Across! Across!"

He looked, and halfway across saw something dark slowly drifting toward the millrace. The major threw off his coat, plunged in, found the water deep enough for swimming, and made straight for the mouth of the millrace, anxious beyond all things to prevent Mark from getting to the waterwheel.

In the meantime, Saffy ran to her mother, while Hester, followed by Vavasor, sped along the bank till she came to the weir. Vavasor laid his hand on her arm to prevent her, but she turned on him with flashing eyes, and lips white with the wrath that has no breath for words. He drew back and dared only follow. The footing was uncertain, with deep water on one side, and a steep descent to more deep water on the other. In one or two spots the water ran over, and those spots were slippery. Hester flew across without a slip, leaving Vavasor behind.

But when they had run along the weir and landed, they were on the slip between the millrace and the river, deep water, therefore, between them and the major, where he was already trying to heave Mark's form onto the bank. The poor man had not swum so far for many years, and was nearly spent.

"Bring him here," cried Vavasor. "The stream is too strong for me to get to you. It will bring you in a moment."

The major uttered an oath, heaved the body half on the

shore, and was then just able to scramble out himself.

When Vavasor looked round, he saw Hester was already almost at the mill. There she crossed the millrace and ran up the other side where the major was doing all he could to bring back life. There was little hope out there in the cold, and Hester caught the child up in her arms and ran with him to the mill. The major followed—running, panting, dripping. When they met Vavasor, he would have taken him from her, but she would not give him up.

"Go back to my mother," she said. "Tell her we have him at the mill. Then go and tell my father, and send for the doctor."

Vavasor obeyed, feeling again a little small.

In a few minutes they had Mark in the miller's blankets with hot water about him, while the major moved the boy's arms and inflated his chest with his own breath.

Vavasor took it upon himself to assure Mrs. Raymount that Mark was safe and would be all right in a little while. She rose then and, with what little help Saffy could give her, managed to walk home. Vavasor ran on to the house and summoned Mr. Raymount, who appeared on the spot just as the first signs of returning animation appeared. The boy opened his eyes, looked at his father, smiled his own heavenly way, and closed them again with a deep sigh. They covered him up warm, and left him to sleep till the doctor should appear.

That same night, as Hester was sitting beside her brother, she heard him talking in his sleep:

"When may I go and play with the rest of the river? Oh, how sweetly it talks! It runs all through me! It was such a nice way, God, of fetching me home! I rode home on a waterhorse!"

He thought he was dead, that God had sent for him home, that he was now safe, only tired. It sent a pang through Hester's heart; what if, after all, he was going to leave them! He had always seemed fitter for being Home than abroad, and any day he might be sent for!

He recovered by degrees, but seemed very sleepy and tired; and when he was taken home, he begged to go to bed. But he never fretted or complained, received every attention with a smile, and told his mother not to mind, for he was not going away yet. He had been told that under the water, he said.

Chapter 30.

AN INVESTIGATION

The major left Yrndale the next morning, saying now there was no Mark to attend to, his room was better than his company. Vavasor, much relieved, said he would stay a day or two longer. He could not go until he saw Mark fairly started on the way of recovery.

But in reality the major went because he could no longer endure the sight of "that idiot" as he called Vavasor, and felt design against him fermenting in his heart.

"The poltroon!" he said. "A fellow like that to marry a grand creature like Hester! Why, rather than wet his clothes, the sneak would have let us both drown after I got him to the bank! Calling me to go to *him*, when I had done my best and was at the last gasp!"

He told them to tell Mark he was gone to fetch tiger skins and a little idol with diamond eyes, and a lot of odd things that he had brought home, and he would tell him all about them, and let him have any of them he liked to keep for his own, as soon as he was well again. So he must make haste, for the moth would get at them if they were long lying about and not seen to.

He told Mr. Raymount that he had no end of business to look after; but now he knew the way to Yrndale, he might be back any day. As soon as Mark was well enough to be handed over to a male nurse, he would come directly. He told Mrs. Raymount that he was going to fetch her some pearls.

He made Hester promise to write to him at the Army and Navy Club every day till Mark was well. And so he departed, much blessed by all the family for saving the life of their precious boy.

When the major reached London he hunted up some of his old friends, and through them sent out inquiry concerning Vavasor. He learned then some few things about him—nothing very bad as things went where everything was more or less bad, and nothing to his special credit. That he was heir to an earldom he liked least of all, for he was only the more likely to marry his beautiful cousin, and her he thought a great deal too good for him—which was truer than he knew.

Vavasor was relieved to find that Hester, while full of gratitude to the major, had no unfavorable impression concerning his own behavior in the sad affair. As the days went on, however, and when he expected enthusiasm to have been toned down, he was annoyed to find that she was just as impressed with the objectionable character of the man who had got the start of him in rendering the family service. If there were any more such relations likely to turn up, the sooner he cut the connection the better!

He could not understand that as to the pure all things are pure, so the common mind sees far more vulgarity in others than the mind developed in genuine refinement. It understands, therefore forgives, nor finds it hard. Hester was able to look deeper than he, and she saw much that was good and honorable in the major, though the bridle of his tongue might be too loose for safe riding in the crowded paths of society. Vavasor took care, however, after hearing the first words of defense which some remark of his brought from Hester, not to go further, and turned the thing he had said aside: where was the use of quarreling about a man he was likely never to set eyes on again?

A day or two before the natural end of his visit, as Mrs. Raymount, Hester, and he were sitting together in the old-fashioned garden, the letters were brought them—one for Vavasor, with a great black seal. He read it through, and said quietly, "I am sorry I must leave you tomorrow, but I ought to be present at the funeral of my uncle, Lord Gartley. He died yesterday. It is a tiresome thing to succeed to a title with hardly enough to pay the servants!"

"Very tiresome," assented Mrs. Raymount, "but a title is not like an illness. If you can live without one, you can live with one."

"True, very true! But society expects so much of a man in my position! What do you think, Miss Raymount?" he asked, turning toward her with a look that seemed to say whatever she thought would always be law to him.

"I think with mama," replied Hester. "I do not see why a mere name should have any power to alter one's mode of life. Of course, if the change brings new duties, they must be attended to, but if the property be so small as you say, it cannot want much looking after."

"I must go a good deal by what my aunt thinks best. She has a sort of right, you see. All her life her one fixed idea, knowing I was likely to succeed, has been the rehabilitation of the earldom, and all her life she has been saving for that."

"Then she is going to make you her heir?" said Hester, who, having been asked her opinion, simply desired the grounds on which to give it.

"My dear Hester!" said her mother.

"I am only too much delighted Miss Raymount should care to ask me anything," said Vavasor. "My aunt does mean to make me her heir, I believe, but one must not depend upon that, because if I were to displease her, she might change her mind any moment. But she has been like a mother to me, and I do not think, for any small provocation such as I am likely to give her, she would yield the dream of her life. She is a kindhearted woman, though a little peculiar; true as steel where she takes a fancy. I wish you knew my aunt, Mrs. Raymount."

"I should be much pleased to know her."

"She would be delighted with this perfect paradise of yours. I feel its loveliness the more that I am so soon to hear its gates close behind me. Happily there is no flaming sword to mount guard against the expelled!"

"You must bring your aunt sometime, Mr. Vavasor. We should make her very welcome," said Mrs. Raymount.

"Unfortunately, with all her good qualities, my aunt is a little peculiar. For one thing she shrinks from making new acquaintances." He should have said "any acquaintances out of her own world." All others, so far as she was concerned, existed only on the sufferance of remoteness.

But by this time Vavasor had resolved to make an attempt to gain his aunt, and thereby Hester. He felt sure his aunt could not fail to be taken with Hester, if only she saw her in fit surroundings; with Miss Vavasor the frame was more than half the picture. He was glad now that she had not consented to call on the family in Addison Square; they would be of so much more importance in her eyes in the setting of Yrndale. He had himself also the advantage of being now of greater importance; he was that Earl of Gartley for whom she had been saving all the time. She must either be of one mind with him now, or lose the cherished purpose of so many years. If he stood out, seeming to prefer poverty and the woman of his choice, she would be compelled to give in.

That same evening he left them in high spirits, and without any pretense of decent regret for the death of one whom he had never seen, and who for many years had lived the life of an invalid and a poor man—neither of much account in his world.

It would be untrue to say that Hester was not interested in the news. They had been so much thrown together of late, and in circumstances so favorable to intimacy, to the manifestation of what of lovable was in him, and to the revelation of how much her image possessed him, that she could hardly have been a woman at all and not care for what might befall him. Neither was she indifferent to the pleasure of wearing a distinguished historical name, or of occupying an exalted position in the eyes of the world. Her nature was not yet so thoroughly possessed with the things that *are* as distinguished from the things that only appear, as not to feel some pleasure in being a countess of this world, while wanting the inheritance of the saints in light. Of course, this was just as far unworthy of her as it is unworthy of anyone who has seen the hidden treasure not to have sold all that he had to buy it—not to have counted, with Paul, everything but dross to the winning of Christ—not even worth being picked up on the way as he presses toward the mark of the high calling.

But she thought of it first of all as a buttressing help to the labors, which, come what might, it remained her chief hope to follow again among her poor friends in London. To be a countess would make things easier for her, she thought. Little she knew how immeasurably more difficult it would make it to do anything whatever worth doing, that, at the very first, she would have to fight for freedom—her own—with hidden crafts of slavery, especially mighty in a region more than any other under the influences of the prince of the power of the air! She had the foolish notion that, thus uplifted among the shows of rule, she would be able with more than mere personal help to affect the load of injustice laid upon them from without, and pressing them earthward. She had not yet sufficiently learned that, until a man has begun to throw off the weights that hold him down, it is a wrong done him to attempt to lighten those weights. Why seek a better situation for the man whose increase of wages will only go into the pocket of the brewer or distiller? While the tree is evil, its fruit will be evil.

So again the days passed quietly on. Mark grew a little better. Hester wrote regular but brief bulletins to the major. The new earl wrote that he had been to the funeral, and described in a would-be humorous way the house and lands to which he had fallen heir. The house might, he said, be made fit to live in, but what was left of the estate was literally a mere savage mountain.

Chapter 31

IN ANOTHER LIGHT

Mr. Raymount went now and then to London, but never stayed long. In the autumn he moved his books to Yrndale. When they were arranged to his mind in the old library, he began, for the first time in his life, to feel he had an abiding place, and talked of selling the house in Addison Square. It would have been greater progress to feel that there is no abiding in place or among things.

In October, Major Marvel again made his appearance at Yrndale, but not quite the same man he was; he had a troubled manner, and the expression on his face of one who had an unpleasant duty to discharge—a thing to do he would rather not do, but which it would cost him far more to leave undone. He had brought the things he promised, every one, and at the sight of them Mark brightened up amazingly. At table the major tried to be merry as before, but failed rather conspicuously, drank more wine than was his custom, and laid the blame on the climate. His chamber was over that of his host and hostess, and they heard him walking about for hours in the night. There was something on his mind that would not let him sleep! In the morning he appeared at the usual hour, but showed plain marks of a sleepless night.

It was a perfect autumn morning, of which everyone except the major felt the enlivening influence—the morning of all mornings for a walk! Just as Hester was leaving, the major humbly requested that she would walk with him alone, as he much wished a private conversation with her. Hester, though with a little surprise, also a little undefined anxiety, at once consented, but ran first to her mother.

"What can he want to talk to me about, mama?"

"How can I tell, my dear?" answered her mother with a smile. "Perhaps he will dare the daughter's refusal too."

"O mama! How can you joke about such a thing!"

"I am not quite joking, my child. There is no knowing what altogether unsuitable things men will do! Who can blame them when they see how women consent to many unsuitable things!"

"But, mama, he is old enough to be my father!"

"Of course he is! Poor man! It would be hard fate to have fallen in love with both mother and daughter in vain! But you need not be much afraid. He is really a gentleman, however easily mistaken for something else. You must not forget how much we owe him for Mark!"

"Do you mean, mama," said Hester, with a strange look out of her eyes, "that I ought to marry him if he asks me?"

Her mother laughed heartily. "What a goose you are, my darling! Don't you know your mother from a miscreant yet?"

But in truth her mother so rarely jested that there was some excuse for her. Relieved from the passing pang of a sudden dread, Hester went and put on her bonnet to go. They set out together, but until they were some distance from the house walked in absolute silence, which seemed to Hester to bode no good. But how changed to poor man was, she thought. It would be pitiful to have to make him still more miserable!

Steadily the major marched along, his stick under his arm like a sword, and his eyes looking straight before him. "Cousin Hester," he asked, "can you imagine a man rendering himself intensely, unpardonably disagreeable, from the very best of motives?"

"I think I could," answered, Hester, wishing neither to lead him on nor deter him. Whatever he had to say, the sooner it was said the better!

"Let me ask you first," he resumed, "whether you are able to trust me a little. I am old enough to be your father—fancy I am your grandfather, wishing you well. Trust me and tell me—what is there between you and Mr. Vavasor? I know ladies think such things are not to be talked about with gentlemen, but there are exceptions to every rule. Are you engaged to Mr. Vavasor?"

"No," answered Hester promptly.

"What is it then? Are you going to be?"

"If I answered that in the affirmative," said Hester, "would it not be much the same as acknowledging myself already engaged?"

"No!" cried the major vehemently. "So long as your word is not passed, you remain free. The two are as far asunder as the pole from the equator. I thank God you are not engaged to him!"

"But why?" asked Hester, with a pang of something like dread. "Why should you be so anxious about it?"

"Has he never said he loved you?" asked the major eagerly.

"No," said Hester hurriedly. But her *no* trembled a little, for the doubt came with it, whether though literally, it was strictly true. "We are friends," she added. "We trust each other a good deal."

"Trust him with nothing, least of all your heart, my dear," said the major earnestly. "Or, if you must trust him, trust him with anything, with everything, except that. He is not worthy of you."

"Do you say that to flatter me or to disparage him?"

"Entirely to disparage him. I never flatter."

"You did not surely bring me out to hear evil of one of my best friends?" said Hester, now angry.

"I certainly did—if the truth be evil—but only for your sake. The man I do not feel interest enough in to abuse even. He is a nobody."

"That only proves you do not know him; you would not speak so if you did," said Hester, widening the space between her and the major.

"I am confident I should have worse to say if I knew him better. It is you who do not know him. It astonishes me that sensible people like your father and mother should let a fellow like that come prowling after you!"

"Major Marvel, if you are going to abuse my father and mother as well as Lord Gartley—" cried Hester, but he interrupted her.

"Ah, there it is!" he exclaimed bitterly. "Lord Gartley! I have no business to interfere—no more than your gardener or coachman! But to think of an angel like you in his arms! Believe me the man is not worthy of you."

147

"What have you got against him? I do hate backbiting! As his friend, I ask you what you have against him."

"I can't tell you anything very bad of him. But he is a man of whom no one has anything good to say—one of whom never a warm word is uttered."

"I have called him my friend!" said Hester.

"That's the worst of it! If it were not for that, he might go to the devil for me! I daresay you think it a fine thing he should have stuck to business for so long! He was put to that before there was much chance of his succeeding; his aunt would not have him on her hands consuming the money she meant for the earldom. His elder brother would have had it, but he killed himself before it fell due. I don't say your *friend* has disgraced himself; he has not, for it takes a good deal for that in his set! But not a soul out of his own family cares twopence for him!"

"There are some who are better liked everywhere than at home, and they're not the better sort," said Hester. "That goes for less than nothing. I know the part of him chance acquaintances cannot know. He does not bear his heart on his sleeve. I assure you, Major Marvel, he is a man of uncommon gifts and—"

"Great attraction, no doubt—to me invisible," blurted the major.

Hester turned from him. "I am going home," she said. "Luncheon is at the usual hour."

"Just one word," he cried, hurrying after her. "I swear I have no purpose or hope in interfering but to save you from a miserable future. Promise me not to marry him, and I will settle on you a thousand pounds a year."

Hester walked faster.

"Hear me," he went on, in an agony of entreaty mingled with something like anger. "I mean it," he continued. "Why should I not for Helen's child?"

He was a yard or two behind her. She turned on him with a glance of contempt. But the tears were in his eyes, and her heart smote her. He had abused her friend, but was plainly honest himself. Her countenance changed as she looked at him. He came up to her. She laid her hand on his arm, and said, "Dear Major Marvel, what would you think of one who took money to do the thing she ought to do? I will not ask you what you would

148

think of one who took money to do the thing she ought not to do! I would not promise not to marry a beggar from the street. It might be disgraceful to marry the beggar; it *must* be disgraceful to promise not!"

"Yes, my dear! You are quite right—absolutely right," said the major humbly. "I only wanted to make you independent. You don't think half enough of yourself. But I will dare one more question; is he going to ask you to marry him?"

"Perhaps. I do not know."

"How could they let you go about with him so much and never ask him what he meant by it?"

"They could easier have asked me what I meant by it!"

"If I had such a jewel, I would look after it!"

"Have me shut up like an Eastern lady, I suppose," said Hester, laughing. "Make my life miserable to make it safe. If a woman has any sense, Major Marvel, she can take care of herself; if she has not, she must learn her need of it."

"Ah!" said the major sadly. "But the thousand pangs and aches and heart-sickenings! I would sooner see my child on the funeral pyre of a husband she loved, than living a merry life with one she despised!"

Hester began to feel she had not been doing the major justice. "So would I!" she said heartily. "You mean me well, and I shall not forget how kind you have been. Now let us go back."

"Just one thing more: if ever you think I can help you, you *will* let me know?"

"That I promise you with all my heart," she answered. "I mean," she added, "if it be a thing I count it right to trouble you about."

The major's face fell. "I see!" he said. "You won't promise anything. Well, stick to that, and don't promise."

"Would you have me come to you for a new bonnet?"

"By George! Shouldn't I be proud to fetch you the best in Regent Street by the next train! But I throw myself on your generosity, and trust you to remember there is an old man that loves you, and has more money than he knows what to do with."

"I think," said Hester, "the day is sure to come when I shall ask your help. In the meantime, if it be any pleasure to you to know it, I trust you heartily. You are all wrong about Lord Gartley though. He is not what you think him."

149

She gave him her hand. The major took it in his own soft small one and pressed it devoutly to his lips.

Now that the hard duty was done, and if not much good yet no harm had resulted, he went home a different man. A pang of fear for Hester in the power of "that ape Gartley" would now and then pass through him, but he had now a right to look after her, and who could tell what might not turn up!

His host congratulated him on looking so much better for his walk, and Hester recounted to her mother their strange conversation.

"Only think, mama!" she said. "He offered me a thousand pounds a year not to marry Lord Gartley!"

"Hester!"

"He does not like the earl, and he does like me, so he wants me not to marry him. That is all!"

"I thought I could have believed anything of him, but this goes almost beyond belief!"

"Why should it, mama? Instead of hating him for it, I like him better than before."

"Are you sure he was not making room for himself?"

"Quite sure. He would have it he was old enough to be my grandfather. But you know he is not that!"

"Perhaps you wouldn't mind if he were a little younger yet," said her mother merrily, "as he is too young to be your grandfather."

"I suppose you had a presentiment I should like him, and left him for me, mama!" returned Hester in like vein.

"But seriously, Hester, is it not time we knew what Lord Gartley means? I cannot help being anxious about you. If he does not love you he has no right to court your company so much."

"I encourage it, mama. I like him."

"That is what makes me afraid."

"It will be time enough to think about it if he comes again, now he has got the earldom."

"Should you like to be a countess, Hester?"

"I would rather not think about it, mama. It may never make any difference whether I should like it or not."

"I can't help thinking it strange he should be so much with you and never say a word!"

150

"Might you not just as well say it was strange of me to be so much with him, or of you, mother dear, to let him come so much to the house?"

"It was neither your part nor mine to say anything. Your father even has always said he would scorn to ask a man his intentions; either he was fit to be in his daughter's company, or he was not. Either he must get rid of him, or leave his daughter to manage her own affairs."

"Don't you think he is right, mother? If I let Lord Gartley come, surely he is not to blame for coming!"

"Only if you should grow fond of him, and it were to come to nothing?"

"It can't come to nothing, mother, and neither of us will be the worse for it, I trust. As to what I think about him at present, I need ask myself. I am afraid you think me very cool, and in truth I don't quite understand myself, but perhaps if one tries to do right as things come up, one may get on without understanding oneself. I will try to do what is right—you may be sure of that, mother."

"I am quite sure of that, my dear, and I won't trouble you more about it. I should not like to see my Hester a lovesick maiden, pining and wasting away!"

"Depend upon it, mama, if I found myself in that state no one else should discover it," said Hester, partly in play, but thoroughly in earnest.

"That only reveals how little you know about such things, my love! You could no more hide it from the eyes of your mother than you could from a husband."

"Such things have been hid before now, mama! And yet why should a woman ever hide anything from one's own mother? No, when I am dying of love, you shall know, mama. But it won't be tomorrow or the next day."

Chapter 32.

THE MAJOR AND THE BOYS

The major was in no haste to leave, but spent most of his time with Mark, and was in nobody's way.

One day he was telling the boy how he had been out alone on a desolate hill all night, how he heard the beasts roaring round him, and not one of them came near him.

"Did you see *Him?*" asked Mark.

"See who, sonny?" returned the major.

"The One between you and them," answered Mark in a subdued tone, and from the tone the major understood.

"No," he answered, and taking into his the spirit of the child, went on. "I don't think anyone sees Him nowadays."

"Isn't it a pity?" asked Mark. Then after a thoughtful pause he resumed. "Well, not see Him just with your eyes, you know! But I fancy sometimes I must have seen Him with my very eyes when I was young, and that's why I keep always expecting to see Him again someday. Don't you think I shall, major?"

"I hope so, indeed, Mark! It would be a bad job if we were never to see Him!" he added, suddenly struck with a new feeling.

"Yes, indeed. That it would!" responded the child. "Why, where would be the good of it all, you know? That's what we came here for—ain't it? God calls children—I know He calls some, for He said, 'Samuel, Samuel!' I wish He would call me!"

"What would you say?" asked the major.

"I would say, 'Here I am, God! What is it?' We mustn't keep God waiting, you know."

The major felt that the child was there to give him apt admonishment. Could God have ever called him and he not have listened? Of course, it was all a fancy! And yet as he looked at the child, and met his simple believing eyes, he felt he had been a great sinner, and the best things he had done were not fit to be looked at. Happily there were no conventional religious phrases in the mouth of the child to repel him; his father and mother had a horror of hypocritical Christianity. They had both seen in their youth too many religious prigs to endure temple-whitewash on their children. Except what they heard at church, hardly a special religious phrase ever entered their ears. Those of the New Testament were avoided from reverence, lest they should grow common and fail of their purpose when the children should read them for themselves. Yet the true teaching for children is persons, history, and doctrine in the old sense— instruction in righteousness, and not human theory about divine facts.

The major was still at Yrndale when Cornelius arrived for his holiday. The major could hardly accept him as one of the family, so utterly inferior did he show. There was a kind of mean beauty about his face and person and an evident varnish on his manners which revolted him. "That lad will bring grief on them!" he said to himself.

Cornelius was more than usually polite to the major—he was in the army, the goal of his aspiration! But he laughed in private at what he called his vulgarity, and delighted to annoy Hester with remarks upon her "ancient adorer." Because he prized nothing of the kind, he could see nothing of his essential worth, and took note merely of his blunders, personal ways, and oddities. The major was not properly vulgar, only ill-bred. Cornelius had learned nothing but manners, and was vulgar with a vulgarity that went miles deeper than that of the major. The major would have been sorry to find he had hurt the feelings of a dog; Cornelius would have whistled on learning that he had hurt the feelings of a woman. If the major was a clown, Cornelius was a cad. The one was capable of genuine sympathy; the other not yet of any. The latter loved his own paltry self, counting it the most precious thing in creation. The major was conceited, but had no lofty opinion of himself. Hence it was that he thought so much of his small successes. He knew they were small things of which he boasted, but he had no other and scorned to invent; his great things, those in which he had shown himself a true and generous man, he looked on as matters of course, nor recognizing anything in them worth thinking of. He was not a great man, but had elements of greatness; he had no vision of truth, but obeyed his moral instincts: when those should blossom into true intents, as one day they must, he would be a great man.

The weeks went on, and all the time the major was studying Cornelius, and saw into him deeper than his mother or Hester—saw a certain furtive anxiety in the youth's eyes, the unrest of trouble he would not show. "The rascal has been doing wrong," he said to himself, "and is afraid of being found out!"

Corney seemed restless for his month to be gone, making no response to the lamentations of the children that Christmas was so near, and Corney not to be with them! He did not show them much kindness, but a little went a great way with them, and they loved him.

As for Mark, he was more than happy when *Majie* was there. They would be together most days all day long, and the number of stories Mark could swallow was amazing.

The family party was about to be broken up—not by subtraction, but by addition. The major had done nothing to spoil the homeness of home, but it was now for a time to be set aside.

Chapter 33

A DISTINGUISHED GUEST

A letter came from Lord Gartley, asking Mrs. Raymount whether he might presume upon her wish to welcome his aunt to the hospitality of Yrndale. "If you have not room for us," he wrote, "or if our presence would spoil your Christmas party, do not hesitate to put us off. I shall understand you, and say nothing to my rather peculiar but most worthy aunt, waiting a more convenient season." The desired invitation was immediately dispatched, with some wry faces on the part of the head of the house, who, however, would not oppose his wife's wishes.

Notwithstanding his knowledge of men, that is, of fundamental human nature, Mr. Raymount was not good at reading a man who made himself agreeable and did not tread on the toes of any of his theories—of which, though mostly good, he made too much, as every man of theory does. He laid too much upon words, attributing more power to them for the regeneration of the world than was reasonable. If he had known how few cared a pin's point for those in which he poured out his mind, just flavored a little with his heart, he would have lost hope altogether. Perhaps the knowledge of how few of those who admired his words acted upon them, would have made him think how little he struggled himself to do those same things. He had not yet believed that to do right is more to do for the regeneration of the world than any amount of teaching can do. It is righteousness—not of words, not of theories, but in being, in vital action—which alone is the power of the spirit.

He did not see through or even into Gartley who was by no means a profound or intentional hypocrite. But Mr. Raymount never started on a new relation with any suspicions. He was too much occupied with what he counted his work—with his theories first, then his writing of them, then the endless defending of them, to care to see beyond the focus of his shortsighted eyes. Vavasor was a gentlemanly fellow and did not oppose him, and that went a long way.

The day before Christmas Eve, the expected visitors arrived just in time to dress for dinner. The family was assembled in the large old drawing room when Miss Vavasor entered. She was tall and handsome and had been handsomer, for she was not of those who, growing within, grow more beautiful without as they grow older. She was dressed in the plainest, handsomest fashion, in black velvet half covered with thick-point lace. The only stones she wore were diamonds. Her features were regular; her complexion was not too sallow for the sunset of beauty; her clear gray eyes were rather large; her expression was very still, self-contained and self-dependent, without being self-satisfied; her hair was more than half gray, but very plentiful. Altogether she was one with an evident claim to distinction, never asserted because always yielded. To the merest glance she showed herself well-born, well-nurtured, well-trained, and well-kept, hence well-preserved. At an age when a poor woman must have been old and wrinkled, and half-undressed for the tomb, she was enough to make any company look distinguished by her mere presence. Her manner was as simple as her dress—without a trace of the vulgarity of condescension or undue stiffness. She spoke with the utmost readiness and simplicity, looked at Hester with interest but without curiosity, had the sweetest smile at hand for use as often as wanted—a modest smile which gleamed but for a moment and was gone. There was nothing in her behavior to indicate a consciousness of error from her sphere. The world had given her the appearance of much of which Christ gives the reality. For the world very oddly prizes the form whose informing reality it despises.

Lord Gartley was in fine humor. He had not before appeared to so great advantage. He had never put off his company manners with Hester's family, but was now almost merry, quite graciously familiar—as if set on bringing out the best points of his friends. But his face when Major Marvel entered! He had even feared his presence. A blank dismay clouded it with an inharmonious expression, which made him look like a discomfited commoner. In a moment he had overcome the unworthy sensation, and was again impassive and seemingly cool. The major did not choose to see him at first, but was presented to Miss Vavasor by their hostess. He appeared a little awed by the fine woman, and behaved like any gentleman used to society. Seated next to her at dinner, he did not once allude to pigsticking or tiger-shooting, to elephants or savages, but talked about the last opera and the last play.

He had been strongly tempted all that day to a very different behavior. He knew at once, when told she was coming, that Lord Gartley was bringing her down with the hope of gaining her consent to his asking Hester to marry him. "The rascal knows," said the major to himself, "that nothing human could stand out against Hester! There is only her inferior position to urge from any point of view!" And therewith arose his temptation: might he not so comport himself before the aunt as to disgust her with the family, and save his lovely cousin from a heartless noodle?

"I'll settle the young ape's hash for him!" he said to himself. "It only wants a little free-and-easyness with my lady to do the deed. It can cost me nothing except her good opinion, which I can afford. What jolly fun it will be to send her out of the house in a rage! And a good deed done too! By George, I'll do it!"

In this resolution he had begun to dress, but before he had finished had begun to have his doubts. Would it not be dishonorable? Would it not bring such indignation upon him that even Mark would turn away? Hester would never accept so much as a postage stamp from him if he brought disgrace on her family, and drove away her suitor! Besides, he might fail! They might come to an understanding and leave him out in the cold! By the time he was dressed he had resolved to leave the fancy alone, and behave like a gentleman. But now with every sip of wine the temptation came stronger and stronger. The spirit of fun kept stirring in him. Not merely for the sake of Hester, but for the joke of the thing, he was tempted, and had to keep fighting the impulse till the struggle was almost more than he could endure. And just from this came the subdued character of his demeanor. What had threatened to destroy his manner for the evening turned out to correct his usual behavior; as an escape from the strife within him, he tried to make himself agreeable. Miss Vavasor was soon interested, and by and by pleased with him. He began to feel pleased with her, and was more at his ease. Therewith came the danger not unforeseen of some at the table—he began to tell one of his stories. But he saw Hester look anxious, and that was enough to put him on his honor. Ere dinner was over he said to himself that if only the nephew were half as good as the aunt, he would have been happy to give the young people his blessing and a handsome present.

"By Jove!" said Lord Gartley. "The scoundrel is not such a low fellow after all! I think I will try to forgive him!"

After dinner, they sat down to whist, of which Miss Vavasor was very fond. When, however, she found they did not play for money, though she praised the asceticism of the manner, she plainly took little interest in the game. The major, who had no scruples either of conscience or of pocket in the matter, suggested that his lordship and Hester should take their places, and proposed cribbage to her, for what points she pleased. The major was the best player in his regiment, but Miss Vavasor had much the better of it, and regretted she had not set the points higher. All her life she had had money in the one eye and the poor earldom in the other. The major laid down his half crowns so cheerfully, with such a look of satisfaction even, that she came quite to like the man, and to hope he would be there for some time. The fear of Lord Gartley as to the malign influence of the major vanished entirely.

And now that he was more at his ease, and saw that his aunt was at least far from displeased with Hester, Lord Gartley began to radiate his fascinations. He grew playful, even teasing; gave quick repartee, and sang well. But when Hester sang, the thing was done, and the aunt was won; she perceived at once what a sensation such a singer would make in her circle! In manner and style, beauty and accomplishments, she would be a decided gain to the family, possessing even in herself a not inconsiderable counterpoise to the title. Then who could tell but that this cousin—who seemed to have plenty of money, he parted with it so easily—might be moved by like noble feelings with her own to make a poor countess a rich one? The thing was settled, so far as the chief family worshiper was concerned.

Chapter 34.

COURTSHIP IN EARNEST

Christmas was a merry day to all but the major, who did not like the idea of an engagement any better than before. He found refuge and consolation with Mark. The boy was merry in a mild, reflected way, because the rest were merry, but preferred his own room with Majie to the drawing room with the grand lady.

Lord Gartley now began to apply his charms to Hester with full intent and purpose. Where men see no reason why a woman should love this or that man, she may see something in him which they do not see, or do not value as she does. Alas for her if she only imagines it! In few cases does the woman see what the men know; for much of that which is manifest to the eyes of the male world, is by the male world scrupulously hidden from the female. And men are more likely never to have thought of than to have forgotten this—that the love which a beautiful woman gives a man is in itself not an atom more precious than that which a plain woman gives. In the two hearts they are the same, if the hearts be like; if not, the advantage may well be with the plain woman. The love of a beautiful woman is no more thrown away than the love of the plainest. The same holds with women of differing intellectual developments or endowment. But when a woman of high hopes and aims—a woman filled with eternal aspirations after life, and unity with her divine original—gives herself to such a one as Lord Gartley, she must have seriously mistaken some things both in him and in herself, the consequence of which requires the correction of suffering.

Hester found her suitor now very pleasant. If sometimes he

struck a jarring chord, she found a way of accounting for it, or explaining it away—if not entirely to her satisfaction, yet so far that she was able to go on hoping everything, and for the present to put off any further consideration of the particular phenomenon to the time when, like most self-deceiving women, she scarcely doubted she would have greater influence over him—namely, the time when as man and wife, they would be one flesh. But where there is not already a far deeper unity than marriage can give, marriage itself can do little to bring two souls together, and may do much to drive them asunder.

She began to put him in training, as she thought, for the help he was to give her with her beloved poor. Lord Gartley had no real conception of her outlook on life, and regarded all her endeavor as born of the desire to perfect his voice and singing. With such teaching he must, he imagined, soon become worthy of her equal. He thought of genius as something supreme in itself, whereas it is altogether dependent on truth in the inward parts. Not millions of years, without an utter regeneration of nature, could make such a man as Gartley sing like Hester. She sang because of the song that was in her soul. Her music came out of her being, not out of her brain and her throat. If such a one as Gartley can sing, there is no reason why he should be kept singing. In all the arts, the man who does not reach to higher things falls away from the things he has.

For Hester the days now passed in pleasure. The closer contact with Lord Gartley influenced the rate of her growth toward the upper regions. We cannot be heart and soul and self in the company of the evil—and the untrue is the evil, however beheld as an angel of light in the mirage of our loving eyes—without sad loss. Her prayers were not so fervent, her aspirations not so strong. Hester was one of those who in their chambers are not alone, but with Him who sees in secret; and not to get so near to God in her chamber did not augur well for the new relationship. But the Lord is mindful of His own. He does not forget because we forget. Horror and pain may come, but not because He forgets—nay, just because He does not forget. That is a thing God never does.

Gartley yielded himself to her with pleasing grace. Inclined to rebel at times when wearied with her demands on his attention and endeavor, he yet condescended to them with something of the playfulness with which one would humor a child; he would have a sweet revenge by and by! His turn would come soon, and he would have to instruct her in many things she was now ignorant of! She had never moved in his great world; he must teach her its laws, instruct her how to shine, how to make the most of herself, how to do honor to his choice! He thought of her relation to the poor as but a passing phase of a hitherto objectless life. Anything beyond a little easy benevolence would be impossible to the wife of Lord Gartley! That she should contemplate the pursuit of her former objects, with even greater freedom and devotion than before, would have seemed to him a thing utterly incredible. And Hester would have been equally staggered to find he had so failed to understand her after the way she had opened her heart to him. To imagine that for anything she would forsake the work she had been sent to do! So things went on upon a mutual misunderstanding, each—in the common meaning of the words—growing more in love with the other every day, while in reality they were separating further and further. An occasional blasting doubt would cross the mind of Hester, but she banished it like an evil specter.

Miss Vavasor continued the most pleasant and unexacting of guests. Her perfect breeding, sustained by a quiet temper and kindly disposition, was easily taken for the sweetness it only simulated. To people like Miss Vavasor does the thought never occur—what if the thing they find it so necessary to simulate should actually in itself be indispensable? What if their necessity of simulating it comes of its absolute necessity?

She found the company of the major agreeable in the slow time she had, for her nephew's sake, to pass with such primitive people. Mr. Raymount would not leave what he counted his work for any goddess in creation, but it was well he did not give Miss Vavasor much of his company; if they had been alone together for a quarter of an hour, they would have parted sworn foes. So the major, instead of putting a stop to the unworthy alliance, found himself actually furthering the affair, doing his part with the lady on whom the success of the enemy depended. He was still now and then tempted to have his hideous revenge, but he was really a man of honor and behaved like one.

So the time went on till after the twelfth night, when Miss Vavasor took her leave for a round of visits, and Lord Gartley

went up to town. He would return to Yrndale in a month, when
the final arrangements for the marriage would be made.

A correspondence naturally commenced, but Gartley's letters
brought Hester the same disappointment as of old. In Hester's
presence, she suggesting and leading, he would utter what she
would have in him; but alone in his room, without the stimulus
of her presence or the sense of her moral atmosphere, the best
things he could write were poor enough. His letters absorbed
her atmosphere, and after each followed a period of mental
asphyxia. Had they been letters of a person indifferent to her,
she would have called them stupid, thrown them down, and
thought no more of them. As it was, she read few of them twice.
But all would be well, she said to herself, when they met again.
It was her absence that oppressed him, poor fellow! He was out
of spirits and could not write. And her father had told her of
men who were excellent talkers, but who could not set thoughts
down with pen in hand.

Yet she *would* have liked a little genuine, definite response to
the things she wrote. He seemed to have nothing to say from
himself. He would only assent and echo, and when she mentioned her work, he always replied as if she meant an undefined
something called *doing good.* He never doubted the failure of her
foolish concert had taught her that whether men be equal in the
sight of God or not, any attempt on the part of their natural
superiors to treat them as such could only be disastrous.

Chapter 35.

CALAMITY

One afternoon the post brought a letter from Lord Gartley, and one in a hand which Mrs. Raymount recognized.

"What can Sarah be writing about?" she said as she read, with a sudden foreboding of evil. "Something has happened to him!" Her face was as white as the paper.

Hester put her arms round her. "Mother! What is it?"

"I thought something would come to stop it all. We were too happy!" she moaned, and began to tremble.

Mr. Raymount's letters had been carried to him in the study, and one of them had put him into like state. He was pacing up and down the room, his pallor that of rage.

"The scoundrel!" he groaned, hurling a chair against the wall. "I suspected he was a mean dog! Now all the world will know it—and that he is my son! What have I done, what has my wife done, that we should give being to a vile hound like this?"

He threw himself in a chair, and wept with rage and shame. He had for years been writing of family and social duties, and now here was his illustration! His books were his words; here were his deeds! How should he ever show himself again! He would leave the country! Damn the property! The rascal should never succeed to it. Mark should have it—if he lived. Hester's engagement must be broken, for Lord Gartley would never marry the sister of a thief!

While he was thus raging, a maid knocked at the door and said, "Please, sir, Miss Raymount says will you come to the mis'ess; she's taken bad!"

This brought him to himself. She must have heard the vile news as well! He followed the maid to the lawn. There stood his wife in his daughter's arms, trembling from head to foot. He asked no questions, but took her in his arms, bore her to her room, laid her on the bed, and sat down beside her, hardly caring if she died, for the sooner they were all dead the better!

Hester had caught up her mother's letter, and now handed it to her father.

"Dear Mistress, it is time to let you know of the goings-on here. I never held with bearing of tales against my fellow servants, and perhaps it's worse to bring tales against Master Cornelius, as is your own flesh and blood, but what am I to do as was left in charge, and to keep house respectable? He's not been home these three nights, and you ought to know as there is a young lady, his cousin from New Zealand, as is come to the house a three or four times since you went away, and stayed a long time with him, though it is some time now that I ain't seen her. She is a pretty, modest looking young lady, though I must say I was ill-pleased when Mr. Cornelius would have her stay all night, and I up and told him if she was his cousin she wasn't his sister, and I would walk out of the house if he insisted on me making up a bed for her. Then he laughed in my face, and told me I was an old fool, and he was only making game of me. I told him if neither he nor the young lady had a character to keep, I had one to lose, and I wouldn't. But I don't think he said anything to her about staying all night, for she came down the stair as innocent as any dove, and bid me good-night smiling, and they walked away together. And I wouldn't have took it upon me to be a spy, but he ain't been home for three nights, and it's my own part to let a mother know her son ain't slept in his own bed for three nights. Oh, why did his father leave him alone in London, with none but an old woman like me, as he always did look down upon, to look after him! Your humble servant for twenty years to command, S.H."

Mrs. Raymount had not read the half of this. It was enough to learn he had not been home for three nights. She concluded her boy had turned into bad ways because left in London, although she knew he had never taken to good ways while they were all with him. If he had never gone right, why should she wonder he had gone wrong?

The doctor had arrived and was sitting by the bedside. Mr. Raymount rose and led Hester from the room—almost sternly, as if she had been to blame for it all. Some people when they are angry, speak as if they were angry with the person to whom they are in fact looking for comfort. But Hester understood her father and did not resent it.

"Is this all your mother knows, Hester?" he asked, pointing to the letter. She told him her mother had read but the first sentence or two.

He returned to the bedside, and stood silent. The life of his dearest had been suddenly withered at the root, and she had not learned the worst!

His letter was from his wife's brother at the bank. A considerable deficit had been discovered in Cornelius' accounts. He had not been to the bank for two days before, and no trace of him was to be found. His uncle, from regard to the feelings of his sister, had not allowed the thing to become public, but would wait his brother-in-law's reply before taking any steps. He feared the misguided youth had reckoned on the forebearance of an uncle, but for the sake of his own future, if for no other reason, the thing could not be passed over!

"Passed over!" Had Gerald Raymount been a Roman with the power of life and death over his children, he would in his present mood have put his son to death with his own hands.

But for his wife's illness he would have been already on the way to London to repay the missing money. Who was there to send? There was Hester! She was a favorite with her uncle. Nor would she dread the interview, which, as the heat of his rage yielded to a cold despair, he felt would be to him an unendurable humiliation. For he had had many arguments, not always quite friendly, with this same brother-in-law concerning the way he brought up his children; they had all turned out well, but here was his own son a miserable felon, disgracing both families!

He led Hester again from her mother's room to his, and gave her her uncle's letter to read. He saw her grow pale, then flush, then turn pale again. At length her face settled into a look of determination. She laid the letter on the table, and rose with a steady troubled light in her eyes.

"Hester," he said, "I cannot leave your mother; you must go for me to your uncle and do the best you can. I would have the rascal prosecuted, but it would break your mother's heart."

Hester wasted no words for reply, though she had often heard him say there ought to be no interference with public justice for private ends. "Yes, papa," she answered. "I shall be ready in a moment. If I ride Hotspur I shall catch the evening train."

"There is time to take the brougham."

"Am I to say anything to Corney, papa?" she asked, her voice trembling over the name.

"You have nothing to do with him," he answered sternly. "Where is the good of keeping a villain from being a villain? I will sign you a blank check, which your uncle can fill up with the amount he has stolen. Come for it as soon as you are ready."

Hester thought as she went whether, if it had not been for the possibility of repentance, the world would ever have been made at all.

On her way to her room she met the major.

"Is your mother in danger?" he asked gently.

"She is very ill," answered Hester. "The doctor has been with her now three hours. I am going up to London for papa. He can't leave her."

"Going up to London—and by the night train!" said the major to himself. "Then there has been bad news! Money matters? No, Helen is not the one to send health after money. That scoundrel Corney has been about some mischief—damn him! I shouldn't be surprised to hear anything bad of him!" he thought. "But what can you do, my dear," he asked aloud. "It's not a fit—" He looked up. Hester was gone.

She put a few things together, obtained the check from her father, and was ready by the time the brougham came to the door. One of the servants opened the carriage door for her, and she was on her way through the gathering dusk to the railway station.

While the lodge gate was being opened, she thought she saw someone get up on the box beside the coachman, and fancied it must be a groom going with them. The drive was a long and anxious one. What might not be happening to Corney! She kept fancying one dreadful thing after another. It was like a terrible dream, only with the assurance of reality in it.

The carriage stopped, the door opened, and there was the major in a huge fur coat, holding out his hand to help her down.

166

It was as great a pleasure as surprise, and she showed both.

"You didn't think I was going to let you travel alone?" he said. "Who knows what wolf might be after my Red Riding Hood!"

Hester was only too glad of his escort. Careful not to seem curious, he seated himself in the farthest corner, and pretended to go to sleep.

And now began Hester's private share in the general misery of the family. In the presence of her suffering father and mother, she put off looking into the mist that kept gathering about her. If this miserable affair should be successfully hushed up, there was yet one who must know it—Lord Gartley. If the love between them had been ideal, would she have been anxious as to how her lover would receive the painful news? But her own mind was made up—if he but hesitated at the news, nothing could make her marry him.

Chapter 36.

IN LONDON

Hester and the major arrived in London, and went to Addison Square. So that she would not be seen at the bank, with the risk of being recognized and rousing speculation, she begged the major to be her messenger to her uncle. The major undertook the commission without question.

Early in the afternoon her uncle came. He was chiefly a man of business, and his very reticence revealed his sympathy with the trouble she and her parents were in. His manner was cold but kind, and had a chilling and hopeless effect upon the ardent mind of the sister. With a slight deprecatory smile and shrug, he took her father's check, and she ventured to ask what he was going to do in regard to her brother.

"This check," answered her uncle, "indicates that I treat the matter as a debt discharged, and leave him entirely in your father's hands. He must do as he sees fit. I am sorry for you all, and for you especially that you should have had to take an active part in the business. I wish your father could have come up himself. My poor sister!"

"My father is so angry with Cornelius that I could almost believe he would have insisted on your prosecuting him. You never saw such indignation as my father's at any wrong done by one man to another. It is a terrible blow! He will never get over it—never, never!"

She broke down and wept bitterly. To think of their family being thus disgraced, with one for its future representative who had not even the commonest honesty! But that his crime had been committed against an indulgent relative, he would assuredly have been prosecuted for felony. It was hard to bear! But to Hester there were considerations far more sad. How was ever such a child of the darkness to come to love the light? He cared so little for righteousness, and would probably only excuse or even justify his crime. How was he to be brought to contrition and rectitude? There was a poor hope in the shame he must feel at the disgrace he had brought upon himself. But if the whole thing was to be kept quiet, and he was not brought to open shame, he would hold his arrogant head as high as ever.

When her uncle left her, she sat motionless a long time, thinking much but hoping little. The darkness gathered deeper around her. The ruin of her own promised history seemed imminent upon that of her family. What sun of earthly joy could ever break through such clouds? There was indeed a sun that nothing could cloud, but it seemed to shine far away. Some sorrows seem beyond the reach of consolation, for their causes seem beyond setting right. They can at best, only be covered over. But the human heart has to go through much before it is able to suspect the superabounding riches of the creating and saving God. The foolish child thinks there can be nothing where he sees nothing; the human heart feels that if it is where it cannot devise help, then there is none possible to God.

It was a sore and dreary time for Hester, alone in the room where she had spent so many happy hours. She sat in a window, looking out upon the leafless trees and the cold gloomy old statue in the midst of them. Frost was upon every twig, and a thin sad fog filled the comfortless air. The fire was burning cheerfully behind her, but her eyes were fixed on the dreary square. She was hardly thinking—only letting thoughts and feelings come and go. What a thing is life and being, when a soul has become but the room in which ghosts hold their reel; when the man is no longer master of himself, can no more say to this or that thought, "Thou shalt come, and thou shalt go," but is a slave to his own existence, and can neither cease to be, nor order his being. Such is everyone parted from the essential life. Although Hester's thoughts now came and went without her, they did not come and go without God, and truth was on its way.

How would her lover receive the news? She would not write, for then she could not know how he received her sad story; and if his mind required making up, which was what she feared, he would have time for it! She must communicate the dread defiling fact with her own lips, and she must see how he took it. If he showed the slightest change toward her, the least tendency to regard their relationship as an entanglement, to regret that he had involved himself with the sister of a thief, marry her he should not! If he was not to be her earthly refuge in this trouble as in any other, she would have none of him! There were worse evils than losing a lover! There was losing a true man—and that he would not be if she lost him!

This feeling of uncertainty with regard to Gartley had been prepared for by things that had passed between them since their engagement, but upon which she had not allowed herself to dwell. She had turned her thought to the time when she imagined she would be able to do so much more for and with him. And now she was almost in a mood to quarrel with him! Brought to moral bay, she stood with her head high, her soul roused, and every nerve strung to defense.

Suddenly came the thought that, after so long a separation, she was at last in the midst of her poor. But how was she to face them now! Who was she to have dared speak to them of the evil of their ways, and the bad influence of an ill-behaved family! But how lightly they bore such ills as that which was now breaking her down with trouble and shame! Even such of them as were honest people would have cousin or uncle or son or husband *in* for so many months, and think only of when they would have him out again! Misfortune had overtaken them, and they loved no less. The man or woman was still mother or husband to them. Nothing could degrade them beyond the reach of their sympathies! They had no pride because they themselves had not transgressed the law, neither drawing back from them with disgust.

So she felt nearer to her poor than ever before, and it comforted her. She was not merely of the same flesh and blood with them, but of the same failing, sinning, blundering breed. Their shame was hers—her brother was a thief! She was and would be more one of them than ever before! The Lord Christ could get nearer to the publican than the Pharisee, to the woman that was a sinner than the self-righteous honest woman! The Pharisee was a good man, but he thought it such a fine thing to be good that God did not like him nearly so well as the other who thought it a sad thing to be bad! Let her but get among her nice, honest, wicked, poor ones, out of this atmosphere of pretense and appearance, and she would breathe again! She dropped upon her knees, and cried to her Father in heaven to make her heart clean altogether, to deliver her from everything mean and faithless, to make her turn from any shadow of ill as thoroughly as she would have her brother repent of the stealing that made them all so ashamed.

And suddenly she perceived that self had been leading her astray; she was tender toward those further from her, hard toward the one nearer to her! It was easy to be indignant toward, those whose evil did not touch herself; to the son of her own mother she was severe and indignant! Corney whom she had nursed as a baby, who used to crow when she appeared—could it be that she who had then loved him so dearly was loving him no more? If God were to do like her, how many would be giving honor to His Son?

But was it possible Corney should ever wake to see how ugly his conduct had been? Perhaps this was one of God's ways—letting him disgrace himself! If he could but be made ashamed of himself there would be hope! And in the meantime she must get the beam out of her own eye that she might see to take the mote or the beam, whichever it might be, out of Corney's! Again she fell upon her knees, and prayed God to enable her. Corney was her brother, and must forever be her brother, were he the worst thief under the sun! God would see to their honor or disgrace; what she had to do was to be a sister. She rose determined that she would not go home till she had done all she could to find him; that the judgment of God should alone drive her, and the judgment of the world be nothing to her forevermore.

Presently she realized that she had in part been drawn toward her lover because of his social position. Had he not been an earl in prospect, were there not some things in him which would have more repelled her? Would she, but for that, have tried so much to like his verses? Clearly she must take her place with the sinners!

Chapter 37

A TALK WITH THE MAJOR

Major Marvel made his appearance. He had been watching outside, saw her uncle go, and an hour after was shown to the room where she still sat, staring out on the frosty trees of the square.

"Why, my child," he said, "your hand is as cold as ice! Why do you sit so far from the fire?"

He put her in an easy chair near the fire, and sat down beside her. Common, pudgy, red-faced, baldheaded as he was, she came to him out of regions of deepest thought with a sense of refuge. He could scarcely have understood one of her difficulties, and would doubtless have judged not a few of her scruples as nonsensical and overdriven. Should her engagement be broken, she knew it would delight the major; yet she was able to look upon him as a friend in whom she could trust. Unity of opinion is not necessary to confidence and warmth.

As they talked, the major, seeing she was much depressed, and thinking to draw her from troubled thought, began to tell her some personal parts of his history. She drew from him much that he would never have thought of volunteering. Before their talk was over, she had come to regard the man in a new light. She had looked upon him as a man of such redeeming qualities, that his faults must be overlooked; but now she felt him a man to be looked up to. It was true that every now and then some remark would reveal in him a less than attractive commonness of thinking, and that his notions in religion were crude, for he regarded it as a set of doctrines—not a few of them very dishonoring to God—yet was the man in a high sense a true man.

Hester began to take him into her confidence. She had received no injunctions to secrecy from her father; both he and her mother knew she was to be trusted as they were themselves. Her father had taken no step toward any effort for the rescue of his son, and she would sorely need help. She would say nothing to the major about Lord Gartley, but might she not ask him to help her to find Corney? He would be prudent and keep quiet whatever ought to be kept quiet. So she told him the whole story. The major said nothing, betrayed nothing, only listened intently.

"My dear Hester," he said solemnly, after a few moments' pause, "the mysteries of creation are beyond me! It's such a mixture! There is your mother, the loveliest woman except yourself God ever made! Then comes Cornelius—well! Then yourself! And then little Mark, a child too good for any of the common uses of this world! I declare I am terrified with him."

"What about him terrifies you?" asked Hester, amused at the idea, in spite of the gnawing unrest at her heart.

"To a saint one must speak the truth; it is simply fear lest I should find I must give up everything and do as I know he is thinking I ought—to turn a saint like him."

"And why should you be afraid of that?"

"Well, I'm not the stuff that good saints are made of; and rather than not be a good one, if I once set about it, I would, saving your presence, be the devil himself."

Hester laughed, yet with some self-accusation. "I think," she said softly, "one day you will be as good a saint as love can wish you to be."

"I would not willingly begin anything I should disgrace, for that would be to disgrace myself. And I do hate humbug, and shall hate it till I die—and so want to steer clear of it."

"I hate it, I hope, as much as you do, Major Marvel," responded Hester. "But, whatever it may be mixed up with, you know that what is true cannot be humbug, and what is not true cannot be anything else than humbug."

"Yes, but how is one to know what is true?"

"The only way to know what is true is to do what is true," replied Hester.

"But you must know what is true before you can do what is true."

"Everybody knows something that is true to do—something he ought to lose no time in setting about. The true thing to any man is the thing that must not be let alone but done. It is much easier to know what is true to do than what is true to think. But those who do the one will come to know the other—and none else, I believe."

The major was silent, and sat looking very thoughtful. At last he rose. "Is there anything you want me to do in this sad affair, cousin Hester?" he said.

"I want your help to find my brother."

"Why? You cannot do him any good!"

"Who can tell that? If Christ came to seek and save His lost, we ought to seek to save our lost."

"Young men don't go wrong for the mere sake of going wrong; you may find him in such a position as will make it impossible for you to have anything to do with him. And you must not expose yourself in such a search to what would be unavoidable."

"Which is in most danger from disease, Major Marvel, the healthy or the sickly?"

"That's a question for the doctor," he answered cautiously, "if even he knows anything about it."

Hester saw it was not for her now to pursue the argument, though it scarcely needed pursuing! For who shall walk safe in the haunts of evil but those upon whom evil has no hold? Sorry one would be, but for the sake of those for whom Christ died, that any woman should be pained with the sight of evil. The true woman may, even like God Himself, know all evil and remain just as lovely and clean.

"What do you think your father would like done?" asked the major.

"I do not know, but as I am Corney's sister, I will venture as a sister may. I think my father will be pleased in the end, but I will risk his displeasure for the sake of my brother."

"I will do what I can for you—though I greatly fear your brother will never prove worth the trouble."

"People have repented who have gone as far as Corney," said Hester, with tears in her voice if not in her eyes.

"True!" responded the major. "But I don't believe he has character enough to repent of anything. He will be fertile

174

enough in excuse! But I will do what I can to find out where he is."

Hester heartily thanked him, and he took his leave.

But if she found Cornelius, was he likely to go home with her? How would he be received if he did go home? And if not, what was she to do with or for him? And what was he to do when the money so vilely appropriated was spent? If want would drive him home, the sooner he came to it the better! For then a first ray of hope begins to break through the darkness of a prodigal's fate.

She wrote to her father and told him what there was to tell. "Tell my darling mother, " she added, "that what a sister can do, up to the strength God gives her, shall be done for my brother. Major Marvel is doing his best to find him."

Next day she heard from her father that her mother was slowly recovering, and on the following day that her letter was a great comfort to her, but beyond this he made no remark. Even his silence was some relief to Hester.

In the meantime she was not idle. Hers was not the nature to sit still, even in grief. The moment she had dispatched her letter, she set out to visit her poor friends. She asked after the Frankses, and was told that they had been seen in the way of their profession, but they were not getting on. Hester was sorry, but had many more she had to think of.

There was much rejoicing at her return. But there were changes—new faces where she had left friends, and not the best news of some who remained. One or two were in prison, of whom when she left she was in great hope. One or two were getting on better in the sense of this world, but she could see nothing in themselves to make her glad of their "good luck." One who had signed the pledge had broken it fearfully, and all but killed his wife. One of whom she had been hopeful had disappeared—it was supposed with another man's wife. In spite of their sufferings, the evil one seemed as busy among them as among the world's elect.

Every day she went among them. Certain women—those who had suffered most with least fault—were as warmly her friends as before. The little ones came about her again, but with less confidence, both because she had been away, and because they had grown more than they had improved.

Chapter 38.

RENCONTRES

There was no news of Cornelius. There was a rumor of a young woman in whose company he had lately been seen, but she too had disappeared from public sight.

Sarah did her best to make Hester comfortable, and behaved the better that she was humbled by the consciousness of having made a bad job of her caretaking with Cornelius.

One afternoon Hester turned into a passage to visit the wife of a bookbinder who had been long laid up with rheumatism and quite unable to work. They had therefore been on the borders of want, and for Hester it was one of those happy cases in which she felt at full liberty to help with money.

The part of the house occupied by them was pretty decent, but the rest of it was in bad repair and occupied by yet poorer people, none of whom she knew much. It was a little way beyond what she had come to count as her limit.

She knocked at the door. It was opened by the parish doctor.

"You cannot come in, Miss Raymount," he said. "We have a very bad case of smallpox here. You good ladies must make up your minds to keep away for a while. Their bodies are in more danger than their souls now."

"That may very well be," replied Hester. "My foot may be in more danger than my head, but I can better afford to lose the one than the other."

The doctor did not see the point, and thought there was none. "You will only carry the infection," he said.

"I will take every precaution," answered Hester. "I always take more, I am certain, than it can be possible for you to take. Why should not I also do my part to help?"

"While the parish is in my care," answered the doctor with some heat, "I must object to increasing the risk of infection. It is hard to have you, even with the best of motives, carrying the seeds from one house to another. I must beg you go away. I shall be compelled to mention in my report how you and other ladies add to our difficulties."

He closed the door. Hester turned and went down the stair, now on her part a little angry. The first thing was to get rid of the anger. She sat down and began to sing; it was not the first time she had sat and sung in a dirty staircase. It was not a wise thing to do, but her anger prevented her from seeing its impropriety.

The children gathered like flies, and in a moment the stair below was half filled with them. Others came in from the street and were pushed up by those who came behind them. The stair and entrance were presently filled with shabby and dirty people listening to the voice of the Singing Lady, as she was called in the neighborhood.

By this time the doctor had finished his visit, and appeared on the stair above. He saw the house was filled with people, and when he saw who the singer was, he lost his temper. He made his way down to Hester, seized her arm from behind, and began to push her down the stair. Some of the faces grew red with anger, and their eyes flamed at the doctor. A loud murmur arose, and several began to force their way up to rescue her, as they would one of their own from the police. Hester rose and began to descend the stair, closely followed by the doctor. It was not easy, and the annoyance of a good many in the crowd gave a disorderly and threatening look to the assemblage.

As she reached the door she saw the pale face and glittering eyes of Mr. Blaney looking at her. The little man was mounted on a box at the door of a shop whose trade seemed to be in withered vegetables and salt fish, and had already had a pint, which was more than he could stand. "Sarves you right, miss," he cried. "You turned me out o' your house for singin', an' I don't see why you should come a singin' an' a misbehavin' of yourself in ourn! Jest you bring her out here, pleeceman, an' let me give her a bit o' my mind. It's time the gentry swells knowed as how we're yuman bein's as well as theirselves, havin' our feelin's hurt for the sake o' what they calls bein' done good to!"

The crowd had been gathering from both ends of the passage, for high words draw yet faster than sweet singing, and the place was so full that it was hardly possible to get out of it. The doctor was almost wishing he had let ill alone, for he was now anxious about Hester. Some of the rougher ones began pushing. The vindictive little man kept bawling, his mouth screwed into the middle of his cheek. The crowd swayed, and Hester spied a face she knew.

"Now we shall have help!" she said. "Mr. Franks!"

The athlete was not far off, and with his great lean muscular arms he sent the crowd right and left like water, and reached her in a moment. He pulled off his fur cap, and making the lowest and politest of stage bows, said, "At your service, Miss Raymount!"

"I am very glad to see you again, Mr. Franks," said Hester. "Do you think you could get us out of the crowd?"

"Easy, miss. I'll carry you out of it like a baby, miss, if you'll let me."

"No, no—that will hardly be necessary," returned Hester, with a smile.

"Go on before, and make a way for us," said the doctor, with an authority he had no right to assume.

"There is not the least occasion for you to trouble yourself about me further, doctor," said Hester. "I am perfectly safe with this man. I know him very well. I am sorry to have vexed you."

Franks looked up sharply at the doctor, then turned to Hester. "Nobody 'ain't been finding fault with you, miss?" he said, a little ominously.

"No more than I deserved," replied Hester. "But come, Franks! Lead the way, or all Bloomsbury will be here, and then the police! I shouldn't like to be locked up for offending Mr. Blaney!"

Those near them heard and laughed. She took Franks' arm, and in a minute they were out of the crowd.

But as if everybody she knew was going to appear, who should meet them as they turned into Steeven's Road, with a fringe of the crowd still at their heels, but Lord Gartley! He had written from town, and Mrs. Raymount had let him know that Hester was in London. He went at once to Addison Square, and had just left the house disappointed when he met Hester on Franks' arm.

"Miss Raymount!" he exclaimed almost haughtily.

"My lord!" she returned, with unmistakable haughtiness, drawing herself up, and looking him in the face, hers glowing.

"Who would have expected to see you here?" he said.

"Apparently yourself, my lord!"

He tried to laugh. "Come then. I will see you home."

"Thank you, my lord. Come, Franks."

As she spoke she looked round, but Franks was gone. Finding she had met one of her own family, as he supposed, he had quietly withdrawn.

Chapter 39.

IN THE HOUSE

The two were silent on their way home, but from different causes. Lord Gartley was uneasy at finding Hester in such a position—led into it by her unreflecting sympathies, no doubt. He had gathered from the looks and words of the remnants of the crowd that she had been involved in some street quarrel. For a woman of her refinement, she had the strangest taste for low company!

Hester was silent, thinking how to begin her communication about Cornelius. Uncomfortable from the incident, as well as from what she had now to do, and irritated by his lordship's expression of surprise, she had felt for a moment as if the best thing would be to break with him at once. She felt for that one moment very plainly that the relation between them was far from the ideal. Another thing was yet clearer; if he could feel such surprise and annoyance at the circumstances in which he had just met her, it would be well to come to a clearer understanding at once concerning her life ideal and projects. But she would make up her mind to nothing till she saw how he was going to carry himself now his surprise had had time to pass off; perhaps it would not be necessary to tell him anything about Corney! They might part upon other grounds!

Not before they reached the house did Lord Gartley speak, and Hester had begun to wonder if he might not already have heard of Cornelius. It was plain he was troubled, and awaiting the coverture of the house to speak. It should be easy for him to get rid of her. He need not be anxious about that!

When they reached the house, instead of ringing the bell, she took a latchkey from her pocket, opened the door herself, and herself closed it behind them. She led the way up the silent stair.

"Did no one come with you?" he asked.

"No one but Major Marvel," she answered, and opened the door of the drawing room. She woke to the consciousness that she was very cross, and in a mood to make her unfair to Gartley. She turned to him and said, "Forgive me, Gartley, I am in trouble; we are all in trouble. When I have told you about it, I shall be more at ease."

She told her story, and could not have done it with greater fairness to her friend; his practiced self-control had opportunity for perfect operation. But the result was more to her satisfaction than she could have dared to hope. He held out his hand with a smile, and said, "I am very sorry. What is there I can do?"

She looked up in his eyes. They were kind and loving.

"Then you don't feel differently toward me?"

"Toward you, my angel?" exclaimed Gartley, and held out his arms.

She threw herself into them, and clung to him. It was the first time either of them had shown anything approaching abandon. Gartley's heart swelled with delight, translating her confidence into his power.

They sat down and talked the whole thing over. Now that Hester was at peace, she began to look at it from Gartley's point of view. "I am so sorry for you!" she said. "It is very sad you should have to marry into a family so disgraced. What *will* your aunt say?"

"My aunt will treat the affair like the sensible woman she is," replied the earl. "But there is no fear of disgrace; the thing will never be known. Besides, where is the family that hasn't one or more such loose fishes about in its pond? The fault was committed inside the family too, and that makes a great difference. It is not as if he'd been betting and couldn't pay up!"

From the heaven of her delight Hester fell prone. Was this the way her almost-husband looked at these things? But how could he help looking at them so? Was it not thus he had been from earliest childhood taught to look at them? The greater was his need of all she could do for him! He was so easy to teach! What she saw clear as day it could not be hard to communicate to one who loved as he loved! She would say nothing now—would let

181

him see no sign of disappointment in her!

"If he doesn't improve," continued his lordship, "we must get him out of the country. In the meantime he will go home, and not a suspicion will be roused. What else should he do, with such a property to look after?"

"My father will not see it so," answered Hester. "I doubt if he will ever speak to him again. Certainly he will not, except he show some repentance."

"Has your father refused to have him home?"

"He has not had the chance. Nobody knows what has become of him."

"He'll have to condone, or compromise, or compound, or what do they call it, for the sake of his family—for your sake, and my sake, my darling! He can't be so vindictive as to expose his own son!"

"If only we could find him!" returned Hester.

"He is not where you would like to find him. Men don't come to grief without help! We must wait till he turns up."

Hester was not inclined to argue the point; she could not expect him or anyone out of their own family to be much interested in the fate of Cornelius. They began to talk about other things, and if they were not the things Hester would most readily have talked about, neither were they the things Lord Gartley had entered the house intending to talk about. To find Hester, the moment she came back to London, yielding afresh to a diseased fancy of doing good—to come upon her in the street of a low neighborhood followed by a low crowd, championed by a low fellow! He had entered the house intending to exact a promise against such follies for the future. But when he heard her trouble and saw how deeply it affected her, he knew this was not the time to say what he had meant.

He had risen to go, and was about to take a loving farewell, when Hester, suddenly remembering, drew back with a guilty look. "O Gartley!" she said, "I ought not to have let you come near me! But you came upon me so unexpectedly!"

"What can you mean, Hester?" exclaimed Gartley.

"There was smallpox in the house I had just left when you met me," she said.

He started back and stood speechless—manifesting therein no more cowardice than everyone in his circle would have justified.

"Has it never occurred to you what you are doing in going to such places, Hester?" he faltered. "It is a treachery against every social claim. I cannot help being surprised at you! I thought you had more sense!"

"I am sorry to have frightened you."

"Frightened!" repeated Gartley, with an attempt at a smile, which closed in a yet more anxious look. "You do indeed frighten me! I should never have thought you capable of showing such a lack of principle. Don't imagine I am thinking of myself— *you* are in most danger! Still, you may carry the infection without taking it yourself!"

"I didn't know it was there when I went to the house—only I should have gone all the same," said Hester. "But if seeing you so suddenly had not made me forget, I should have had a bath as soon as I got home. I *am* sorry I let you come near me!"

"One has no right either to take or carry infection," insisted Lord Gartley, perhaps a little glad of the height upon which an opportunity of finding fault set him above her. "But there is no time to talk about it now. I hope you will use what preventives you can. It is very wrong to trifle with such things!"

"Indeed it is!" answered Hester. "And I say again I am sorry I forgot. It was you made me forget!"

But his lordship was by no means now in a smiling mood. He bade her a somewhat severe good-night, and with a solemn bow he turned and went, his mind full of conflicting feelings and perplexing thoughts. What a glorious creature she was, and how dangerous! What a spirit she had, but so ill-directed! It was horrible to think of her going into such abominable places, and all alone too! How ill she had been trained! In such utter disregard of social obligation and the laws of nature! He little thought what risks he ran when he fell in love with her. If he got off now without an attack he would be lucky; but if she were to take it herself, to die, or lose her complexion! Would honor compel him to marry her if she were horribly pockmarked? Those dens ought to be rooted out! Philanthropy was gone mad! It was strict repression that was wanted!

Chapter 40

THE MAJOR AND
THE SMALLPOX

His lordship was scarcely gone when the major came; perhaps the major had seen his lordship enter the house, and had been waiting and watching till he was gone. But Hester was not yet to be seen: she had no fear of the worst smallpox could do to her, yet was taking what measures appeared advisable for her protection. Her fearlessness came from no fancied absence of danger, but from an utter disbelief in chance. The same and only faith that would have enabled the major to face the man-eating tiger enabled her to face the smallpox; if she did die by going into such places, it was all right.

The major sat down and waited.

"I am at my wits' end!" he said, when she entered the room. "I can't find the fellow! Don't you think you had better go home? I will do what can be done, you may be sure!"

"I *am* sure," answered Hester, "but mama is better. So long as I am away papa will not leave her, and she would rather have papa than a dozen of me."

"But it must be so dreary for you—here alone all day!" he said, with a touch of malice.

"I go about among my people," she answered.

"Ah!" he returned. "Then I hope you will be careful, for I hear the smallpox is in the neighborhood."

"I have just come from a house where it is now," she answered. The major rose in haste. "But," she went on, "I have changed my clothes, and had a bath since."

The major sat down again. "My dear young lady!" he said,

the roses a little ashy on his cheekbones. "Do you know what you are about? What is to become of us if you take the smallpox? Why, my dear cousin, you might lose every scrap of your good looks!"

"And then who on earth would care for me anymore!" said Hester, with mock mournfulness, which brought a glimmer of the merry light back to the major's face.

"But really, Hester," he persisted, "this is most imprudent. It is also your life you are periling!"

"Perhaps," she answered.

"And the lives of us all!" added the major.

"Is the smallpox worse than a man-eating tiger?"

"Ten times worse," he answered. "You can fight the tiger, but you can't fight the smallpox. You really ought not to run such fearful risks."

"How are they to be avoided? Every time you send for a doctor you run a risk! You can't order a clean doctor every time!"

"A joke's all very well, but it is our duty to take care of ourselves."

"In reason, yes," replied Hester.

"You may think," said the major, "that God takes special care of you because you are about His business—and far be it from me to say you are not about His business or that He does not take care of you—but what is to become of me and the likes of me if we take the smallpox from you?"

Hester had it on her lips to say that if he was meant to die of the smallpox, he might as well take it of her as of another; but she said instead that she was sure God took care of her, but not sure she would not die of the smallpox.

"How can you say God takes care of you if He lets you die of the smallpox?"

"No doubt people would die if God forgot them, but do you think people die because God forgets them?"

"My dear cousin Hester, if there is one thing I have a penchant for it is common sense, and not a paradox!"

"Did God take care of Jesus?"

"Of course! But He wasn't like other men, you know."

"I don't want to have more of God's care than He had."

"I don't understand you. I should think if we were sure God

185

took as good care of us as of Him—" But there he stopped, for he began to see where she was leading him.

"Did He keep Him what you call safe?" said Hester. "Did He not allow the worst man could do to overtake Him? Was it not the very consequence of His obedience?"

"Then you have decided to die of the smallpox?"

"Only if it be God's will," replied Hester. "To that, and that alone, have I made up my mind. If I die of the smallpox, it will not be because it could not be helped, or because I caught it by chance; it will be because God allowed it as best for me and for us all. It will not be a punishment for breaking His laws. He loves none better, I believe, than those who break the laws of nature to fulfill the laws of the spirit."

"I haven't a notion what you mean," said the major, "though I don't doubt you mean well, and that you are a most courageous and heroic young woman. Yet it is time your friends interfered, and I shall let your father know how you are misbehaving yourself."

"They will not believe me quite so bad as I fear you will represent me."

"I don't know. I must write anyhow."

"That they may order me home to give them the smallpox? Wouldn't it be better to wait and be sure I had not taken it already? Your letter might even carry the infection. I think you had better not write."

"You persist in making fun of it! It is not a thing to be joked about," remarked the major, looking red.

"I think," returned Hester, "that whoever lives in terror of infection had better take it and have done with it. I know I would rather die than live in the fear of death. It is the meanest of slaveries. To live a slave to one's fears is next worst to living a slave to one's likings. Do as you please, Major Marvel, but if you interpose—even for kindness—I will never ask you to help me again."

She held out her hand to him, adding with a smile, "Is it for good-bye, or a compact?"

"But just look at it from my point of view," said the major, disturbed by the appeal. "What will your father say if he finds me aiding and abetting?"

"You did not come up at my father's request, or from the least desire on his part to have me looked after. You were not put in charge of me, and have no right to suppose me doing anything my parents would not like. They never objected to my going among my friends as I thought fit. Possibly they had more faith in my good sense, knowing me better than Major Marvel does."

"I give in," said the major with a sigh, "and will abide by the consequences."

"But you shall not needlessly put yourself in danger. If you hear anything of Corney, write, please."

"You don't imagine," cried the major, firing up, "that I am going to turn tail where you advance? I'm not going to run from the smallpox any more than you. So long as it doesn't get on my back to hunt other people, I don't care. By George, you women have ten times more courage than we men!"

"What we've got to do we just go and do, without thinking about danger. I believe it is often the best wisdom to be blind and let God be our eyes as well as our shield. But would it be right of you, not called to the work, to put yourself in danger because you would not be out where I am in? I could admire you, of course, but never quite justify you."

"You're fit for a field marshal, my dear!" said the major enthusiastically, adding, as he kissed her hand, "I will think over what you have said, and at least not betray you without warning."

"That is enough for the present," returned Hester, shaking hands with him warmly.

The major went away filled with admiration. "By Jove," he said to himself, "it's a confounded good thing I didn't marry Helen; she would never have had a girl like that if I had! The world needs a few such in it—even if they be fools—though I suspect they will turn out the wise ones, and we the fools for taking such care of our precious selves!"

Chapter 41.

DOWN AND DOWN

The Frankses went down the hill and down to the shores of the salt sea, where the flowing life is dammed into a stagnant lake, a dead sea growing more and more bitter with separation and lack of outlet. Mrs. Franks had come to feel the comforting of her husband a hopeless thing, and had all but ceased to attempt it. He grew more helpless for the lack of what she thought moved him no more, and when she ceased to comfort him, the fountain of her own hope began to fail; in comforting him she had comforted herself. The boys grew more gloomy, but had not begun to quarrel, for that evil the father had sternly crushed.

They had reached at last the point of being unable to pay for their lodging. The day came when they must go forth like Abraham without a home, but not like Abraham with a tent and the world before them to set it up in, with camels and donkeys to help them along. The weakly wife had to carry the sickly baby, who had been slowly pining away. The father went laden with the largest portion of their remaining goods, and led the Serpent of the Prairies by the hand. The other boys followed, bearing the small stock of implements belonging to their art.

They had delayed their departure till it was more than dusk, shrinking from being seen of men's eyes. The world held only the hope of an occasional rest on a doorstep or the edge of the curbstone when the policeman's back was turned. They set out to go nowhere—to tramp on and on. Is it any wonder, and does it imply wickedness beyond that lack of trust in God which is at the root of all wickedness, if the thought of ending their troubles

188

by death crossed Franks' mind? But the sad eyes of his wife turned him from the thought, and he would plod on, thinking, as near as possible, about nothing.

They wandered to a part where seemed to be only small houses and mews. Presently they found themselves in a little lane with no thoroughfare, at the back of some stables, and had to return along the rough-paved, neglected way. Such was the quiet and apparent seclusion of the spot, that it struck Franks they had better find its most sheltered corner, in which to sit down and rest awhile. They spied a narrow path between some kind of warehouse and the wall of the next property. Scarcely had they turned into it when the Serpent disappeared with a little cry, and a whimper ascended through the darkness.

"John!" cried the mother in an agonized whisper. "He's fallen down a sewer! O my God! He is gone forever!"

"Hold your n'ise," said Franks, "an' let's all go down after him! It's better down anywheres than up where there ain't nothing to eat an' nowheres to lie down in."

" 'Tain't a bad place," cried a little voice in a whisper broken with repressed sobs. "Only I broke one o' my legs; it won't move to fetch of me up again."

"Thank God, he's alive!" cried the mother.

Franks went down a few steps and found his child, where he half lay, half sat upon them. But when he lifted him, he gave a low cry of pain. It was impossible to see where or how much he was hurt. The father sat down and took him on his knees.

"You'd better come an' sit here, wife," he said in a dull voice. "The boy's a bit hurt, an' here you'll be out of the wind."

They all got as far down the stair as its room would permit— the elder boys with their heads hardly below the level of the wind. By and by one of them crept down past his mother, feebly soothing the whimpering baby, and began to feel what sort of a place they were in.

"Here's a door, father!" he said.

"Well, what o' that?" returned his father. " 'Tain't no door open to us but the door o' the grave."

"Perhaps this is it, father," said Moxy.

"If it be," answered his father with bitterness, "we'll find it open, I'll be bound."

The boy's hand had come upon a latch; he lifted it, and

pushed. "Father," he gasped, *"it is open!"*

"Here, you come an' take the Sarpint," returned the father, with faintly reviving hope, "an' I'll see what sort of place it is. If it's any place at all, it's better than bein' i' the air all night at this freezin' time!"

Ready as he had been a moment before for the grave, he was careful in stepping into the unknown dark. Feeling with foot and hand, he went in. He trod upon an earthen floor, and the place had a musty smell—it might be a church vault. With sliding foot on the soundless floor, and sliding hand along the cold wall, he passed on round two corners, a closed door, and back to that by which he had entered.

"Wife," he said, "we can't do better than to take the only thing that's offered. The floor's firm, an' it's out o' the air. It's some sort of a cellar and it do look as if it wur left open jest for us! You *used* to talk about *Him* above, wife!"

He took her by the hand and led the way into the darkness. Feeling about, one of the boys came upon a large packing case; having laid it down against the inner wall, Franks sat, and made his wife lie upon it, with her head on his knees, and took Moxy again in his arms, wrapped in one of their three thin blankets. The boys stretched themselves on the ground, and were soon fast asleep. The baby moaned by fits all the night long.

In about an hour the sleepless Franks heard the door open softly and stealthily, and knew a presence besides themselves in the place. But when the slow dawn light crept through the chinks of the door, they were quite alone.

It was a large dry cellar, empty save for the old packing case. They must use great caution, and do their best to keep hold of this last retreat! Misfortune had driven them into the earth; it would be fortune to stay there.

When his wife awoke, he told her what he had been thinking. He and the boys would creep out before it was light, and return after dark. She must not put even a finger out of the cellar door all day. He laid Moxy down beside her, woke the two elder boys, and went out with them. For many days Franks and the boys gained bread enough to keep them alive, though it may well seem a wonder they did not perish with cold.

190

Chapter 42.

DIFFERENCE

About noon the next day, Lord Gartley called at Addison Square. Hester was very glad to see him again.

"I think I am a safe companion today," she said. "I have not been out of the house yet. But till the bad time is over among my people, we had better be content not to meet, I think."

Lord Gartley mentally gasped. He stood for a moment speechless, gathering his thought. "Do I understand you, Hester?" he said. "It would trouble me to find I do."

"I fear I understand you, Gartley!" said Hester. "Is it possible you would have me abandon my friends to the smallpox, as a hireling his sheep to the wolf?"

"There are those whose business it is to look after them."

"I am one of those," returned Hester.

"Well," answered his lordship, "for the sake of argument we will allow it *has* been your business. But how can you imagine it your business any longer?"

Indignation, a fire always laid in Hester's bosom, but seldom yet lighted by Lord Gartley, burst into flame. "I am aware, my lord," she said, "that I must by and by have new duties to perform, but I have yet to learn that they must annihilate the old. The claims of love cannot surely obliterate those of friendship! The new should make the old better, not sweep it away."

"But my dear girl, you will enter on a new life! The duties of a wife are above those of an unmarried woman."

"But the duties of neither can supercede those of a human being. If the position of a wife is higher than that of an unmar-

191

ried woman, it must enable her to do yet better things than were her duty as a human being before."

"It is impossible you should perform the duties of the station you are about to occupy, and continue to do as you are doing now."

"You set me thinking of too much to manage all at once," she replied in a troubled way. "I must think."

"All I want of you is to think. If you do, your good sense will convince you I am right. Just think what it would be to have you coming home to go out again straight from one of these kennels of the smallpox. The idea is horrible! Wherever you were suspected of being present, the house would be shunned like the gates of death."

"In such circumstances I should not go out."

"The suspicion of it would be enough. And in your absence, as certainly as in your presence, though not so fatally, you would be neglecting your duty to society."

"Then," said Hester, "the portion of society that is healthy, wealthy, and merry has stronger claims than the portion that is poor and sick and in prison!"

Lord Gartley could scarcely believe she actually meant that those to whom she alluded were to be regarded as a portion of the same society that ruled his life. He thought another moment, then said, "There are the sick in every class; you would have those of your own to visit. Why not leave others to visit those of theirs?"

"Then of course you would have no objection to my visiting a duchess with the smallpox?"

"There could be no occasion for that," he said. "She would have everything she could want."

"And the others are in lack of everything! To desert them would be to desert the Lord. He will count it so."

"Well, certainly," said his lordship, returning on the track, "there would be less objection in the case of the duchess, inasmuch as every possible precaution would in her house be taken against the spread of the disease. It would be horribly selfish to think only of the person affected."

"The poor should not be deserted by the rich in their bitter necessity! Who among them is able to take the right precautions against the spread of the disease? And if it spread among them, there is no security against its reaching those who take every possible care of themselves and none for their neighbors. You do not imagine, because I trust in God and do not fear what the smallpox can do to me, I would therefore neglect any necessary preventive! That would be to tempt God; means as well as results are His. They are a way of giving us a share in His work."

"Then you mean to give up society for the sake of nursing the poor?"

"Only upon occasion, when there should be a necessity—such as an outbreak of infectious disease."

"And how, pray, should I account for your absence—not to mention the impossibility of doing my part without you? I should have to be continually telling stories, or people would avoid me too as if I were the pest itself!"

It was to Hester as if a wall rose suddenly across the path that had been stretching before her in long perspective. It was clear that he and she had been going on without any real understanding of each other's view in life. Her expectations tumbled about her like a house of cards. If he wanted to marry her, full of designs and aims in which she did not share, and she was going to marry him, expecting sympathies and helps which he would not give her, where was the hope for either of anything worth calling success?

"Do you mean then, Gartley," she said, "that when I am your wife, if ever I am, I shall have to give up all the friendships to which I have devoted so much of my life?"

"I would not for a moment act the tyrant, or say you must never go into such houses again. Your own good sense, the innumerable engagements you will have, the endless calls upon your time and accomplishments, will guide you—and I am certain will guide you right as to what attention you can spare to the claims of benevolence. But in the circle to which you will belong, nothing is considered more out of place than any affectation of enthusiasm. I do not care to determine whether your way or theirs is the right one; but as the one thing to be avoided is peculiarity, you should not speak of these persons, whatever regard you may have for their spiritual welfare, as *your friends*. One cannot have so many friends—not to mention that a unity of taste and feeling is necessary to friendship. You know well enough such persons cannot be your friends."

Hester broke out with a vehemence for which she was afterward sorry, though nowise ashamed of. "They *are* my friends. Twenty of them would do more for me than you would."

Lord Gartley rose, hurt. "Hester," he said, "you think so little of me or my anxiety about your best interests, that it must be a relief to you if I go."

She answered not a word—did not even look up, and his lordship walked gently but unhesitatingly from the room.

"It will bring her to her senses!" he said to himself. "How grand she looked!"

Long after he was gone, Hester sat motionless. What she had vaguely forboded was come! They were not, never had been, never could be one! He was a mere man of this world, without relation to the world of truth! And yet she loved him—would gladly die for him, but not to give him his own way, to swell his worldly triumphs, and help gild the chains of his slavery. But to save him from himself, and give him God instead—that would be worth dying for! It was one thing to die that a fellow creature might have all things good, and another to live a living death that he might persist in the pride of life. It was a sad breakdown of the hopes that had clustered about Gartley!

But did she not deserve it? Therewith began a self-searching which did not cease until it had prostrated her in sorrow and shame before Him whose charity is the only pledge of ours.

To forget her friends that she might go into *society* a countess! She would leave such ambition to women who devoured novels and studied peerage. One loving look from human eyes was more to her than the admiration of the world! She would go back to her mother as soon as she had found Corney, and had seen her people through the smallpox. If only the house was her own, that she might turn it into a hospital to which anyone might flee for shelter. She would be more than ever the sister and helper of her own—cling faster than ever to the skirts of the Lord's garment, that the virtue going out of Him might flow through her to them! She would be like Christ, a gulf into which wrong should flow and vanish—a sun radiating an uncompromising love.

Easy is the thought of the loveliest devotion, but hard is the doing of the thought in the face of a thousand unlovely difficulties! Hester knew this but—God helping—she was determined not to withdraw hand or foot or heart. She rose, and having prepared herself, set out to visit her people. First of all she would go to the bookbinder's and see how his wife was attended to.

The doctor not being there, she was readily admitted. The poor husband, unable to help, sat a picture of misery by the scanty fire.

"Won't you sing to her a bit, miss?" beseeched the husband. "It'll do her more good than the doctor's stuff. She'll hear it like in a dream, an' she'll think it's the angels a singin', and that'll do her good."

Hester yielded and sang, thinking all the time how the ways of the open-eyed God look to us like things in a dream because we are only in the night of His great day, asleep before the brightness of His great waking thoughts. The woman had been tossing and moaning in discomfort, but as Hester sang, she grew still, and soon lay asleep.

"Thank you, miss," said the man. "You can do more than the doctor, as I told you! When he comes, he always wakes her up; you make her sleep true!"

Chapter 43.

DEEP CALLS UNTO DEEP

Yet worse trouble came upon the poor Frankses. About a week after they had taken possession of the cellar, little Moxy became seriously ill. Yet they dared not get a doctor to him for fear of being turned out to the workhouse.

They had made the cellar a little more comfortable. They managed to get some straw, and with two or three old sacks made a bed for the mother and the baby and Moxy on the packing case. They got also some pieces of matting, and put up a screen between the bed and the rickety door. By the exercise of their art, they had gained enough to keep them in food, but never enough to pay for the poorest lodging. They counted themselves, however, better off by much than if they had been crowded with all sorts in such lodging as a little more might have enabled them to procure.

The parents loved Moxy more tenderly than either of his brothers, and it was with sore hearts they saw him getting worse. The sickness was a mild smallpox, yet more than Moxy could bear, and he was gradually sinking. When this became clear to the mother, then indeed she felt the hand of God heavy upon her.

Religiously brought up, she had through the ordinary troubles of a married life sought help from the God in whom her mother believed; but with every fresh attack of misery, every step down on the stair of life, she thought she had lost her last remnant of hope, and knew that up to that time she had hoped, while past seasons of failure looked like times of blessed prosperity. No man, however little he may recognize the hope in him, knows what it would be to be altogether hopeless. Now Moxy was about to be taken from them, and no deeper misery seemed possible!

How little hope there is in the commoner phrases of religion! The message grounded on the uprising of the crucified Man has as yet yielded but little victory over the sorrows of the grave, and small anticipation of the world to come; not a little hope of deliverance of hell, but scarce a foretaste of a blessed time at hand when the heart shall exult and the flesh be glad. In general there is at best but a sad looking forward to a dreary and shadowy region. When Christ comes, shall He find faith in the earth—even among those who think they believe that He is risen indeed? Margaret Franks, in the cellar of her poverty, the grave yawning below it for her Moxy, felt as if there was no heaven at all, only a sky.

The child seemed to know that he was dying. One morning he suddenly cried out in a tone most pitiful, "Mother, don't put me in a hole."

The words went like a knife to the heart of the mother. She was unable to speak, nor knew what to answer. Most mothers would have sought to soothe the child, their own hearts breaking the while, with the assurance that no one should put him into any hole, or anywhere he did not want to go. But this mother could not lie in the face of death, nor had it ever occurred to her that no *person* is ever put into a hole, though many a body.

Again came the cry, this time in despairing though suppressed agony, "Mother, don't let them put me in a hole!"

The mother gave a cry like the child's, and her heart within her became like water.

"O God," she gasped, and could say no more. But with the prayer—for what is a prayer but a calling on the name of the Lord?—came to her a little calm, and she was able to speak. She bent over him and kissed his forehead.

"My darling Moxy, mother loves you," she said. What that had to do with it she did not ask herself. The child looked up in her face with dim eyes. "Pray to the Heavenly Father, Moxy, and tell Him that you don't want to be put in a hole, and tell Him that mother does not want you to be put in a hole. For she loves you with all her heart."

"Don't put me in the hole," said Moxy, now using the definite article.

"Jesus Christ was put in the hole," said the voice of the next elder boy from behind his mother. It was Sunday, and he had strolled into a meetinghouse and had heard the wonderful story of hope. "But He didn't mind it much, and soon got out again!"

"Ah, yes, Moxy!" said the poor mother. "Jesus died for our sins, and you must ask Him to take you up to heaven."

But Moxy did not know anything about sins, and just as little about heaven. What he wanted was an assurance that he would not be put in the hole. And the mother, now a little calmer, thought she saw what she ought to say.

"It ain't your soul, it's only your body, Moxy, they put in the hole," she said.

"I don't want to be put in the hole," Moxy screamed.

The poor mother was at her wit's end. But here the child fell into a troubled sleep, and for some hours a silence as of the grave filled the dreary cellar.

The moment he woke the same cry came from his fevered lips. "Don't put me in the hole," and at intervals, growing longer as he grew weaker, the cry came all the day.

Chapter 44.

DELIVERANCE

Hester had been to church, and then had visited some of her people, carrying them words of comfort and hope. They received them from her hand, but none of them, had they gone, would have found them at church. How seldom is the man in the pulpit able to make people feel that the things he is talking about are things at all! Neither when the heavens are black with clouds and rain, nor when the sun rises glorious in a blue perfection, do many care to sit down and be taught astronomy! But Hester was a live gospel to them—and most when she sang. Even the name of the Saviour came nearer to them when she sang than when she spoke it. She often felt, however, as if some new, other kind of messengers than she must one day be sent them; for there seemed a gulf between their thoughts and hers, such as neither they nor she could pass.

The Sunday was a close, foggy, cold, dreary day. The service at church had not seemed interesting. The heart seemed to have gone out of the world, as if God had gone to sleep, and His children had wakened before Him and found dismal gray of the world's morning full of discomfortable ghosts. She tried her New Testament, but Jesus too seemed far away—nothing left but the story about Him, as if He had forgotten His promise, and was no longer in the world. She tried some of her favorite poems, but each and all were infected with the same disease— commonplace nothingness. They seemed all made up—words, words, words! Nothing was left her in the valley but the shadow, and the last weapon, prayer. She fell upon her knees and cried to God for life. "My heart is dead within me," she said, and poured out her lack into the hearing of Him from whom she had come that she might have Himself. She did not dwell upon her sorrows; even they had sunk and all but vanished in the gray mass of lost interest.

But even in her prayers Hester could not get near Him. It seemed as if His ear were turned away from her cry. She sank into a kind of lethargic stupor, until she rose from her knees in a kind of despair, almost ready to think that either there was no God, or He would not hear her. An inaccessible God was worse than no God at all!

It had been dark for hours, but she had lighted no candle, and sat in bodily as in spiritual darkness. She was in her bedroom on the second floor at the back of the house, looking out on the top of the gallery that led to the great room. She had no fire, though one was burning away unheeded in the drawing room below. She was too miserable to care whether she was cold or warm. When she had found some light for her body, then she would go and get warm!

It was about ten o'clock. The streets were silent, the square deserted. The evening was raw and cold, and drove everybody indoors that had doors to go in at.

Through the cold and darkness came a shriek that chilled her with horror, yet it seemed as if she had been expecting it—as if the day's gathering cloud of misery had at length reached its fullness, and burst in the lightning of that shriek. It was followed by another and yet another. Whence did they come? Not from the street, for all beside was still. Even the roar of London was hushed. They rose in the house! Was Sarah being murdered?

The house seemed unnaturally still as she descended. At the top of the kitchen stairs she called aloud to Sarah, with a certain tremor in her throat. There came no reply, so down she went to face the worst. Hester was a woman of true courage—that is, a woman whom no amount of apprehension could deter when she knew she ought to seek the danger.

In the kitchen stood Sarah, motionless, frozen with fear. A lighted candle was in her hand. "It's in the coal cellar, miss!" she gasped. "There's something buried in them coals!"

"Nonsense!" returned Hester. "Who could scream like that from under the coals? Come, we'll go and see what it is."

"Laws, miss, don't you go near it now. It's too late to do anything. Either it's the woman's sperrit as they say was murdered there, or it's a new one."

"And you would let her be killed without interfering?"

"Oh, miss, all's over by this time!" persisted Sarah.

"Then you are ready to go to bed with a murderer in the house?" asked Hester.

"He's done his business now, an' 'll go away."

"Give me the candle. I will go alone."

"You'll be murdered, miss—as sure's you're alive!"

Hester took the light from her, and went to the coal cellar. The old woman sank on the chair.

The subterranean portion of the house extended under the great room. A long vault, corresponding to the gallery above, led to these cellars. It was a rather frightful place; its darkness was scarcely affected by the candle, and seemed only to blind her. She held it above her head, and then she could see a little. The black tunnel stretched on and on, like a tunnel in a feverish dream, a long way before the cellars began to open from it. She advanced, not fearless, but therefore only the more brave.

She reached the coal cellar and looked in. The coal heap was low, and the place looked large and very black. She went in and moved about until she had thrown light into every corner: no one was there. But she heard a moan, followed by a succession of low sobs. Her heart began to beat violently, but she stopped to listen. The light of her candle fell upon another door, a pace or two from where she stood. She laid her ear against it, and listened. The sobs continued a while, ceased, and left all silent. Then clear and sweet, but strange and wild, came the voice of a child. "Mother," it rang out, "you *may* put me in the hole."

And the silence fell deep as before.

Hester stood for a moment horrified, then went back to the kitchen. "Where does the door beyond the coal cellar lead to?" she asked Sarah.

"Not out to nowhere, miss. That's a large cellar as we never use. I ain't been into it since the first day, when they put some of the packing cases there."

"Give me the key," said Hester. "Something is going on there we ought to know about."

"Then pray send for the police, miss!" answered Sarah, trembling. "It ain't for you to go into such places!"

"What? Not in our own house?"

"It's the wicked as is in it, I fear, miss."

"It's those that weep anyhow, and they're our business, if it's only to weep with them. Quick! Give me the key."

Sarah noted the coolness with which her young mistress took the key, gathered courage, and followed a little way behind.

When Hester reached the door, she found it secured by only the bolt of the lock. She set the candle on the floor, and put in the key as quietly as she could. It turned without much difficulty, and the door fell partly open with a groan of the rusted hinge. She caught up her light, and went in.

It was a large, dark, empty place, but she spied a group of faces, looking white through the blackness, their eyes fixed in amazement, if not in terror, upon her. She advanced toward them, and immediately recognized them, but felt as if surrounded by the veiling shadows of a dream. Whose was that palled little face whose eyes were not upon her with the rest? It stared straight on into the dark, as if it had no more to do with the light!

When the eyes of the mother saw the face of her Moxy who had died in the dark, she threw herself in a passion of tears and cried upon her dead. But the man knelt upon his knees, and when Hester turned in pain from the agony of the mother, she saw him with lifted hands of supplication at her feet. A torrent of divine love and passionate pity filled her heart, breaking from its deepest God-haunted caves. She stooped and kissed the man upon his upturned forehead.

Franks burst out crying like the veriest child. All at once in the depths of hell the wings of a great angel were spread out over him and his! No more starvation and cold for his poor wife and baby! The boys would have plenty to eat now! Surely the God his wife talked about must have sent her to them! Did He think they had borne enough now? Only he had borne it so ill! Thus thought Franks, in dislocated fashion, and remained kneeling.

Hester was now kneeling also, with her arms round her whose arms were about the body of her child. She did not speak to her, did not attempt a word of comfort, but wept with her: she too had loved the little Moxy! She too had heard his dying words— glowing with reproof to her faithlessness who cried out like a baby when her father left her for a moment in the dark! In the midst of her loneliness and seeming desertion, God had these people already in the house for her help! The back door of every tomb opens on a hilltop.

With awestruck faces the boys looked on. They too could now see Moxy's face. They had loved Moxy—loved him much more than they knew yet.

The woman at length raised her head, and looked at Hester. "O miss, it's Moxy!" she said, and burst into a fresh passion of grief. "Who's to look after him now?"

"There will be plenty to look after him. You don't think He who provided a woman like you for his mother before He sent him here, would send him there without having somebody ready to look after him?"

"Well, miss, it wouldn't be like Him—I don't think!"

"It would *not* be like Him," responded Hester, with self-accusation. Then she asked them a few questions about their history since last she saw them, and how it was they had sunk so low, receiving answers more satisfactory than her knowledge had allowed her to hope.

"But O miss!" exclaimed Mrs. Franks. "You ought not to ha' been here so long: the little angel there died o' the smallpox, an' it's no end of catching!"

"Never mind me," replied Hester. "I'm not afraid. But," she added, rising, "we must get you out of this."

"O miss! Where would you send us?" said Mrs. Franks in alarm. "There's nobody as'll take us in! An' it would break both our two hearts—Franks' an' mine—to be parted at such a moment, when us two's the father an' mother o' Moxy. An' they'd take Moxy from us, an' put him in the hole he was so afeared of!"

"You don't think I would leave my own flesh and blood in the cellar!" answered Hester. "I will go and make arrangement for you above and be back presently."

"Oh, thank you, miss!" said the woman, as Hester set down the candle beside them. "I do want to look on the face of my blessed boy as long as I can! He will be taken from me altogether soon!"

"Mrs. Franks," rejoined Hester, "you mustn't talk like a heathen. Don't you know that Jesus died and rose again that we might be delivered from death? Don't you know it's He and not death has got your Moxy? He will take care of him for you till you are ready to have him again. If you love Moxy more than Jesus loves him, then you are more like God than Jesus was!"

"O miss, don't talk to me like that! The child was born of my own body!"

"And both you and he were born of God's own soul; if you know how to love, He loves ten times better."

"You know how to love anyhow, miss! The Lord love you! An angel o' mercy you been to me an' mine."

"Good-bye then for a few minutes," said Hester. "I am only going to prepare a place for you."

Only as she said the words did she remember who had said them before her. And as she went through the dark tunnel she sang with a voice that seemed to beat at the gates of heaven, "Thou didst not leave His soul in hell."

Mrs. Franks threw herself again beside her child, but her tears were not so bitter now; she and hers were no longer forsaken!

"And she'll come again and receive us to herself!" she said. "An' Christ'll receive my poor Moxy to Himself!"

The bereaved mother lay with her arm over the lovely body of her child. He lay like the sacrifice that sealed a new covenant between his mother and her Father in heaven. We have yet learned but little of the blessed power of death. We call it an evil! It is a holy, friendly thing. We are not left shivering all the world's night in a stately portico with no house behind it; death is the door to the temple-house, whose God is not seated aloft in motionless state, but walks about among His children, receiving His pilgrim sons in His arms, and washing the sore feet of the weary ones. Either God is altogether such as Christ, or the Christian religion is a lie.

The hearts of husband and wife were too full for speech, but their hands found and held each other.

Chapter 45.

ON THE WAY UP

Sarah ventured near enough to the door to hear something of what was said. Set at rest by finding but a poor family that had sought refuge in the cellar, she was ready to help. More than sufficiently afraid of robbers and murderers, she was not afraid of infection. "What should an old woman like me do taking the smallpox! I've had it bad enough once already!" She was rather staggered, however, when she heard Hester's plan.

Nothing more, since the night of the concert, had been done to make the great room habitable by the family. It had been well cleaned out and that was all. What better place, thought Hester, could there be for a smallpox ward! There she would convey her friends rescued from the slimy embrace of London poverty.

She told Sarah to light a great fire while she settled what could be done about beds. Almost all in the house were old-fashioned wooden ones, hard to take down, heavy to move, and hard to put up again. It would be better to hire iron beds which would be easily purified—only it was Sunday night, and late! But she knew the broker in Steeven's Road—she would go and see him.

She had to ring his bell a good many times before the door opened, for it was now eleven o'clock. He was not well pleased at being taken from his warm bed to go out and work—on such a night too! He more than hinted his surprise that Hester would ask him to do such a thing on Sunday. She told him it was for some who had nowhere to lay their heads, and in her turn more than hinted that he could hardly know what Sunday meant if he did not think it right to do any number of good deeds on it. The man assented to her argument, and went to extract two bedsteads from the disorganized heaps in the back of his shop. He and Hester together proceeded to carry them home—no very light job. It was long after midnight before the beds were ready and a meal spread in the great room. Then at last Hester went back to the cellar.

"Now, come," she said, taking up the light, unresisting baby. Franks rose from the edge of the packing case, on which lay the body of Moxy, with his mother yet kneeling beside it, and put his arm round his wife to raise her. She yielded, and he led her away after their hostess, the boys following hand in hand. But when they reached the cellar door, the mother gave a heartbroken cry, and ran and threw herself again beside her child.

"I can't!" she cried. "I can't leave my Moxy lyin' here all alone! He's never once slep' alone since he was born. I can't bear to think o' that lovely look o' his, lost on the dark night—not a soul to look down an' see it!"

"What makes you think there will not be a soul to see it?" said Hester. "The darkness may be full of eyes! And the night itself is only the black pupil of the Father's eye. But we're not going to leave the darling here. We'll take him too, and find him a good place to lie in."

The mother was satisfied, and the little procession passed through the dark way and up the stair.

The boys looked pleased at the sight of the comforts that waited them, but a little awed with the great lofty room. Over the face of Franks passed a gleam of joy mingled with gratitude, despite his little Serpent of the Prairies having crept away through the long tangled grass of the universe. Much was now begun to be set to rights between him and the high government. But the mother's mind was with the little body lying alone in the cellar. Suddenly with a wild gesture she made for the door.

"O miss!" she cried. "The rats!" and would have darted from the room.

"Stop, dear Mrs. Franks!" cried Hester. "Here, take the baby. Sarah and I are going immediately to bring him away, and lay him where you can see him when you please."

Again she was satisfied. She took the baby, and sat down beside her husband.

In the low-pitched room under the great one, Hester had told Sarah to place a table covered with white. They would lay the body there in such a fashion as would be a sweet remembrance to the mother. She now went to see whether this was done.

But on the way she met Sarah coming up with ashy face. "O miss!" she said. "The body mustn't be left a minute. There's a whole army of rats in the house already! As I was covering the table with a blanket, there got up all at once behind the wainscot the most hurry-scurry o' them horrid creatures!"

"Come," said Hester, and led the way. She looked first into the narrow room to see that it was properly prepared, and heard a strange sound behind the wainscot.

"There, miss!" said Sarah.

Hester saw that little Moxy should not be left alone. Her heart trembled a little at the thought, but she comforted herself that Sarah would not be far off, and that the father and mother of the child would be immediately over her head. The same instant she was ashamed of having found this comfort first, for was He not infinitely nearer to her who is Lord of life and death?

"But how," said Hester on the way to the cellar again, "can the Frankses have got into the place?"

"There is a back door to it, of course!" answered Sarah. "But master wouldn't have it used. He didn't like a door to his house he never set eyes on, he said."

"But how could it have been open to let them in?"

When they reached the cellar, Hester took the candle and went to look at the door. It was pushed to, but not locked, though in the lock was the key. She turned the key, took it out, and put it in her pocket.

Then they carried up the little body, washed it, dressed it in white, and laid it straight in its beauty, the little hands folded on the breast under the well-contented face, repeating the calm expression of that conquest over the fear of death, that submission to be "put in the hole," with which the child-spirit passed into wide spaces. They lighted six candles, three at the head and three at the feet, that the mother might see the face of her child, and because light, not darkness, befits death. To Hester they symbolized the forms of light that sat, one at the head and one at the foot, of the place where the body of Jesus had lain.

Then they went to fetch the mother, who was washing the supper things. The boys were already in bed. Franks was staring into the fire: the poor fellow had not even looked at one for

207

some time. Hester asked them to go and see where she had laid
Moxy, and they went with her. The beauty of death's courtly
state comforted them.

"But I can't leave him alone!" said the mother. "I know he
won't wake up no more, only you know, miss—"

"Yes, I know very well," replied Hester. "You are both worn
out and must go to bed. I will stay with the beautiful thing, and
see that no harm comes to it."

After some persuasion they consented, and in a little while the
house was quiet. Hester threw a fur cloak round her, and sat
down in the chair beside the dead. When she had sat some time,
the persistent stillness of the form beside her began to fill her
heart with a gentle awe. The awe gradually grew to dismay, and
inexplicable, unreasonable fear began to invade her. She knew
at once that she must go to the truth for refuge, for it is little use
telling one's self that one's fear is silly.

She prayed to the Father, awake with her in the stillness, and
then began to think about the dead Christ. Would the women
who waited for the dawn, because they had no light by which to
minister, have been afraid to watch by that body all the night
long? Oh, to have seen it come to life, to move and wake and rise
with the informing God! Every dead thing belonged to Christ,
not to something called death! This dead thing was His. It was
dead as He had been dead! There was nothing dreadful in
watching by it, any more than in sitting beside the cradle of a
child yet unborn! He had abolished death!

Thus thinking, she lay back in the chair, closed her eyes, and
thanking God, fell fast asleep.

She started suddenly awake, roused by the opening of a door.
In the wall opposite stood the form of a man! She neither cried
out nor fainted, but sat gazing, dumb with wonder. In that wall
was the door said to lead into the next house: for the first time
she saw it open. A smile she seemed to have seen before broke
gradually from the man's lips and spread over his face. The next
moment he stepped from the wall and came toward her.

It was Dr. Christopher! She rose, and held out her hand.

"You are surprised to see me!" he said. "And well you may be!
Am I in your house? And I seem to recognize the child's sweet
face! I must have seen you and it together before. Yes, it *is*
Moxy!"

"You are right, Dr. Christopher," she answered. "Dear little Moxy died of the smallpox in our cellar. He was just gone when I found them there."

"Is it wise of you to expose yourself so much to the infection?" said the doctor.

"Is it worthy of you to ask such a question?" returned Hester. "We have our work to do; life or death is the care of Him who sets the work."

The doctor bent his head low before her. Nothing moves a man more than to recognize in another his own principles. "I put the question to know on what grounds you based your action," he replied, "and I am answered."

"Tell me then," said Hester, "how you came to be here. It seemed to my sleepy eyes as if an angel had melted his own door through the wall! Are you free of ordinary hindrances?"

"I came a simple way," he said, "though I am no less surprised than you to find myself in your presence. I was called to see a patient. When I went to return as I came, I found the door by which I had entered locked. I then remembered that I had passed a door on the stair, and went back to try it. It was bolted on the side to the stair. I withdrew the bolts, opened the door gently, and beheld a most impressive sight.

"I saw the light shining in the darkness, and the darkness comprehending it not—six candles, and only the upturned face of the dead, and the downturned face of the sleeping! I seemed to look into the heart of things, and see the whole waste universe waiting for the sonship, for the redemption of the body, the visible life of men! I saw that love, trying to watch by death, had failed, because the thing that is not needs not to be watched. Then you woke."

Hester's face alone showed that she understood him. She turned and looked at Moxy to calm her emotion.

Dr. Christopher stood silent, as if brooding on what he had seen. She could not ask him to sit down, but she must understand how he had come into the place. Was his patient in the next house? That door must be secured on their side, for their next midnight visitor might not be so welcome as this, whose heart burned to the same labor as her own! "But what we really want," she thought, "is to have more of our doors open, if they be but the right ones for the angels to come and go!"

209

"I never saw that door open before," she said, "and none of us knew where it led. We took it for granted it was into the next house."

"It goes into no lady's house," he said. "The stair leads to a garret, much higher up."

"Would you show me how you came in?" said Hester.

"With pleasure," he answered, and taking one of the candles, led the way.

"I would not let the young woman leave her husband to show me out," he went on. "When I found myself a prisoner, I thought I would try this door before periling the sleep of a patient in the smallpox. You seem to have it all round you here!"

Through the door so long mysterious Hester stepped on a narrow, steep stair. Christopher turned downward, and trod softly. At the bottom he passed through a door admitting them to a small cellar, a mere recess. Thence they issued into that so lately occupied by the Frankses. Christopher went to the door Hester had locked, and said, "This is where I came in. I suppose one of your people must have locked it."

"I locked it myself," replied Hester, and told him in brief the story of the evening.

"I see!" said Christopher. "We must have passed through just after you had taken them away."

"Who can be in our house without our knowledge?" asked Hester. "The stair is plainly in our house."

"Beyond a doubt," said Christopher. "But how strange it is you should know your own house so imperfectly! I fancy the young couple, having got into some difficulty, found entrance the same way the Frankses did. Only they went farther and fared better! There is something peculiar about them—I can hardly say in a word."

"Could I not go up with you tomorrow and see them?"

"That would hardly do, I fear. I could be of no further use to them were they to suppose I had betrayed them. You have a perfect right to know what is going on in your house, but I would rather not appear in the discovery. One thing is plain, you must either go to them, or unlock the cellar door. You will be taken with the young woman. She is a capable creature—an excellent nurse. Shall I go out this way?"

"Will you come tomorrow?" said Hester. "I am alone, and

cannot ask anybody to help me because of the smallpox, and I shall want help for the funeral. You do not think me troublesome?"

"Not in the least. It is all in the way of my business. I will manage for you."

"Come then. I will show you the way out. This is Number 18 Addison Square. You need not come in the cellar next time."

"If I were you," said Christopher, "I would leave the key in that cellar door. The poor young woman would be terrified to find they were prisoners."

She replaced the key.

"Now let us fasten up the door I came in by," said Christopher. "I have a screw in my pocket, and I never go without my pocketknife." This was soon done, and he went.

What a strange night it had been for Hester. For the time she had forgotten her own troubles. Ah, if she had been of one mind with Lord Gartley, those poor creatures would be now moaning in darkness by the dead body of their child, or out with it in their arms in the streets, or parted asunder in the casual wards of some workhouse! Certainly God could have sent them other help than hers, but where would *she* be then—a fellow worker with his lordship, and not with God. Woe for the wife whose husband has no regard to her deepest desires, her highest aspirations! Who loves her so that he would be the god of her idolatry, not the friend and helper of her heart, soul, and mind!

Many of Hester's own thoughts were revealed to her that night by the side of the dead Moxy. It became clear to her that she had been led astray, in part by the desire to rescue one to whom God had not sent her, in part by the pleasure of being loved and worshiped, and in part by worldly ambition. Would God have her give herself to one who would render it impossible for her to make her life more abundant to others? Was a husband to take the place of Christ, and order her life for her? It came to this: was he or God to be her master? There could be no relation of life over which the Lord of life was not supreme!

When the morning came, she sent Sarah to take her place, and went to get a little rest.

Chapter 46.

MORE YET

But Hester could not sleep. She rose, went back to the room where Moxy lay, and sent Sarah to get breakfast ready. Then came upon her an urgent desire to know the people who had come, like swallows, to tenant without leave the space overhead. She undid the screw, opened the door, and stole gently up the stair, steep, narrow, and straight, which ran the height of the two rooms between two walls. A long way up she came to another door which must admit to the small orchestra high in the end wall of the great room. Probably then the stair and the room below had been an arrangement for the musicians.

Higher yet, near the roof, the stair brought her to a door. She knocked, and after some little delay it was opened by a young woman, with her finger on her lips, and a scared look in her eye. She had expected to see the doctor, and started and trembled at the sight of Hester. There was little light where Hester stood.

The girl came out on the landing and shut the door behind her. "He is very ill," she said, "and he hears a strange voice even in his sleep. A strange voice is dreadful to him." Her voice was not strange, and the moment she spoke it seemed to light up her face.

"Amy!" Hester said.

"O Miss Raymount!" cried Amy Amber joyfully. "Are you come at last? I thought I would never see you anymore!"

"You bewilder me," said Hester. "How do you come to be here? I don't understand."

"*He* brought me here."

"*Who* brought you here?"

"Why, miss!" exclaimed Amy, as if hearing the most unexpected of questions. "Who should it be?"

"I have not the slightest idea," returned Hester. But a mingled feeling of alarm, discomfort, indignation, and relief crossed her mind.

Through her whiteness Amy turned whiter still, and she turned a little away, like a person offended. "There is but one, miss!" she said coldly. "Who should it be but him?"

"Speak his name," said Hester almost sternly. "This is no time for hide-and-seek. Tell me who you mean."

"Are you angry with me?" faltered Amy. "O Miss Raymount, I don't think I deserve it!"

"Speak out, child! Why should I be angry with you?"

"Do you know what it is? He is dying!" She sank on the floor, and covered her face with her hands. Hester looked at her weeping, her heart filled with sad dismay, mingled with a kind of wan hope. Then softly and quickly she opened the door of the room and went in, followed by Amy, who pled with her not to wake him.

It was a great room, but the roof came down to the floor nearly all round. It was lighted only with a skylight. Hester crept gently toward a screen in the far corner and peeped behind it. There lay a young man in a troubled sleep, his face swollen and red and blotched with the smallpox, but through the disfigurement she recognized her brother. Her eyes filled with tears, and she stole out again as softly as she came in. Outside, Amy again closed the door.

"You *will* forgive him, won't you, miss?" she said pitifully.

"What do you want me to forgive him for, Amy?" asked Hester, supressing her tears.

"I don't know, miss. You seemed angry with him. I don't know what to make of it. Sometimes I feel certain it must have been his illness coming on that made him weak in the head and talk foolishness, and sometimes I wonder whether he has really been doing anything wrong."

"He must have been doing something wrong, else how should *you* be here, Amy?" said Hester, with hasty judgment.

"He never told me, miss, or of course I would have done what I could to prevent it," answered Amy, bewildered. "We were so

213

happy, miss, till then, and we've never had a moment's peace since! That's why we came here where nobody would find us. I wonder how he came to know the place!"

"Do you not know where you are then, Amy?"

"No, miss. I only know where to buy the things we need. He has not been out once since we came."

"You are in our house, Amy. What will my father say! How long have you—have you been—" Something in her heart or her throat prevented Hester from finishing the question.

"How long have I been married to him, miss? You surely know that as well as I do, miss!"

"My poor Amy! Did he make you believe we knew about it?"

Amy gave a cry, but after her old way instantly crammed her handkerchief into her mouth, and uttered no further smallest sound.

"Alas!" said Hester, "He has been more wicked than we know! Amy, he has done something else very wrong."

Amy covered her face with her apron, through which Hester could see her soundless sobs.

"I have been doing what I could to find him," continued Hester, "and here he was close to me all the time! But it adds greatly to my misery to find you with him, Amy!"

"Indeed, miss, I may have been silly, but how was I to suspect he was not telling me the truth? I loved him too much for that! I told him I would not marry him without his father's leave. And he said he had it, and read me such a beautiful letter from his mother!"

A new fear came upon Hester. Had he deceived the poor girl with a pretended marriage? Was he bad through and through? What her father would say to a marriage was hard to think; what he would say to a deception, she knew!

Amy said, in a voice of terror, "Please, miss, do not let him see you till I have told him you are here."

"Certainly not," answered Hester, "if you think the sight of me would hurt him!"

"Thank you, miss. I am sure it would," whispered Amy. "He is frightened of you."

"Frightened of me!" said Hester to herself, repeating Amy's phrase when she was gone in, leaving her at the head of the stair. "I should have thought he only disliked me!"

214

Now first it began to dawn upon Hester that there was in her a certain hardness of character, distinct from that unbending devotion to the right which is imperative—belonging in truth to the region of her weakness—that self which fears fear itself, and is of death, not of life. But she was one of those who, when they discover a thing in them that is wrong, take refuge in the immediate endeavor to set it right—with the conviction that God is on their side to help them, for is He not God our Saviour?

She went down to the house to seek things to make the garret more comfortable. It would be long before Cornelius could be moved. In particular she sought out a warm fur cloak for Amy. Poor Amy was but the shadow of her former self, yet a shadow very pretty and pleasant to look on. Hester's heart was sore to think of such a bright, good honest creature married to a man like her brother. But she was sure however credulous she might have been, she had done nothing to be ashamed of. Where there was blame it must all be Corney's!

She carried everything she could at the time up the stair, then gave herself to the comfort of her other guests.

Left alone in London, Corney had gone idly ranging about the house when another man would have been reading, or doing something with his hands. Curious in correspondent proportion to his secrecy, for the qualities go together, the moment he happened to cast his eyes on the door in the wainscot of the low room, no one being in the house to interfere with him, he proceeded to open it. He little thought then what his discovery would be to him, for at that time he had done nothing to make him fear his fellowmen. But he kept the secret after his kind.

Contriving often to meet Amy, he had grown rapidly more and more fond of her—became indeed as much in love with her as was possible to him; and though the love of such a man can never be of a lofty kind, it may yet be the best thing in him, and the most redemptive power upon him. Without a notion of denying himself anything he desired and could possibly have, he determined she should be his, but avoided the direct way of gaining her. The straight line would not, he judged, be the shortest; his father would never, or only after unendurable delay, consent to his marriage with a girl like Amy! So he contrived to persuade her to a private marriage—contrived also to prevent her from communicating with Hester.

His desire to please Amy, his passion for showing off, and the preparations his designs rendered necessary, soon brought him into straits for money. He could not ask his father, who would have insisted on knowing how it was that he found his salary insufficient, seeing he had only to buy his clothes. He went on and on, borrowing small sums from those about him, till he was ashamed to borrow more. The next thing was to borrow a trifle of what was passing through his hands. He was merely borrowing, and of his own uncle! It was a shame his uncle should have so much and leave him in such straits—be rolling in wealth and pay him such a contemptible salary! It was the height of injustice! Of course, he would replace it long before anyone knew. Thus by degrees the poor weak creature, deluding himself with excuses, slipped into the consciousness of being a rogue. There are some who fall into vice from being so satisfied with themselves that they think it impossible they should ever do wrong.

He went on taking until at last there was no possibility of making restoration. Then in cold despair, he laid hold of a large sum and left the bank an unconvicted felon. By some story he convinced Amy of the necessity for concealment, and brought her to their refuge by the back way. She went and came only through the cellar, and knew no other entrance. When they found that others had taken refuge in the cellar, they dared not warn them off the premises, for fear of attracting attention to themselves.

Chapter 47

AMY AND CORNEY

The great room was given over to the Frankses. There they rested until the funeral was over, and then Hester would have father and sons go out to follow their calling, while the mother did what she could for the ailing baby, who could not linger long behind Moxy.

She would not let them move from the house; she must have them in better condition first, and with a little earned money in their own pockets. And the very first day, though they went out with heavy hearts, and could hardly have played with much spirit, they brought home more money than any day for weeks before. And Franks, as he walked home weary, took some comfort that his Moxy was not with him to trouble his mother with his white face and drawn looks.

The same day Lord Gartley called, but was informed by Sarah, who opened the door but a chink, that the smallpox was in the house, and that she could admit no one but the doctor. Her young mistress was perfectly well, but could and would see nobody—was in attendance upon the sick. So his lordship was compelled to go without seeing her, with a haunting doubt that he was being played upon.

As had happened before, the major soon made his appearance. To him Sarah gave the same answer, adding that there was no longer any need to seek Cornelius, for it was all explained, and her mistress would write to him.

But what was Hester to tell her father and mother? Until she knew with certainty the truth of the "marriage," she shrank from mentioning Amy, and at present it was impossible to find out anything from Cornelius. She merely wrote, therefore, that she had found him, but very ill, that she would take the best care of him she could, and as soon as he was able to be moved she would bring him home to be nursed by his mother.

She did her best to help Amy without letting her brother suspect her presence, and by degrees she got the room more comfortable for them. Corney had indeed taken a good many things from the house to make habitable the waste expanse, but had been careful not to take anything Sarah would miss.

He was covered with the terrible eruption, and if he survived, would be much changed, for Amy could not keep his hands from his face. In trifles the lack of self-restraint is manifested, and its consequences are sometimes grievous.

Hitherto Hester had not let her parents know how ill he was, not to save them from any anxiety, but to save her mother from hearing her father say the best thing Corney could do would be to die. Nor was she mistaken; many a time had her father said so to himself. It was simply impossible, he said, that he should ever again speak to him or in any way treat him as a son. He had by his vile conduct ceased to be a son, and he was nowise bound to do anything more for him; though, from mere compassion, he would keep him from starving till he found some employment for which no character was necessary.

Corney began at last to recover, but it was long before he could be treated other than a child—feeble and unreasonable. The first time he saw and knew Hester, he closed his eyes and turned away his head. She retired, but watched, and presently saw him, in his own sly way, look through half-closed lids to know whether she was gone. When he saw Amy where Hester had stood, his face beamed up. "Amy," he said, "come here," and when she went, he took her hand and laid it on his cheek, little knowing what a disfigured cheek it was.

"Thank God!" said Hester to herself; she had never seen him look so sweet or loving or lovable, despite his disfigurement. But she did not show herself again till he should be a little accustomed to the idea of her presence.

The more she saw of Amy the better she liked her. She treated her patient with so much good sense, showed such readiness to subordinate her ignorance to the wisdom of others, and such careful obedience to the directions of the doctor, that she rose every day in Hester's opinion, as well as found a yet deeper place in her heart.

His lordship wrote, making an apology for anything he had said, from anxiety about one whom he loved to distraction, in which he might have presumed on the closeness of their relation to each other. He would gladly talk the whole matter over with her. He had no doubt that her good sense—relieved from the immediate pressure of her feelings, which were in themselves but too divine for the needs of this world—would convince her of the reasonableness of all he had sought to urge upon her. As soon as she was able, and judged it safe to admit a visitor, his aunt would be happy to call upon her. For the present, as he knew she would not admit him, he would content himself with frequent and most anxious inquiries after her, reserving argument and expostulation for a happier and, he hoped, not very distant time.

Hester smiled a curious smile at the prospect of a call from Miss Vavasor; was she actually going to plead her nephew's cause?

As her brother grew better and things became easier, the thought of Lord Gartley came oftener, with something of the old feeling for the man himself, but mingled with sadness and a strange pity. She would never have been able to do anything for him! It had been spiritual presumption to think she could save him by the preciousness of her self-gift to him and the strength of her power over him!

If God cannot save a man by all His good gifts, not even by the gift of a woman offered to his higher nature but by that refused, then the woman's giving of herself a slave to his lower nature can only make him the more unredeemable. Yet the withholding of herself *may* do something—may one day wake in him some sense of what a fool he has been. The man who would go to the dogs for lack of the woman he fancies, will go to the dogs when he has her, and may possibly drag her to the dogs with him.

Hester began to see something of this. She recalled how she had never once gained from him a satisfactory reply to anything she said worth saying; she had foolishly supplied from her own imagination the defective echoes of his response! Love had

made her apt and able to do this, but now doubt made her see
many things differently.

And it was her brother now she had to save! His dear little
wife was doing all she could for him, but it would take sister and
mother and all to save him. She could not do so much for him as
Amy now, but by and by there would be his father to mediate
with: to that she would give her energy!

But would his poor mother recognize him—so terribly scarred
and changed? Some men are as vain as any women, and Corney
was one of those some. While pretending to despise the kindest
word concerning his good looks, he had taken the greatest
pleasure in them; and the first time he saw himself in a mirror, a
look of dismay, of despairing horror, came over his face. He had
been accustomed to regard himself as superior on most
grounds, on that of good looks in particular—and now he had to
admit that he was nothing less than unpleasant to behold, even
to those who loved him! It was a pain that in itself could do little
to cast out the evil spirit that possessed him; but it was something that that evil spirit, while it remained in him, should be
deprived of one source of its nourishment. It was a good thing
that from any cause the transgressor should find his ways hard.
He dashed the glass from him, and burst into tears which he did
not even try to conceal.

From that time he was more dejected and less peevish. He had
always been peevish at home, where he never thought of cultivating the same conception of himself as before the eyes of the
world. Much of supposed goodness is merely an imitating of the
thing men would like to be considered—originating in admiration or a vague wish to be that thing, but without desire or
strength enough to rouse the smallest endeavor after being it.
Still Hester found it difficult to bear with his remaining peevishness and bad temper; but at such hard moments, she had the
good sense to leave him to the soothing ministrations of his wife.
Amy never set herself against him; she would show him she
understood what was troubling him, then would say something
sympathetic or petting or coaxing, and always had her way with
him.

He had never quarreled with Amy, and that gave a ground of
hope for her influence with him that his sister had long lost. So
Hester learned from the sweetness of Amy, as Amy from the

unbending principle of Hester.

Hester at last decided to take Cornelius home without giving her father the opportunity of saying he should not come. She would presume he must go home after such an illness; the result she would wait! The meeting could in no case be a happy one, but if he were not altogether repulsed, if the mean devil in Corney was not thoroughly roused by the harshness of his father, she would think much had been gained!

With gentle watchfulness she regarded Amy, and was more and more satisfied that, whatever might be wrong, she had had a share in it not as one who did wrong, but as one who endured it. And she could not believe that Amy would have married him knowing what kind of person he was. She did not think how nearly the man she had once accepted stood on the same level of manhood.

When he was able to be moved, Hester brought them down into the house, and placed them in a comfortable room. She then moved the Frankses into the garret. With their own entrance through the cellar, they were to live there after their own fashion, and follow their own calling, only they were to let Hester know if they found themselves in any difficulty. And now for the first time in her life she wished she had some means of her own, that she might act with freedom. She had seen hope of freedom in marriage, but now she wished it in independence.

Chapter 48.

MISS VAVASOR

About three weeks after Lord Gartley's call, during which he had left a good many cards in Addison Square, Hester received a letter from Miss Vavasor. "My dear Miss Raymount, I am very anxious to see you, but fear it is hardly safe to go to you yet. You with your heavenly spirit do not regard such things, but I am not so much in love with the future as to risk my poor present for it; neither would I willingly bear infection into my own circle. But speak with you I must, for your own sake as well as Gartley's, who is pining away for lack of the sunlight of your eyes."

Hester pondered well her answer. She could hardly say, she replied, that there was no danger, for her brother was yet in the house. She suggested that they should meet in some quiet corner of one of the parks. She need hardly add she would take every precaution against carrying infection.

The proposal proved acceptable to Miss Vavasor; a time and place were agreed upon, and so they met.

Hester appeared on foot, having dismissed her cab at the gate. Miss Vavasor, who had remained seated in her carriage, got down as soon as she saw her, sent it away, and advanced to meet her with a smile: she was perfect in skin hospitality.

"How long is it now," Miss Vavasor began, "since you saw Gartley?"

"Three weeks or a month," replied Hester.

"I am afraid you cannot be much of a lover, not to have seen him for so long and look so fresh!" smiled Miss Vavasor. She

222

followed the words with a sigh, as if *she* had memories of a different complexion.

"When one has one's work to do," began Hester.

"Ah, yes!" returned Miss Vavasor, not waiting for the sentence. "Those peculiar ideas about work are spreading in our circle too. I know many ladies who visit the poor. They complain there are so few unobjectionable tracts to give them. I fear they will upset everything before long. No one can tell where such things will end."

"We know nothing about the ends of things," said Hester, "only the beginnings."

There had been an air of gentle raillery in Miss Vavasor's tone, and Hester used the same, for she had no hope of coming to an understanding with her about anything.

"Then the sooner we do know the better! I don't see how else things are to go on at all!" said Miss Vavasor.

"When the Master comes He will stop a good deal," thought Hester, but she did not say it.

"You and Gartley had a small misunderstanding, he tells me, the last time you met," continued Miss Vavasor.

"I think I understood him very well," answered Hester.

"My dear Miss Raymount, you must not be offended with me. I am an old woman, and have had to compose differences between goodness knows how many couples. I have had considerable experience in that sort of thing."

"I do not doubt it," said Hester. "What I do doubt is that you have had any experience of the sort necessary to set things right between Lord Gartley and myself. The fact is that I saw then—for the first time plainly—that to marry him would be to lose my liberty."

"Not more, my dear, than every woman does who marries at all. I presume you will allow marriage and its duties to be the natural calling of a woman?"

"Certainly."

"Then she cannot complain of the loss of her liberty."

"Not so much as is naturally involved in marriage, I allow."

"Then why draw back from your engagement?"

"Because he requires me to turn away at once, and before any necessity shows itself, from the exercise of a higher calling yet. God has given me gifts to use for my fellows, and use them I must till He, not man, stops me."

"But you know that of necessity a woman must give up a good many things when she accepts the position of a wife, and possibly the duties of a mother."

"The natural claims upon a wife or mother I would heartily acknowledge."

"Then of course to the duties of a wife belong the claims Society has upon her as a wife."

"So far as I yet know what is meant in your circle by such claims, I count them the merest usurpation. I will never subject myself to such—never put myself in a position where I should be expected to obey a code of laws not merely opposed to the work for which I was made, but to all the laws of the relations of human beings to each other as human beings. I simply do not belong to your set."

"But you are about to belong to it, I hope."

"I hope not."

"You are engaged to marry my nephew."

"Not irrevocably, I trust."

"You should have thought of all that before you gave your consent. Gartley thought you understood. Certainly our circle is not one for saints."

"Honest women would be good enough for me. But I thought I had done and said more than was necessary to make Gartley understand my ideas of what was required of me in life, and I thought he would help me. Now I find that he never believed I meant what I said, but all the time intended to put a stop to the aspiration of my life the moment he had it in his power to do so."

"Ah, my dear young lady, you do not know what love is!" said Miss Vavasor, and sighed again as if *she* knew what love was. And in truth she had been in love at least once in her youth, but had yielded when her parents objected to her marrying three hundred pounds a year. She saw it was reasonable—what fellowship can light have with darkness, or love with starvation? "A woman really in love," she went on, "is ready to give up *everything* for the man she loves. She who is not equal to that does not know what love is."

"Suppose he should prove unworthy of her?"

"That would be positively nothing. If she had once learned to love him, she would see no fault in him."

"*Whatever* faults he might have?"

"Whatever faults. Love has no second thoughts."

"Suppose he showed himself heedless of her best welfare, caring for her only as an adjunct to his display?"

"*If she loved him,* she would be proud to follow in his triumph. His glory is hers."

"Whether it be real or not?"

"If he counts it so. A woman who loves gives herself to her husband to be molded by him."

"I fear that is the way men think of us," said Hester sadly, "and no doubt there are women whose behavior would justify them in it. With all my heart I say a woman ought to be ready to die for the man she loves—but that she should fall in with all his thoughts, feelings, and judgments whatever, even such as in others she would most heartily despise—that she should act as if her husband and not God made her, and his whims, instead of the lovely will of Him who created man and woman, were to be to her the bonds of her being—that surely no woman could grant who had not first lost her reason."

"You won't lose yours for love at least," concluded Miss Vavasor, who could not help admiring her ability, though she despised the direction it took. "I see," she said to herself, "she is one of the strong-minded who think themselves superior to any man. Gartley will be well rid of her! I think I have done nearly all he could require of me."

"I tell you honestly," continued Hester, "I love Lord Gartley so well that I would gladly yield my life to do him any worthy good. But I would do that to redeem any human creature from the misery of living without God. I would even marry Lord Gartley, if only I knew that he would not try to prevent me from being the woman I ought to be and have to be. But I for one will not take an enemy into the house of my life. I grant you a wife must love her husband grandly and passionately, but there is One to be loved immeasurably more grandly and passionately— He whose love creates love. Can you for a moment imagine, when the question came between my Lord and my husband, I would hesitate?"

" 'Tis a pity you were not born in the Middle Ages," said Miss Vavasor, smiling, but with gentle scorn in her superior tone.

"You would certainly have been canonized!"

"But now I am sadly out of date—am I not?" returned Hester, trying to smile also. "I could no more consent to live in God's world without minding what He told me, than I would marry a man merely because he admired me."

"Heavens!" exclaimed Miss Vavasor to what she called herself. "What an extravagant young woman! She won't do for us! You'll have to let her fly, my dear boy!"

To Hester she said, "My dear, you have just confessed that that kind of thing is out of date. And when a thing is once of the past, it cannot be called back, do what you will. It is all very well to go to church and that sort of thing; I should be the last to encourage the atheism that is getting so frightfully common. But really, it seems to me such extravagant notions about religion as you have been brought up in must have not a little to do with the present sad state of affairs—must in fact go far to make atheists. Civilization will never endure to be priest-ridden."

"It is my turn now," said Hester, "to say that I scarcely understand you. Do you take God for a priest? Do you object to atheism, and yet regard obedience to God as an invention of the priests? Was Jesus Christ a priest? Or did He say what was not true when He said that whoever loved anyone else more than Him was not worthy of Him? Or do you confess it true, yet say it is of no consequence? If you do not care about what He wants of you, I simply tell you that I care about nothing else."

"It is very plain," said Miss Vavasor, "that you do not love my nephew as he deserves to be loved. A woman should fashion herself upon her husband, fit her life to his life, her thoughts to his thoughts, her tastes to his tastes."

"You are right," said Hester. "I do not love Lord Gartley sufficiently for that! Thank you, Miss Vavasor, you have helped me to the thorough conviction that there could never have been any real union between us. Can a woman love a man who has no care that she should attain to the perfect growth of her nature? He would have been quite content I should remain forever the poor creature I am—would never by word or wish or prayer have sought to raise me above myself! The man I shall love as I could love must be a greater man than Lord Gartley! He is not fit to make any woman love him so. If she were so much less than he as to have to look up to him, she would be too small to have any devotion in her. No! I will be a woman and not a countess! I wish you good morning, Miss Vavasor."

She held out her hand. Miss Vavasor drew herself up, and looked a cold annihilation into her eyes. The warm blood rose from Hester's heart to her brain, but she quietly returned her gaze, nor blenched a moment. Miss Vavasor felt as if she were looking a far-off idea in the face—as if Hester were telling her what a poor miserable creature of money and manners, ambitions and expediencies she thought her. Miss Vavasor, unused to having such a full strong virgin look fixed fearless, without defiance, but with utter disapproval, upon her, quailed.

Hester smiled at last and said, "I am glad you are not going to be my aunt, Miss Vavasor."

"Thank goodness, no!" cried Miss Vavasor, with a slightly hysterical laugh.

Despite her educated self-command, she cowered before the majesty of Hester, for woman was face to face with woman, and the truth was stronger than the lie. It was very hard that she, who desired only to set things right, looking for no advantage to herself, should have been so ignominiously foiled. It did not occur to her that there was a power here altogether different from any she had before encountered—a soul possessed by truth and clad in the armor of righteousness. When faced with a girl who did not acknowledge the jurisdiction of society's law, she was out of her element.

Now she had to go back to her nephew and confess that she had utterly failed. She had to tell him that his lady was the most peculiar, most unreasonable young woman she had ever dealt with; and that she was not only unsuited to him, but quite unworthy of him!

She turned and walked away, attempting a show of dignity, but showing only haughtiness. Hester turned and walked in the opposite direction, feeling that one supposed portion of her history was now but a closed episode.

She did not know that, both coming and going, she was attended at a distance by the major. He had beheld her interview—but by no means overheard her conversation—and had seen with delight the unmistakable symptoms of serious difference. He did not approach her, but as he followed her to Addison Square, his heart was beating with exultant hope that the rascal nobleman had been dismissed.

Next day the major found a summons from Hester waiting him at his club. She had thought it better to prepare him for what she was about to ask of him, therefore mentioned in her note that in a day or two she was going to Yrndale with her brother and his wife.

"Whew!" exclaimed the major when he read it. "Wife! This complicates matters! If he were not such a confounded ape I should pity him. But the smallpox and a wife may perhaps do something for him!"

When he reached the house, Hester received him warmly, and requested that he go down to Yrndale with them. He agreed, but thought she had better not say he was coming, as in the circumstances he could hardly be welcome. They made their arrangements, and he left her, yet more confirmed in a new respect for her. The one most deficient thing in him was reverence, and he was now having a strong lesson.

Chapter 49

DR. CHRISTOPHER

On the Sunday evening, the last before she was to leave for Yrndale, Hester had gone to see a poor woman. She was walking homeward again when she heard the voice of Dr. Christopher, and discovered that it came from a nearby room half underground. She went to the door, and heard that familiar voice pleading with his fellows not to be miserable and die, but to live and rejoice. Now for all Hester's true liberality, she had never entered any place of worship that did not belong to the established church. But as the poor would not go to church, a layman like Dr. Christopher might surely give them of the good things he had! So she went in for a moment.

It was a low room, and though not many were present, the air was stifling. The doctor stood at the far end. Hester could hardly say she saw among his shabby congregation much sign of listening. Most of the faces were just as vacant as those to be seen in the most fashionable churches, with but one or two in some kind of sympathetic relation with the speaker. The speaker's eyes were glowing, his face was gleaming with a light of its own, and his hands were often clenched hard. The whole rough appearance of the man was elevated into dignity. He was not self-possessed, but God-possessed. He said the simplest things to them, telling them that they were like orphan children, hungry in the street, raking the gutter for what they could get, while behind them stood a grand beautiful house where their Father lived! There He sat in a beautiful room, waiting for any of them who would to turn round, run in, and up the stairs to Him.

"But you will ask," he went on, "why He does not send out a message to them, to tell them He is waiting there for them. But that is just what He does do. He is constantly sending out messengers to tell them to come in. But they mostly laugh and make faces. *They* won't be at the trouble to go up those stairs! 'It's not likely,' they say, 'that He would trouble His head about us, even if we were His children!' But some do listen and hear and go in; and some of them come out again, and say they find it all true. Very few believe them a bit, or mind in the least what they say. They are not miserable enough yet to go back to the Father who loves them, who would be as good to them as the bird that covers her young ones all over with her wings, or the mother who wraps her shawl round her child.

"Some of you are thinking now, '*We* wouldn't do like that! *We* should be only too glad to get somebody who would make us comfortable without any trouble on our parts!' Ah, there's the rub! You won't take any trouble about it! I am one of those who have been into the house, and have found my Father—oh, so grand, and so good to me! And I am come out again to tell you it is so, and that if you will go in, you will have the same kindness I have had. All the servants of the house even will rejoice over you with music and dancing—so glad that you are come home. Is it possible you will not take the trouble to go? Certain things are required of you when you go, but perhaps you are too lazy or too dirty in your habits to like doing them! Some refuse to scrape their shoes, or rub them on the doormat when they go in, and then complain loudly that they were refused admittance. A fine house would such keep for their Father, for they would make it unfit for any decent person to live in. A few months and they would have the grand beautiful house as wretched and mean and dirty as the houses they live in now. Such persons keep grumbling that they are not rich. They want to loaf and drink and be a nuisance to everybody, like some of the rich ones. They think it hard they should not be able to do just as they please with everything that takes their fancy, when they would do nothing but break and spoil it, and make it no good to anyone. Their Father, who can do whatever He sees fit, is not one to let such disagreeable children work what mischief they like! He is a better Father than that, for a father who lets them be dirty and rude just as they like, is one of the worst enemies of his children. And the day is coming when, if God can't get them to mind Him any other way, He will put them where they will be ten times more miserable than ever they were at the worst time of their lives, and make them mind. Out of the same door whence came the messengers to ask them in, He will send dogs and bears and lions and tigers and wildcats out upon them.

"Some of you will say, 'Ah, we know what you mean; but that's not the sort of thing we care for, so you needn't go on about it.' I know it is not the sort of thing you care for, else you might have been in a very different condition by this time. And I know the low, dirty things you do care for; you are like children who prefer mud and the gutter to all the beautiful toys in the shop. But though these grand things are not the things you want, they are the things you need, and the time is coming when you will say, 'Ah me! What a fool I was not to look at the precious things, and see how precious they were, and put out my hand for them when they were offered me!' "

In this simple way, the man freed his soul of the message he had to give. After about twenty minutes, he ceased, and they sang a hymn. Then he prayed for two or three minutes and sent them away. Hester, near the door, went out with the first of them, and walked home full of pleasure in the thought of such preaching. If only her friends could hear it! She was near the turning to her square when she was overtaken by Dr. Christopher.

"I was ever so glad to see you!" he said. "I was able to speak the better, for I was sure then of some sympathy in the spiritual air. It is not easy to go on when you feel all the time a doubt whether your words are more than mere words to those present; or, if they have some meaning to any, whether that meaning is not something very different from your meaning."

"I do not see," said Hester, "how anyone could misunderstand, or indeed avoid understanding what you said."

"The one incomprehensible thing is ignorance!" he returned. "To understand why another does not understand seems beyond the power of humanity. As God only can understand evil, while we only can be evil, so God only can understand ignorance, while we only can be ignorant. I have tried for months to teach those people, and I am not sure that a single thought has passed from my mind into one of theirs. I sometimes think I am but beating the air."

"I was surprised," said Hester, "to find you taking the clergy-man's part as well as the doctor's."

"I took no clergyman's part. I took but the part of a human being, bound to share with his fellows. What could make you think so? Did I preach like one?"

"Not very," she answered.

"I am glad of that," he returned, "for such a likeness would not help me with those people. I see no reason why a layman, as was our Lord, should not speak to his fellows. I do whatever seems to me a desirable action, so long as I see no reason for not doing it. I hold the customs of society in mere and simple contempt—at least where they would hamper my freedom. I have another Master, and they who obey higher rules need not regard lower judgment."

"You interest me much," she said. "Would you mind telling me how you, whose profession has to do with the bodies of men, have come to do more for their souls?"

"You would find it, I fear, a long story if I were to tell it in full. I studied medicine that I might have a good reason for going among the poor. I am bound to do all I can for their bodies, for no one who has not been among them knows their sufferings—borne by some of them without complaint for the sad reason that complaining is of no use. But it was not primarily from the desire to alleviate their sufferings that I learned medicine, but in the hope to start them on the way toward victory over all evil. I saw that the man who brought them physical help had a chance with them such as no clergyman had."

"How well I understand you!" said Hester. "I began because I saw how miserable so many people were, and longed to do something to make life a better thing for them."

"That was not quite the way with me," replied Christopher. "I must explain first that my father died when I was a child. Then my grandfather died and left me both the family business and a good deal of money. Though I was then at school preparing for Oxford, it was necessary that I should look into the affairs of the business. Now my grandfather was not counted a bad man, but stood high in the world's opinion. Yet I came across things in the books, all fair and square in the judgment of the trade itself, which were truly unfair and dishonest. I asked myself, 'Am I to use the wages of iniquity as if they were a clean God-gift? Wrong demands reparation. I cannot look on this money as mine, for part of it ought not to be mine.' I saw that my business in life must be to send the money out again into the channels of right. It was impossible to return more than a small portion of the sums rightly due; therefore a large something else must be done.

"But it grew clear that there could be no real good but oneness with the will of God; that man's good lay in becoming what the Inventor of him meant in the invention of him. I came to see that if the story of Christ was true, then the God that made me was inconceivably lovely, and that the very flower of existence must be to live as the heir of all things, at home with the Father. Next came the perception that my brothers and sisters of the same Father must be, next to the Father Himself, the very atmosphere of life; and that perfect misery must be to care only for one's self. I felt the only thing worth giving the energy of life to was the work that Christ gave Himself to—the delivery of men out of their lonely devotion to themselves, into the glorious liberty of the sons of God, whose joy and rejoicing is the rest of the family. Then I saw that here the claim upon my honesty met the highest calling of man, and gave me the glimmer of a way to use grandfather's money altogether worthily. I keep thinking in order to find it all out, and it will one day be revealed to me. God who has laid the burden on me will enable me to bear it until He shows me how to unpack and disperse it.

"First I spent a portion in further study, and especially the study of medicine, for God might be pleased if I should heal a little by the doctor's art. I would learn how to spend the money upon humanity, repaying what had been wrongfully taken from its individuals. And while so doing, I should also fill up what was left behind for me of the labors of the Master.

"That is my story. I am now trying to do as I have seen, working steadily, without haste, with much discouragement, and now and then with a great gladness and hope. Though I have here and there a new idea, I have not much hope from money. If it were not that I cannot help having it, and am bound to spread it, I would not trouble myself about any scheme to which it was necessary. I know the feeling is wrong and faithless; for money is God's as certainly as the earth in which the crops grow, though He does not care so much about it."

"I know what I would do if I had money!" said Hester. "I would have my own house, one of refuge to which anyone might run for cover or rest or warmth or food or medicine or whatever he needed. I would have it like the porch of heaven itself. It should be a refuge for the needy, from the artisan out of work to the child with a cut finger or cold-bitten feet. I would take in the weary-brained prophet, the worn curate, or the shadowy needle-woman. I would not take in drunkards or ruined speculators—not before they were very miserable indeed. Their suffering is the only desirable consequence of their doing, and to save them from it would be to take from them their last chance."

"It is a lovely idea," said Christopher. "One of my hopes is to build a small hospital for children in some lovely place."

"Is it not delightful to know that you can start anything when you please?"

"Anybody can do that who will begin at the beginning. Nothing worth calling good can or ever will be started full-grown. The larger you begin, the less room you leave for the life to extend itself. Small beginnings with slow growings have time to root themselves thoroughly in wisdom. God's beginnings are imperceptible, whether in the region of soul or of matter. Besides, I believe in no good done save in person, for it is our personality alone that can work with God's perfect personality.

"How the devil would laugh at the idea of a society for saving the world! But if he saw *one* take it in hand, one who would do the will of God with all his heart and soul, and cared for nothing else, then he might tremble for his kingdom! It is the individual Christians, forming the church by their obedient individuality, that have done all the good done since men for the love of Christ began to gather together. It is individual ardor alone that can combine into larger flame. There is no true power but that which has individual roots. Neither custom nor habit nor law nor foundation is a root. The real roots are an individual conscience that hates evil, an individual faith that loves and obeys God, and an individual heart with its kiss of charity."

They had walked twice round the square, and had now the third time reached the house. He went in with her and saw his patient, then took his leave to go home to his Greek Testament—for the remainder of the evening if he might.

234

Chapter 50.

AN ARRANGEMENT

Second causes are God's as much as first, and Christ made sure of them as His Father's way. It were a sad world indeed if God's presence were only interference, that is, miracle. The round-about common ways of things are just as much His as the straight, miraculous ones—more His, in the sense that they are plainly the ways He prefers. We are always disbelieving in Him because things do not go as we intend and desire them to go. We forget that God has larger ends for us than we can see, so His plans do not fit ours. If God were to answer our prayers as we want them answered, He would not be God our Saviour, but the ministering genius of our destruction.

Hester decided it would now be safe to visit her friend Miss Dasomma, having much to say to her and ask of her. First she told her of herself and Lord Gartley. Miss Dasomma threw her arms about her, and broke into a flood of congratulations. Hester looked a little surprised, and was indeed a little annoyed at the vehemence of her pleasure.

Miss Dasomma hastened to excuse herself. "My dear, the more I saw and thought and heard of that man, the more I marveled you should ever have taken him for other than the most worldly, shallow, stunted creature. It was the very impossibility of your understanding such a man that made it possible for him to gain on you. If you had married him, you would have been sick and hopeless of him in six weeks."

"There was more and better in him than you imagine," returned Hester, hurt that her friend should think so badly of the

235

man she loved, but not certain that she was wrong.

"That may be," answered her friend. "But if you had married him, you could have done him no good."

Then Hester went on with her tale of trouble. Her brother Cornelius had been behaving very badly, she said, and had married a young woman without letting them know. Her father and mother were unaware of the fact as yet, and she dreaded having to tell them. He had been very ill with the smallpox and she must take him home, but what to do with his wife until she had broken the matter to them, she did not know. She knew her father would be very angry, and until he should get over it a little she dared not have her home.

"*Are* they married?" asked Miss Dasomma.

"I am not sure, but I am sure she believes they are." Then she told her what she knew of Amy.

Miss Dasomma thought, and then asked, "Could I see her?"

"Surely, any time," replied Hester, "now that Corney is so much better."

Miss Dasomma called, and was so charmed with Amy that she proposed to Hester she should stay with her. This was just what Hester wished but had not dared propose.

Now came the painful necessity not only of breaking to Amy that she must be parted from her husband for a while, but worse, of revealing that he had deceived her.

Had Cornelius not been ill, helpless, and characterless, he would probably have refused to go home; but he did not oppose Hester's determination. He knew she had not told Amy anything, but saw that, if he refused, she might judge it necessary to tell her all. And notwithstanding his idiotic pretense of superiority, he had a kind of thorough confidence in Hester. In his sickness something of the old childish feeling about her as refuge from evil had returned upon him, and he was now nearly ready to do and allow whatever she pleased, trusting her to get him out of the scrape he was in!

"But now tell me, on your word of honor," she said to him that same night, happening to find herself alone with him, "are you really and truly married to Amy?"

She was delighted to see him blaze up in anger.

"Hester, you insult us both!" he said.

"No, Cornelius," returned Hester. "I have a right to distrust you—but I distrust only you. Whatever may be amiss, I am certain you alone are to blame—not Amy."

Then Cornelius vowed that Amy was his lawful wife.

"Then what is to be done with her when you go home? You cannot expect she will be welcomed. I have not dared tell them of your marriage—only of your illness."

"I don't know what's to be done with her. How should I know?" answered Cornelius with a return of his old manner. "I thought you would manage it all for me! This cursed illness—"

"Cornelius," said Hester, "this illness is the greatest kindness God could show you."

"Well, we won't argue about that! Sis, you must get me out of the scrape!"

Hester's heart swelled with delight at the sound of the old loving nursery word. She turned to him and kissed him. "I will do what I honestly can, Cornelius," she said, "but we must not take Amy down with us. She must wait till I have told."

"Then my wife is to be received only on sufferance!"

"You can hardly expect to be otherwise received yourself. You have put your wife at no end of disadvantage by making her your wife without the knowledge of your family. And you have taken money not your own, and torn the hearts of your mother and father with anguish. If you have any love for poor Amy, you will not dream of exposing her to the first outbreak of shocked judgment."

"Then I'm not going. Better stay here and starve!"

"If so, I must tell Amy what you have done. I will not have our parents supposed guilty of cruelty. Amy must know all about it someday, but it ought to come from you—not from me. You will never be fit for honest company till for very misery you have told your wife."

Hester would not let him fancy things were going back into the old grooves—that his crime would become a thing of no consequence, and pass out of existence, ignored and forgotten. Evil cannot be destroyed without repentance.

"So now," said Hester, "will you, or must I, tell Amy that she cannot go home?"

He thought for a moment. "I will," he said.

Hester left him and sent Amy to him. In a few minutes she returned. She had wept, but was now, though looking very sad, quite self-possessed.

"Please, miss," she said, but Hester interrupted her.

"You must not call me *miss*, Amy," she said. "You must call me Hester. Am I not your sister?"

A gleam of joy shot from the girl's eyes, like the sun through red clouds. "Then you have forgiven me!" she cried, and burst into tears.

"No, Amy, not that! I should have to know something to forgive first. You may have been foolish; everybody can't always be wise, though everybody must try to do right. But now we must have time to set things straighter, without doing more mischief, and you mustn't mind staying a little while with Miss Dasomma."

"Does she know all about it, miss—Hester?" asked Amy, and as she called her new sister by her name, her blood rushed into her face.

"She knows enough not to think unfairly of you."

"And you won't be hard upon him when he hasn't me to comfort him, will you, Hester?"

"I will think of my new sister who loves him," replied Hester. "But you must not think I do not love him too. And Amy, you must be very careful over him. No one can do with him what you can. You must help him to be good, for that is the chief duty of a wife to her husband."

Chapter 51.

THINGS AT HOME

Meanwhile, things had been very gloomy at Yrndale. Mrs. Raymount was better in health but hardly more cheerful. How could she be? Sorrow was now the element of her soul, for Cornelius had destroyed the family heart. But what most oppressed her was to see the heart of his father so turned from the youth. What could become of them if essential discord invaded their home! The way her husband took their grief made them no more a family, but a mere household, for they did not share sorrow as they had shared joy.

Her husband went about listless and sullen. He wrote no more. How could one thus disgraced in his family presume to teach the world anything! How could he ever hold up his head? Cornelius' very being cast doubt on all he had ever said or done! He had been proud of his children, but they were like those of any common stock! For hours he sat with his hands in his pockets, scarcely daring to think, for the misery of the thoughts that came crowding out the moment the smallest chink was opened in their cage. He had become short in his speech to his wife. He would break into sudden angry complaints against Hester for not coming home, but stop dead in the middle, as if nothing was worth being angry about now, and turn away with a sigh that was almost a groan.

The sight of the children was a pain to him. Saffy did not understand much grief beyond her own passing troubles, and her mother feared she saw in her careless glee the same root which in her brother flowered in sullen disregard.

239

Mark was very different. The father would order Saffy away, but the boy might come and go as he pleased, although he scarcely took any notice of him. Mark had been told nothing of the cause of his parent's evident misery. When the news came of Corney's illness, his mother told him of that, but he perceived that there must be something more amiss; if this were all, they would have told him of it when first they began to be changed! And when the news came that Corney was getting better, his father did not seem the least happier! Mark would sometimes stand and gaze at his father, but the solemn, far-off, starry look of the boy's eyes never seemed to disturb him. He loved his father as few boys love, and yet had a certain dread of him and discomfort in his presence, which would vanish at once when he spoke to him.

Mark had never recovered from his near drowning, and his mother began to doubt if ever he would be well again. He had grown a good deal thinner; his food did not seem to nourish him; and his being seemed slipping away from the hold of the world. He was full of dreams and fancies, all of the higher order of things where love is law. He would spend happy hours alone, seeming to be doing nothing, because his doing was with the unseen. Children do not drop haphazard into this world, neither are they kept out of the next one by any care or any power of medicine; all goes by heavenly will and lovely ordinance. Some of us will have to be ashamed of our outcry after our dead.

At last came a letter from Hester saying that in two days she hoped to bring Corney home. The mother read the letter, and with a faded gleam of joy on her countenance, passed it to her husband. He took it, glanced at it, threw it from him, rose and left the room.

He took his hat and stick and went out. Had Corney been returning in tolerable health the father might possibly have kicked him out of the house for his impudence in daring to show his face there; but even this wrathful father, who thought he did well to be angry, could not turn from his sickly child, let him be the greatest scoundrel under the all-seeing sun. But not therefore would he receive or acknowledge him! His son, having unsonned himself, should no more be treated as a son. He should be in the house on sufferance—in no right of sonship, and should be made to understand it was so! Swine were the natural companions of the prodigal, and the sooner he was among them the better! There was truth in the remark, but hell in the spirit of it, for the heart of the father was turned from his own son. The Messiah came to turn the hearts of the fathers to their children—strange it should ever have wanted doing! But it wants doing still!

Gerald Raymount went walking through the pinewoods on his hills. Little satisfaction lay in land to which such a son was to succeed! No! Not an acre, not as much as would bury him, should the rascal have! He had taken honesty as a matter of course in *his* family. Were they not *his* children? He had not thought of God as the bond of life between him and them, nor sought to nourish the life in them. He was their father and was content with them. He had pondered much the laws by which society proceeds and prospers, but the relation between himself and his children had been left to shift for itself.

He had never known anything of what was going on in the mind of his son. He had never asked himself if the boy loved the truth, or if his consciousness was anything better than the wallowing of a happy-go-lucky satisfaction in being. And now he was astonished to find *his* boy no better than the common sort of human animal! Few understand that the true end is not to keep their children from doing what is wrong, though that is on the way to it, but to render them incapable of doing wrong.

But the heart of the mother was longing after her boy. He had sinned, he had suffered, and was in disgrace—good reasons why her arms should long to enfold him! Was he unlovely? She must love him the more! Was he selfish and repellent? She must get the nearer to him! Everything was reason to her for love and more love. Corney could not keep his mother out of his heart now! Now that sickness had reduced his strength and shamed his proud spirit, love would have room to enter and minister! When, oh when would he appear, that her heart might go out to meet him!

Chapter 52.

THE RETURN

The day came in London as the invalid was carefully wrapped up for the journey. Hester, the major, and Miss Dasomma followed the young couple to the station. There the latter received the poor wife, and when the train was out of sight, took her home with her.

Thus Hester, escorted by the major, bore her lost sheep home to Yrndale—in little triumph and much anxiety. But when they stopped at the door it was night, and no one was on the outlook for them—the hall was not lighted and the door was locked. The major rang the bell, and when the door was opened by one of the servants, he took Corney in his arms and carried him into the dining room.

There seemed no light in the house. Hester and the major spoke together, then she hurried from the room and returned in a moment. "I was sure of it," she whispered to the major. "There is a glorious fire in his room, and everything ready for him. The house is my father, but the room is my mother, and my mother is like God."

The major carried him up the stair—so thin and light he was. The moment they passed the door of her room, out came the mother behind them in her dressing gown, and glided pale and noiseless as the disembodied after them. Hester looked round and saw her, but she laid a finger on her lips, and followed without a word. When they were in the room, she came to the door, looked in, and watched them, but did not enter. Cornelius did not open his eyes as the major laid him down on the sofa near the fire. A gleam of it fell on his face, and the mother drew a sharp quick breath and pressed her hands against her heart; there was his sin upon his face, branding him that men might know him. But then came a fresh rush from the inexhaustible fountain of mother-love. She would have taken him into her anew, with all his sin and pain and sorrow, to clear away in herself brand and pollution, and bear him anew—even as God bears our griefs, carries our sorrows, destroys our wrongs, takes their consequences on Himself, and gives us the new birth from above.

With wounded heart she went back to the room where her husband sat with hopeless gaze fixed on the fire. She reached the side of the bed, and fell senseless upon it. He started up with a sting of self-accusation; he had killed her, exacting from her a promise that by no word would she welcome the wanderer that night! She had promised, for she would not have her husband imagine in his bitterness that she loved the erring son more than the father whose heart he had all but broken. She was, in truth, nearly as anxious about the one as the other, for was not the unforgivingness of the one even worse than the theft of the other?

He lifted her to the bed and administered the familiar restoratives; soon her eyelids began to tremble. "My baby!" she murmured, and the tears began to flow.

"Thank God!" he said as she fell asleep from the exhaustion that followed excess of feeling. But for all his stern fulfillment of duty, he did not feel fit to lie down by his wife. He would watch: she might have another bad turn! So he sat watchful by the fire. She was his only friend, he said, and now she and he were no more of one mind! Never until now had they differed!

Hester and the major put Corney to bed, and instantly he was fast asleep. The major arranged himself to pass the night by the fire, and Hester went to see what she could do for her mother. Knocking softly at the door and receiving no answer, she peeped in: there sat her father and there slept her mother. She would not disturb them but, taking her share in the punishment of him she had brought home, retired without welcome or good-night. She too was presently fast asleep. There was no gnawing worm of duty undone or wrong unpardoned in her to keep her awake. Sorrow is sleepy, while pride and remorse are wakeful.

243

Chapter 53.

A HEAVENLY VISION

The night began differently for the two watchers. The major was troubled at what seemed the hard-heartedness of the mother, for he loved her with a true brotherly affection. He had not seen her look in at the door, nor did he know the cause of her appearing so withdrawn and unmotherly. He brooded over the thing, saying that he could not endure the low-minded cub himself, and would gladly, if only the wretch were well enough, give him a sound horsewhipping. But to see him so treated by father and mother was more than he could bear, and he began to pity a lad born of parents so hard-hearted. What would have become of himself, he thought, if his mother had treated him so? He had never, to be sure, committed any crime against society worse than shocking certain ridiculously proper people; but if she had made much of his foibles and faults, he might have grown to be capable of doing how could he tell what? Who would turn out a mangy dog that was his own dog?

As the major sat thinking, the story came back to him which his mother had so often told him and his brothers, all now gone but himself, as they gathered round her on the Sunday evenings in the nursery—about the prodigal son.

The story father had spied his son coming a great way off, and knew him at once, and ran to meet him, and fell on his neck and kissed him. But this father would not even look at the son that had just escaped the jaws of death! True, the prodigal came home repentant, but the father did not wait to know that, but ran to meet him!

244

As the major thus reflected, he drew nearer to the individual "I" lurking at the keyhole of every story. Only he had to go home, else how was his Father to receive him? The major, there in the middle of the night, went down on his knees, and as he had not done since the eve of his last battle, tried to say the prayers his mother had taught him. Presently he found himself saying things she had not taught him, and spoke from his heart as if One was listening, One who in the dead of the night did not sleep, but kept wide awake lest one of His children should cry.

In his wife's room, Gerald Raymount sat on into the dead waste of the night. No such comfort had come to him as to his friend. He had been much more of a religious man than the major—had his theories concerning both the first and the second Table of the Law; nor had he been merely a talker, though his talk, as with all talkers, was constantly ahead of his deed. Well it is for those whose talk is not ahead of their endeavor! It was the *idea* of religion, and the thousand ideas it broods, more than the religion itself, that was his delight. He philosophized well of the relations between man and Maker, of the necessity to human nature of belief in God, of the disastrous consequences of having none, and such like things; but having such an interest is a very different thing from being in such relations with the Father that the thought of Him is an immediate and ever-returning joy and strength. He was so busy understanding with his intellect that he missed the better understanding of heart and imagination.

Thus the present trial found him no true parent. The youth of course could not be received either as clean-handed or as repentant; but love is at the heart of every true treatment of the sinner, even in the very refusal of external forgiveness. That the father should not have longed for his son's repentance; that he should not have met even his seeming return; that he should have nourished resentment because the youth had sinned against *his* family; that he should care to devise no measures for generating a sense of the evil he had done, and aiding repentance as makes forgiveness a necessary consequence; that he should, instead, seek to make his son feel most poignantly his absolute scorn and loathing—this made the man a kind of paternal Satan who sat watching by the repose of the most Christian, most loving, most forgiving, most self-forgetting mother. He stirred up in himself fresh whirlwinds of indignation at the incredible thing which had become the fact of facts, lying heaviest, stinging deepest, seeming unchangeable. That it might prove a blessing he would have spurned as a degrading and absurd suggestion.

He rose, and treading softly lest he should wake the only being he *felt* love for now, and whom he was loving less than before, he left the room and went to his study. He sat down with a book to turn his thoughts from his misery. But it was no use, for his thoughts could hold no company with other thoughts. The world of his kind was shut out; he was a man alone, because unforgiving and unforgiven. His soul slid into the old groove of miserable self-reiteration, and the night slid away.

The morning was near when the door to the study opened softly, and a child in a long white gown stood by his side. Mr. Raymount started violently. It was Mark—but asleep! He had seen his mother and father even more than usually troubled all day, and their trouble had haunted him in his sleep; it had roused him without waking him from his dreams, and the spirit of love had directed his feet to the presence of his father. He stood a little way from him, his face white as his dress, silent, and haunted by a smile of intense quiet, as of one who, being comforted, would comfort. His soul was not precisely with his body; his thoughts, though concerning his father, were elsewhere, and his eyes, although open, evidently saw nothing.

There had never been tender relations between Mark and his father. Mark loved his father, yet was a little afraid of him—never went to him with confidence, never snuggled close to him, never sat down by his side to read his book in a heaven of peace. He would never have gone to his father's room for refuge from sleeplessness.

His father was surprised and indeed annoyed as well as startled to see him. He was in no mood for such a visit, and felt strangely afraid of the child. Wretched about one son, he was dismayed at the nocturnal visit of the other.

Suddenly the child stretched out his hands to him, with an upcast, beseeching face. Anxious to prevent him from waking, he took the child softly in his arms, lifted him to his knees, and held him gently. An expression of supreme delight came over the boy's face, a look of absolute contentment mingled with hope. He put his thin hands together, palm to palm as if praying, and lifted his countenance to his father, though his gaze was still to the infinite. And now he began to murmur, praying to a Father closer to him than the one upon whose knees he sat.

"Dear God," said Mark, "I don't know what to do, for I am afraid papa and Corney are both naughty. I don't know what it is, and I think Corney must be more to blame than my dear papa, but when he came home tonight he did not go to papa, and papa did not go to him. But I am always wanting to come to You, God, to see You. You are our big Papa! Please put it all right. I don't know how, or I would tell You, but it doesn't matter—You would only smile at my way, and take a much better one of Your own. But please, dear God, make papa and Corney good, and make their naughtiness just nothing at all. You know they must love one another, and I know You will do just what I want. Good-bye, God. I'm going to bed now—down there. I'll come again soon."

With that he slipped from his father's knee, and walked from the room with slow stately step.

By this time the heart of the strong man was swelling with the love which, in it all along, was now awake. He could not weep, but sobbed dry, torturing sobs that seemed as if they would kill him. But he must see that the boy was safe in bed, and so rose and left the room.

In the corridor he breathed more freely. Through an old window, the bright moon, shining in peace with nobody to see, threw partly on the wall and partly on the floor a shadow-cross. He found himself on his knees in the passage before the shadow—not praying, not doing anything he knew, but under some spiritual influence known only to God.

When the strange passion for the time was over, when the rush of the huge tidal wave of eternity had subsided, and his soul was clearing of the storm that had swept through it, he rose from his knees and went up to Mark's room. The moonlight was there too, and the father saw his child's white bed glimmering like a tomb. He drew near, but could not rightly see the face of his boy; and for an eternal, awful moment he felt as if he had lost him—he had been lifted straight from the study to the bosom of the Father to whom he had prayed! But slow through the dusk dawned his face; he had not then been taken bodily. The father gazed in fascinated fear, and then saw that his son breathed.

The boy was sleeping peacefully and dreaming pleasantly, for the ghost of a smile glinted about his lips. Then upon the father came the wonder of watching a dreamer: what might not be going on within that brain, inaccessible as the most distant star? Splendrous visions might be gliding through the soul of the sleeper—his child, born of his body and his soul—and not one of them was open to him! Could they be more divided if the child were dead?

But how much nearer to him in reality was the child when awake and about the house? How much more did he know then of the thoughts, the loves, the imaginations, the desires, the aspirations, that moved in the heart and brain of the child? For all that his contact with him came to, he might as well be dead! The boy was sickly, and might be taken from him before he had made any acquaintance with him!

He turned away and went back to his room. There, in deepest loneliness, he went down on his knees to beg the company of the great Being whose existence he had so often defended, but whom he had so little regarded as actually existent that he had not yet sought refuge with Him. Raymount knelt before the living Love and Source of his life, and of all the love that makes life a good thing, and rose from his knees a humbler man.

Chapter 54.

A SAD BEGINNING

Toward morning Mr. Raymount went to bed, and slept late—heavily and unreposefully; but when he woke, there was the old feeling again! How *could* he forgive the son that had so disgraced him! He tried to persuade himself on philosophical grounds that it was better to forgive his son; that it was the part of the wise man to abstain from harshness, and not drive the youth to despair. But anger and pride were too much for him.

His breakfast was taken to him in the study, and there Hester found him, an hour after, with the food untouched. He submitted to her embrace, but scarcely spoke, and asked nothing about Corney. Hester felt sadly chilled, and very hopeless. She had begun to learn that one of the principal parts of faith is patience, and that the setting of wrong things right is so far from easy that not even God can do it all at once. Yet time lies heavy on the young especially, and Hester left the room with a heavy heart.

Mr. Raymount strove hard to reconcile the memories of the night with the feelings of the morning—strove to realize a state of mind in which forgiveness to his son blended with satisfaction to the wounded pride of his paternal dignity. How could he take his son to his bosom as he was? He asked—but did not ask how he was to draw him to repentance! He did not think of the tender entreaty with which God pleads with His people to come back to Him. If the father, instead of holding out his arms to the child he would entice to him, folds them and turns his back—expectant, but giving no sign of expectancy—the child will hardly suppose him longing to be reconciled.

For a father not to forgive is far worse than for a son to need forgiveness; and such a father will go from bad to worse as well as the son, except he repent. The shifty, ungenerous spirit of compromise awoke in Raymount. His forgiveness he would postpone, but he would be very good, very gentle, very kind to everyone else in the house! He would walk softly, but he was not ready to walk uprightly. He knew his feelings toward Corney were wearing out the heart of his wife, yet he would not yield! But there was little Mark; he would make more of him, know him better, and make the child know him better!

He went to see his wife. Finding her a trifle better, he felt a little angry and not a little annoyed: what added to his misery was a comfort to her! She was the happier for having her worthless son! In the selfishness of his misery he looked upon this as a lack of sympathy with himself. He did not allude to Cornelius, but said he was going for a walk, and went to find Mark, with a vague hope of consolation in the child who had clung to him so confidently in the night. He had forgotten it was not to him *Mark's soul* had clung, but to the Father of both.

Mark was in the nursery, as the children's room was still called. When Mark heard his father's step, he bounded to meet him; and when his sweet moonlit face appeared at the door, the gloom on his father's yielded a little, and he said kindly, "Come, Mark, I want you to go for a walk with me."

"Yes, papa," answered the boy.

But Mr. Raymount was not doing the right thing in taking him out. The boy was not able for anything to be called a walk, and neither was the weather fit for his going out. But absorbed in his own trouble, the father did not think of his weakness, and away they went.

With his heart in such a state, the father naturally had next to nothing to say to his boy. Their silence did not affect Mark; he was satisfied to be with his father, and was too blessed in the long silences between him and God to dislike silence. It was no separation so long as like speech it was between them. But Mark was growing tired, and could scarcely put one leg past the other.

The sun had been shining when they started, but now it was clouded and threatened rain. They were in the middle of a bare, lonely moor, and the wind had begun to blow cold. Sunk in his miserable thoughts, the more miserable that he had now yielded even the pretense of struggle, the father saw nothing of his child's failing strength, but kept trudging on. All at once he became aware that the boy was not by his side. Alarmed, he stopped, turned, called his name aloud, and retraced his steps.

Some five hundred yards back, he came to a hollow, where on a tuft of brown heather sat white-faced Mark. His anxiety relieved, the annoyed father berated the little fellow for stopping.

"I wasn't able to keep up, papa," replied Mark. "So I thought I would rest here, and meet you as you came back."

"You ought to have told me. I shouldn't have brought you had I known you would behave so. Come, we must go home."

"I'm very sorry, papa, but I think I can't."

"Nonsense!" said his father, frightened. Mark had never shown himself whimsical. But he stooped to lift him, and began walking homeward with him.

The next moment Mark spied the waving of a dress. "Oh," he cried, "there's Hessie! She will carry me!"

"You little goose!" said his father tenderly. "Can she carry you better than I can?"

"She is not stronger than you, papa, because you are a big man; but I think Hessie has more carry in her!"

Hester was running, and when she came near was quite out of breath. She had feared much when she found the two had gone for a walk, and was angry as she hurried to meet her father. When, however, she saw the boy's arms round his father's neck, and his suffering face laid against his, her anger went from her, and she was sorry and ashamed.

"Let me take him, papa," she said.

The father had no intention of giving up the child. But Mark stretched out his arms to Hester, and wriggled into hers. Instinctively trying to retain him, he hurt him, and the boy gave a little cry. With a new pang of pain, and a new sting of resentment, he let him go and followed in distressed humiliation.

By and by Hester found, with all her good will, that her strength was of the things that can be shaken, and was obliged to yield him to her father again. It was much to his relief, for a sense of moral weakness had invaded him as he followed his children. He had become a nobody in his family!

When at length they reached home, Mark was put to bed and the doctor sent for.

Chapter 55.

MOTHER AND SON

In the meantime Cornelius kept his bed. The moment her husband was gone, his mother rose and hastened to her son. For the first time since their marriage, she was glad her husband was gone that she might do what was right without annoying him. With all her strength of principle, she felt too weak to go openly against him, though she never dreamed of concealing what she did. She tottered across her son's floor, threw herself on the bed beside him, and took him to her bosom.

With his mother Corney had never pretended to the same degree as with other people, and his behavior to her was now more genuine than to any but his wife. He clung to her and felt that, let his father behave to him as he might, he had yet a home. All the morning he had been fretting, in the midst of Hester's kindest attentions, that he had not his wife to do things for him as he liked them done. But now that Cornelius had his mother, he was more content, or rather less discontented. She was greatly consoled, and he felt so happy with her that he began to wish that he had not kept a secret from her; for the first time in his life he was sorry to have one. He grew anxious that she should know it, but not anxious that he should have to tell her.

She had been thinking of the Corney she had lost, and the Corney that had come home to her instead; she was miserable over the altered looks of her disfigured child. The truest mother can hardly be expected to reconcile herself with ease to a new face on her child; she has loved him in one shape, and now has to love him in another! She would gaze intently in his face, and then clasp him to her heart as if seeking a shorter way to his presence than through the ruined door of his countenance.

Hester, who had never received from her half so much show of tenderness, could not help, like the elder brother in the divine tale, a little choking at the sight; but she soon consoled herself that the less poor Corney deserved it, the more he needed it. Hester could not with any confidence look on this prodigal as a repentant one, and she feared all this tenderness would do him harm, causing him to think less of his crime, and blinding him to his low moral condition. But she thought also that God would do what He could to keep the love of such a mother from hurting; and it was not long before she was encouraged by a softness in Corney's look, and a humid expression in his eyes which she had never seen before. In former days he would have turned from such overflow of love as womanish gush; but disgraced, worn out, and even to his own eyes an unpleasant object, he was not so much inclined to repel the love of the only one knowing his story who did not feel contempt for him.

Something was slowly working on him—now in the imagined judgment of others, now in the thought of his wife, now in the devotion of his mother. Little result was there for earthly eye, but the mother perceived or imagined a difference in him. If only she could see something plain to tell her husband! If the ice that froze up the spring of his love would but begin to melt! For to whom are we to go for refuge from ourselves if not to those through whom we were born into the world, and who are to blame for more or less of our unfitness for a true life? "His father *must* forgive him!" she said to herself. She would go down on her knees to him. Their boy should *not* be left out in the cold! The mother still carried in her soul the child born of her body, preparing for him the new and better, the all-lovely birth of repentance unto life.

Hester had not yet said a word about her own affairs. No one but the major knew that her engagement to Lord Gartley was broken. She was not willing to add disappointment to the grief of the household.

The major learned of Mark's condition from Hester, and insisted on taking charge of him. She might trust him to his care! Hester could not be other than pleased, and so the major took the position of head nurse.

Hester's mind was almost constantly occupied with thinking how she was to let her father and mother know what they must know soon, and ought to know as soon as possible. But she could not see how to set about it. She had no light, and seemed to have no leading—and so waited as she ought, for much harm comes of the impatience that outstrips guidance. People are too ready to think something must be done, and forget that the time for action may not have arrived, that there is seldom more than one thing fit to be done, and that the wrong thing must in any case be worse than nothing.

Cornelius grew gradually better, and at last was able to go downstairs. But he had not yet seen his father, and his dread of seeing him grew to a terror. He never went down until he knew he was not in the house, and then would sit at some window that commanded the door by which he was most likely to enter. He enticed Saffy to be his scout, and bring him word in what direction his father went. This did the child incalculable injury. The father was just as anxious to avoid Cornelius, fully intending, if he met him, to turn his back upon him. But it was a rambling and roomy old house, and there was plenty of space for both. A whole week passed and they had not met—to the disappointment of Hester, who cherished some hope in a chance encounter.

She had just one consolation—with Cornelius safe under her wing, the mother was manifestly improving. But even this was a source of dissatisfaction to the brooding selfishness of the unhealthy-minded father. He thought to himself, "Here have I been heart and soul nursing her through the illness he caused her, and all in vain till she gets the rascal back, and then she begins at once to improve! She would be perfectly happy with him if she and I never saw each other again!"

The two brothers had not yet met. Corney disliked the major, and the major objected to a visit. He felt Corney's disfigurement would distress Mark, and retard the possible recovery of which he was already in great doubt.

Chapter 56

MISS DASOMMA AND AMY

Miss Dasomma was pleased with Amy. She found her very ignorant in the regions of what is commonly called education, but
very quick in understanding where human relations came in.
And she was teachable, coming largely of her trustfulness. Thus
had Corney gained his influence over her: superior knowledge
was to her a sign of superior goodness.

Miss Dasomma began at once to teach her music. Here also
she understood quickly, but found the doing very hard—the
more so that her spirit was but ill at ease. Corney had deceived
her, and had done something wrong besides; she was parted
from him—all was very different from what she had expected in
marrying her Corney! Then Hester's letters made her uncomfortable. They were no nearer a solution of their difficulty than
when they parted at the railway; Hester did not even know yet
what she was going to do in the matter! Unable yet to tell her
parents all the uncomfortable truth, there rose a hedge and
seemed to sink a gulf between her and Amy. Amy naturally
surmised that the family was not willing to receive her, and that
the same unwillingness was in Hester also. Yet it was not, for
Hester knew that the main hope for her brother lay in his love
for Amy and her devotion to him—in her common sense, her
true, honest, bright nature. She was only far too good for
Corney!

And Amy noted that Miss Dasomma did not read to her every
word of Hester's letters. Once she stopped suddenly in the
middle of a sentence, and after a pause went on with another!

Something was there she was not to know! Was Corney worse and they afraid to tell her, lest she should go to him? Perhaps they were making his life miserable because she had married him! It explained his deceiving her, for if he had told them, they would not have let her have him at all! By excusing her husband all she could, she was in danger of lowering her instinctively high sense of moral obligation.

She brooded over the matter, threw herself on her knees, and begged her friend to let her know what the part of her sister's letter she had not read to her was about.

"But, my dear," said Miss Dasomma, "Hester and I have long been friends, and may have things to say to each other alone. A lady must not be inquisitive, you know."

"I know that, and I never did pry into other people's affairs. Tell me it was nothing about my husband, and I shall be content."

"But think a moment, Amy!" returned Miss Dasomma, who began to find herself in a difficulty. "There might be things between his family and him, who have known him longer than you, which they were not quite prepared to tell you all about before knowing you better. Some people in the way they treated you would have been very different from that angel sister of yours! There is nobody like her—that I know!"

"I love her with my whole heart," sobbed Amy, "next to Cornelius. But even she must not come between him and me. If it is anything affecting him, I have a greater right than anyone else to know about it, and no one has a right to conceal it from me!"

"Why do you think that?" asked Miss Dasomma, agreeing that she had a right to know, but thinking also that one might have a right to conceal it. She did not see how to answer her appeal. She could not tell her a story, and she did not feel at liberty to tell her the truth—yet if she declined to answer her question, the poor child might imagine something dreadful.

"Why, miss," answered Amy, "we can't be divided! I must do all I can for him, and I have a right to know what there is to be done for him."

"But can you not trust his own father and mother?" said Miss Dasomma, her conscience accusing her.

"Yes, surely," replied Amy, "if they were loving him, and not angry with him. But I have seen even that angel Hester look very vexed with him sometimes, and when he was ill too! I know what your own people can do to make you miserable!"

Miss Dasomma looked with admiration at the little creature—showing fight like a wren for her nest. How rapidly she was growing! How noble she was and free! She was indeed a treasure! The man she had married was little worthy of her; but if she rescued him—not from his parents, but from himself—she might perhaps have done as good a work as helping a noble-hearted man.

"I've got him to look after," Amy resumed, "and I will. He's mine, miss! If anybody's not doing right by him, I ought to be by and see him through it."

It stung Miss Dasomma to hear her friends suspected of behaving unjustly. "That's all you know, Amy!" she blurted out—and bit her lip in vexation with herself.

Amy was upon her like a cat upon a mouse. "What is it?" she cried. "I must know! You shall *not* keep me in the dark! If you do not tell me, I will go to him."

Miss Dasomma faltered, reddened, and betrayed considerable embarrassment. A prudent person lapsing into a dilemma is specially discomfitted. Amy saw, and was the more convinced and determined. She persisted, but Miss Dasomma recovered herself a little. "How can you wonder," she said with confused vagueness, "when you know he deceived you, and never told them he was going to marry you?"

"But they know nothing of it yet—at least from the way Hester writes!"

"Yes, but one who could behave like that would be only too likely to give other grounds of offense."

"Then there *is* something more!" exclaimed Amy. "I suspected it the moment I saw Hester's face at the door! I may be young and silly, but I care for nothing but my husband, and I can do more for him than anybody else can. Know all about it I will! It is my business!"

Miss Dasomma had waked a small but active volcano, and must either answer her questions or persuade her not to ask any.

"I beg, Amy," she said with entreaty, "you will do nothing rash. Can you not trust friends who have proved themselves faithful?"

"Yes, for myself," answered Amy, "but it is my *husband!*" She almost screamed the word. "And I will trust nobody to take care enough of *him*. They can't know how to treat him or he would love them more, and would not have been afraid to let them know he was marrying a poor girl. Miss Dasomma, what have you got against him? I have no fear you will tell me anything but the truth!"

"Of course not!" returned Miss Dasomma, offended, but repressing it. "Why then will you not trust me?"

"I will believe whatever you say, but I will not trust even you to tell or not to tell me as you please where my husband is concerned. That would be to give up my duty to him. Tell me what it is, or—"

She did not finish the sentence. The postman's knock came to the door, and she bounded off to see what he had brought, leaving Miss Dasomma in fear lest she should appropriate a letter not addressed to her. She returned with a look of wild exultant triumph.

"Now I shall know the truth!" she said. "This is from him!" And with that she flew to her room. It was Corney's first letter to her. It was filled not with direct complaints, but a general grumble. "I do wish you were here, Amy, my own dearest! I love nobody like you, nobody but you. If I did wrong in telling you a few tales, it was because I loved you so I could not do without you. And what comforts me for any wrong I have done is that I have you. That would make up to a man for anything short of being hanged! My mother is very kind to me, of course—much better company than Hester! She never looks as if a fellow had to be put up with, or forgiven, or anything of that sort, in her high and mighty way. But you do get tired of a mother always keeping on telling you how much she loves you. You can't help thinking there must be something behind it all. Depend upon it she wants something of you—wants you to be good—to repent, as they call it! They're all right, I suppose, but it ain't nice for all that. And Hester has never told my father yet.

"I haven't even seen my father. He has not come near me once! Saffy wouldn't look at me for a long time—that's the last of the litter; she called me 'Ugly Corney'! But I've got her under my thumb at last, and she's useful. Then there's that prig Mark! I always liked the little wretch, though he is such a precious humbug! He's in bed, and never had any stamina in him. They won't let me go near him for fear of frightening him! But that braggart Major Marvel comes to me sometimes, and makes me hate him—talks as if I wasn't as good as he, as if I wasn't even a gentleman! I long to be back in the horrid garret alone with my little Amy!"

So went the letter.

When Amy next appeared before Miss Dasomma, her eyes were red with weeping, and her hair was in disorder. She had been lying now on the bed, now on the floor, tearing her hair, and stuffing her handkerchief in her mouth.

"Well, what is the news?" asked Miss Dasomma kindly, as if she saw nothing particular in her appearance.

"You must excuse me," replied Amy, with the stiffness of a woman of the world resenting intrusion. "But there is nothing, positively nothing, in the letter interesting to anyone but myself."

Though anxious about the letter, Miss Dasomma would not risk a single question more. Perhaps she herself was going to escape without further questioning!

Corney's letter, in conjunction with the word Miss Dasomma let slip, had at last begun to open Amy's eyes to the character of her husband. She had seen a good deal of his family, and found it hard to believe they would treat him unkindly—but his father had not been once to see him since his return! Corney had not mentioned that he himself had avoided meeting his father. If they did not yet know he was married, then that other, unknown thing must be a very serious one! There must be something to explain it, something to show it not altogether the monstrous thing it seemed!

Of course, it must be the same thing that made him hide in the garret! She was convinced now that he had done something hideously wrong, and saw with absolute clearness what she must do. "I must know all about it," she said to herself, "or how am I to help him?" It seemed to her the most natural thing that when one has done wrong, he should confess it as wrong—so have done with it, disowning and casting away the cursed thing. This, alas, Cornelius did not seem inclined to do! But was she, of all women in the world, to condemn him without knowing what he had to say for himself? She was bound to learn the truth of the thing, if only to give her husband fair play.

By degrees her mind grew calm in settled resolve. It might, she reasoned, be very well for husband and wife to be apart while they were both happy; but when anything was troubling either, still more when it was anything *in* either, then it was horrible and unnatural that they should be parted. What could a heart then do but tear itself to pieces?

All her indignant strength and unalterable determination rose up. She would see who would keep them asunder now she had made up her mind! She would walk her way, work her way, or beg her way, if necessary, but nothing should keep her from Corney!

Not a word more concerning their difference passed between her and Miss Dasomma. They talked cheerfully, and kissed as usual when parting for the night.

The moment she was in her room, Amy packed a small carpetbag, made a small bundle of cloak and shawl, and lay down in her clothes. Long before dawn she crept softly down the stairs, and stole out. For the second time was she a fugitive—then *from,* now *to.*

Miss Dasomma, discovering her absence the next morning, did not suspect at first where she had gone, but concluded that Corney's letter had announced that their marriage was not a genuine one; and that, in the dignity of her true heart, she had at once and forever taken her leave of Cornelius. Miss Dasomma wrote to Hester, but the post would not arrive till the afternoon of the next day.

Amy reached the station in time for the first train of the day. Without a moment's hesitation, though it left her almost penniless, she bought a ticket for Yrndale.

Chapter 57

THE SICK ROOM

At Yrndale things went on in the same dull way, anger burrowing like a mole in the heart of the father, a dreary spiritual fog hanging over all the souls, and the mother weary for some glimmer of a heavenly dawn. Hester felt she could not endure it much longer, as if the place were forgotten of God, and abandoned to chance.

But there was one dayspring in the home yet—Mark's room, where the major sat by the bedside of the boy, reading to him, telling him stories, and listening to him as he talked childlike wisdom in childish words. Saffy came and went, by no means so merry now that she was more with Corney. Infected by Corney's fear, she like him began to watch to keep out of their father's way.

And the weather had again put on a wintry temper. Sleet and hail, and even snow fell, alternated with rain and wind, day after day for a week.

One afternoon the wind rose almost to a tempest. The rain drove in sheets against the windows of Mark's room. It was a cheerful room, with colored prints on the walls, and the fire burning in the grate shone on them. The major was reading in his easy chair, but very sleepy, and longing for a little nap. In a moment he was far away, following an imaginary tiger, when the voice of Mark woke him.

"What kind of thing do you like best in all the world, Majie?" he asked. "Things around you, I mean."

The major sat bolt upright, rubbed his eyes, stretched himself quietly, and answered, "Well, Mark, I don't think we can beat this very room here, can we?"

"Let's see what makes it so nice!" returned Mark. "First of all, you're there, Majie!"

"And you're there, Markie," said the major.

"Yes, that's all right! Next there's my bed for me, and your easy chair for you, and the beautiful fire for us both! And the sight of your chair is better to me than the feel of my bed! And then there are the shines of the fire all about the room. What a beautiful thing a shine is, Majie! I wish you would put on your grand uniform, and let me see the fire shining on the gold lace and the buttons and the epaulets and the hilt of your sword!"

"I will, Markie."

"Your sword is beautiful, Majie. Can you tell me why a thing for killing should be so beautiful?"

The major thought, and replied, "It must be that it is not made for the sake of the killing, but for the sake of the right that would else be trodden down! Whatever is on the side of the right ought to be beautiful."

"But ain't a pirate's sword beautiful, with precious stones? That's not for the right, is it now, Majie?"

The boy was gradually educating the man without either of them knowing it, for the major had to think in order to give reasonable answers to Mark's questions.

"Anything," he said at last, "may be turned from its right use, and then it goes all wrong."

"But a sword looks all right—it shines—even when it is not put to a wrong use!"

"For a while," answered the major. "It takes time for anything that has turned bad to lose its good looks."

"But how can a sword ever grow ugly?"

Again the major had to think. "When people put things to a bad use, they are not good themselves, or they are lazy and neglect things. When a soldier takes to drinking or cruelty, he neglects his weapons, and the rust begins to eat them, and at last will eat them up."

"What is rust, Majie?"

"It is a sword's laziness, making it rot. A sword is a very strong thing, but if not taken care of will not last so long as a silk handkerchief."

Mark, however, had not lost sight of their first subject, and did not want to leave it yet.

"But, Majie," he replied, "we haven't done with what we like best! We hadn't said anything about the thick walls round us, while the rain is beating and the wind blowing all about, but can't come at us! I fancy sometimes, as I lie awake in the night, that the wind and the rain are huge packs of wolves howling in a Russian forest, but not able to get into the house to hurt us. Then I feel so safe! And that brings me to the best of all. It is in fancying danger that you know what it is to be safe."

"But, Mark, you know some people are really in danger!"

"Yes, I suppose so. I know that I am not in danger, because He is between me and all the danger!"

"How do you know He is between you and *all* danger?"

"I don't know how I know it; I only know that I'm not afraid," Mark answered. "I feel so safe! God can't forget me or you, Majie, more than any one of the sparrows. Jesus said so, and what Jesus said lasts forever. His words never wear out, or need to be made over again. Majie, I do wish everybody was as good as Jesus! He won't be pleased till we all are. If I thought He did not care whether everybody was good or not, it would make me so miserable that I should like to die and never come to life again. He will make Corney good, won't He, Majie?"

"I hope so, Markie," returned the major.

"But don't you think we ought to do something to help to make Corney good? You help me to be good, Majie—every day, and all day long! I know Mother teaches him, for he's her firstborn! Just like Jesus is God's firstborn! But I don't think we ought to leave Corney to Mother all alone; she's not strong enough! Corney never was willing to be good. Why shouldn't he like to be good? It's surely good to be good!"

"Yes, Mark, but some people like their own way when it's ever so nasty, better than God's way when it's ever so nice!"

"But God must be able to let them know what foolish creatures they are, Majie!"

It was on the major's lips to say, "He has sent you to teach it to me, Mark!" but he thought it better not to say it. The major had grown quite knowing in what was lovely in a soul—could see the same thing lovely in the child and the Ancient of Days.

"You see, Majie," Mark went on, "it won't do for you and me

to be so safe from all the storm and wind, wrapped in God's cloak, and poor Corney out in the wind and rain, with the wolves howling after him! You may say it's his own fault—it's because he won't let God take him up and carry him. That's very true, but then that's just the pity of it! It is so dreadful! I can't understand it."

The boy could understand good, but was perplexed with evil.

While they talked thus in their nest of comfort there was one out in the wind and rain, all but spent with their buffeting, who hastened with what poor remaining strength she had to the doing of His will. Amy, left at the station with an empty purse, had set out to walk through mire and darkness and storm, up hill and down dale, to find her husband—the man God had given her to look after.

Chapter 58.

VENGEANCE IS MINE

That same morning, Mr. Raymount had chosen to imagine it necessary to start pretty early for the country town, on something he called business, and was not expected home before the next day. Assuming heart in his absence, Cornelius freely wandered about the house, and lunched with his mother and Hester and Saffy like one of the family. His mother, wisely or not, did her best to prevent his feeling any difference from old times; where the father erred so much on the side of severity, the mother erred on that of leniency. Perhaps she ought to have justified her husband's conduct, to the extent to which it would bear justification, by her own. But who shall be sure what would have been right for another where so much was wrong and beyond her setting right? If what is done be done in faith, some good will come out of our mistakes even; only let no one mistake self-will for that perfect thing faith!

Their table talk was neither very interesting nor very satisfactory. How could it be? Well might the youth long for his garret and the company of the wife who had nothing for him but smiles and sweetest attentions!

After dinner he sat for a time at the table alone. He had been given wine during his recovery, and was already in some danger of adding a fondness for that to his other weaknesses. He was one of those slight natures to which wine may bring a miserable consolation. But the mother was wise, and kept in her own hands the administrating of the medicine. Today, however, she had not put away the decanter, and Cornelius had several times filled his glass before she thought of her neglect. When she reentered the dining room, the decanter revealed what had taken place. The mother blamed herself, and thought it better to say nothing.

Cornelius left the room in a somewhat excited mood, and sauntered into his father's study. Coming there upon a volume by a fashionable poet of the day, he lighted the lamp which no one used but his father, and threw himself into his father's chair. He began to read, but from weariness and wine he was presently overcome with sleep. His mother came and went and would not disturb him, vexed that she had failed in her care over him. Her satisfaction in having him under her roof was beginning to wane in the continual trouble of a presence that showed no signs of growth any more than one of the dead. But her faith in the Father of all was strong, and she waited in hope.

Up above, the major and Mark talked of sweet heavenly things, and down below the youth lay snoring, where, had his father been at home, he would not have dared show himself. The mother was in her own room, and Hester in the drawing room. The house was quiet but for the noise of the wind and the rain, and those Cornelius did not hear.

He started awake and sat up in terror. A hand gripped his shoulder like a metal instrument, and not a thing of flesh and blood. The face of his father stared at him through the lingering vapors of his stupid sleep.

Mr. Raymount had started out with a certain foolish pleasure in the prospect of getting wet through, and being generally ill-used by the weather, preferring such accompaniment for his thoughts than any blue sky and sunshine. The road was very bad, and the mud drew off one of his horse's shoes, but he did not discover the loss until the poor animal fell suddenly lame on a piece of newly mended road. There was a roadside smithy a mile or two farther on, and dismounting, he made for that. He left his horse in the smithy, walked to an inn yet a mile or two farther on, and there dried his clothes and had some refreshment. By the time his horse was brought him and he was again mounted, the weather was worse than ever; he had had enough of it, and it was too late to do business in town. He gave up his journey, and returned to Yrndale.

He was annoyed, even angry, to find his unpleasant son

asleep in *his* chair! "The sneak!" he said. "He dares not show his face when I'm at home, but the minute he thinks himself safe, gets into my room and lies in my chair! Drunk too!" he added, as a fume from the sleeper's breath reached the nostrils beginning to dilate with wrath. "What can that wife of mine be about, letting the rascal go on like this! She is faultless except in giving me such a son—and then helping him to fool me! The snoring idiot!" he growled. He seized his boy by the shoulder and the neck and roughly shook him awake.

The father had drunk just enough to add to the fierceness of his wrath, and make him yet more capable of injustice. He had come into the study straight from the stable, and when Cornelius looked up half awake, and saw his father standing over him with a heavy whip in his hand, he was filled with a paralyzing terror. He sat and stared with white, trembling lips, red, projecting eyes, and a look that confirmed the belief of his father that he was drunk, whereas he had only been, like himself, drinking more than was good for him.

"Get out of there, you dog!" cried his father, and hurled him from the chair to the floor, where he lay in weakness mixed with cowardice. When Raymount saw the creature who had turned his hitherto happy life into a shame and a misery lying abject at his feet, he heaved his arm aloft and brought the whip down with a fierce lash on the quivering flesh of his son. Cornelius richly deserved the punishment, but God would not have struck him that way. There was the poison of hate in the blow. He again raised his arm, but as it descended, the piercing shriek that broke from the youth startled him, and the violence of the blow was broken. But the lash of the whip found his face, and marked it for a time worse than the smallpox.

And while the cry of his son yet sounded in his ears, another cry like its echo rang ghastly through the storm like the cry of a banshee. A spectral face flitted swift as a bird up to the window, and laid itself close to the glass of the French window. The glass burst with a great clang and clash and wide tinkle of shivers, and a small figure leaped into the room with a second cry that sounded like a curse in the ears of the father. Amy threw herself on the prostrate youth, and covered his body with hers, then turned her head and looked up at the father with indignant defiance in her flashing eyes. Cowed with terror, and smarting with keenest pain, the youth took his wife in his arms and sobbed like the beaten thing he was.

The father stood over them like a fury, fixed there by the shock of the girl's cry, and her stormy entrance like an avenging angel. But he recovered his senses, and concluded that here was the cause of all his misery—some worthless girl that had drawn Cornelius into her toils, and ruined him and his family forever! The thought set the geyser of his rage roaring and spouting in the face of heaven. He heaved his whip, and the blow fell upon her. But instead of a shriek, there came nothing but a shudder and a silence and the unquailing eye of the girl fixed like that of a specter upon her assailant. He struck her again, and again came the shivering shudder and the silence; the sense that the blows had not fallen upon Corney upheld the brave creature. Cry she would not, if he killed her! She never took her eyes from his face, but lay expecting the next blow. Suddenly the light in them began to fade, and went out; her head dropped like a stone upon the breast of her cowardly husband, and there was no more defiance.

What if he had killed the woman! An inquest! A trial for murder! In lowest depths Raymount saw a lower deep, and stood looking down on the pair with subsiding passion.

Amy had walked all the long distance from the station and more, for she had lost her way. Wet through and through, buffeted by the wind, having had nothing but a roll to eat, and cold to the very heart, she struggled on to Yrndale. She was just going up to the door when she heard her husband's cry. She saw the lighted window, flew to it, dashed it open, and entered. It was the last expiring effort of the poor remnant of her strength. She had not life enough left to resist her father-in-law's blows.

While still the father stood looking down on his children, the door softly opened, and the mother entered. She knew nothing, not even that her husband had returned, came merely to know how her unlovely but beloved child was faring in his heavy sleep. She saw what looked like a murdered heap on the floor, and her husband standing over it, like the murderer beginning to doubt whether the deed was as satisfactory as the doing of it.

But behind her came Hester, and peeping over her shoulder understood at once. She pushed her mother aside as she sprang to help, though her father would have prevented her. "No, father!" she said. "It is time to disobey." A pang as of death went through her at the thought that she had not before spoken. All was clear: Amy had come, and died defending her husband from his father! She put her strong arms round the dainty little figure, and lifted it like seaweed hanging limp, its long wet hair continuing the hang of the body and helpless head. Hester gave a great sob. Was this what Amy's lovely brave womanhood had brought her to! What creatures men were! As the thought passed through her, she saw on Amy's neck a frightful swollen welt. She looked at her father, with the whip in his hand! "O papa!" she screamed, and dropped her eyes for her shame through him. And then she saw Cornelius open his eyes.

"O Corney!" said Hester, in the tone of an accusing angel, and ran with Amy from the room.

The mother darted to her son, but the wrath of the father rose afresh. "Let the hound lie!" he said, and stepped between them.

"You've killed him, Gerald! Your own son!" said the mother, with a cold, still voice. She staggered, and would have fallen, but the arm that through her son had struck her heart, now caught and supported her. The husband bore the wife once more to her chamber, and the foolish son, the heaviness of his mother, was left alone on the floor, smarting, ashamed, and full of fear for his wife, yet in ignorance that his father had hurt her.

Cornelius rose, but the terror of his father which had filled him was gone. They had met; his father had put himself in the wrong; he was no more afraid of him. It was not hate that cast out fear. He had been accustomed to look vaguely up to his father as a sort of rigid but righteous divinity; and in a disobedient, self-indulgent, poverty-stricken nature like his, reverence could only take the form of fear. But now that he had seen his father in a rage, the feeling of reverence had begun to give way, and with it the fear; they were more upon a level. It consoled him that he had been hardly used by his father; his father's unmerciful use of the whip on him seemed a sort of settling of scores, a breaking down of the wall between them. He seemed thereby to have even some sort of claim upon his father; so cruelly beaten, he seemed now near him. A stone weight was lifted from his mind by this violent blowing up of the horrible negation that had been between them so long. As when punished in boyhood, he felt as if the storm had passed, and the sun had begun to appear.

He did not yet know where or how his wife was, only that she was safe with Hester. He stole, smarting and aching, yet cherishing his hurts like a possession, slowly to his room. There he tumbled himself into bed and longed for Amy to come to him. In a few minutes he was fast asleep.

When Mrs. Raymount came to herself, she looked up at her husband, who stood expecting her reproach. But she stretched out her arms to him, and drew him to her bosom. Her pity for the misery which could have led him to behave so ill, joined to her sympathy for the distressing repentance which must have already begun in him, made her treat him much as she treated her wretched Corney. In his sense of degradation—not for striking his son, who he thought entirely deserved it, but for striking a woman—his wife's embrace was like balm to a stinging wound.

But then he suddenly recognized that the girl had been Amy, and the beneficient iron spearhead of remorse entered his soul. His crime brought back to Mr. Raymount's mind the vision of the bright girl he used to watch in her deft and cheerful service, and with that vision came the conviction that not she but Corney must be primarily to blame. He had twice struck the woman his son had grievously wronged! He must make to her whatever atonement was possible—first for having brought the villain into the world to do her such wrong, then for his own cruelty to her in her faithfulness! He pronounced himself the most despicable and wretched of men. He had lifted his hand against a woman who had only been following his son, and had been ready to die for him!

Chapter 59

FATHER AND DAUGHTER-IN-LAW

Hester carried Amy to her own room, laid her on her own bed, and did for her all one child of God could do for another. With tender hands she undressed her, bathed her, then put her to bed. Amy lay like one dead, seeming to care for nothing, though she smiled a pitiful smile to Hester. Her brain was haunted with the presence of Corney's father. He seemed ever to be standing over her and Corney with that terrible whip. All her thought was how to get away from the frightful place. Hester did her best to reassure her, telling her Corney was fast asleep and little the worse, and a little after midnight Amy fell asleep. Then Hester lay down on the sofa, sorely exhausted.

In the gray of morning Mr. Raymount woke, and was aware of a great hush about him. The stillness awed, almost frightened him; his very soul seemed hushed, as if in his sleep the Voice had said, "Peace! Be still!" He felt like a naughty child, who, having slept, seems to have slept away his naughtiness. Yesterday seemed far away, but he knew if he began to think it would be back with its agony. Had it been but hinted before that he should behave so to a woman as to Amy, he would have scorned the idea, for he had always thought himself a chivalrous gentleman! This was the end of his faith in himself!

He would still be able to do something for Amy, and must make atonement for treating her so brutally! And he must see Cornelius and tell him he was sorry he had struck him. Hope dawned feebly on his murky horizon, as in the yet dark gray of the morning he went to his son's room.

When he reached his son's open door he heard a soft voice persuading within. It was Amy's voice! In his house! In his son's room! And after the lesson he had given them the night before! This was too bad! He pushed the door open and looked in. The dainty little figure that had haunted his dreams was half lying on the bed with her arm thrown round his son. He could not see her face, but could hear perfectly the words.

"Corney, darling!" she said. "You must get up and come away. Here I am to take you from them. I came because I was sure they were not treating you well! I did not know how cruel they were, or I would have come long ago. But, Corney, you must have done something very wrong to make your father so angry with you! And you cannot have said you were sorry, or he would have forgiven you! He can't be a bad man—though he does hurt dreadfully!"

"He is a very good man!" muttered Corney from the pillow.

"But I'm afraid," continued Amy, "if he hasn't been able to make you sorry before, he will never be able now! To beat you as he did last night will never make you repent."

"Oh, he didn't hurt me much! You don't think a fellow would mind that sort of thing from his own father? Besides, Amy, I only gave him too good reason."

"Come, then, we will go somewhere. I want to make you think the right way about the thing; and when you are sorry, we will come back and tell him so. Then perhaps he will forgive me."

The cunning creature! This was her little trick to entice him from his home, and just as the poor boy was beginning to repent too! She would fall in with his better mood and pretend goodness—would help him to do what he ought, and be his teacher in righteousness! No doubt the fellow was just as bad as she, but he must do what he might for the redemption of his son!

But it smote him that Cornelius could not but prefer going with one who loved him, and talked to him like that, let her be what she might, to staying with a father who treated him as he had been doing! But he must interfere now, cost what it might!

He pushed the door wide and went in. Amy raised herself from the bed, stood upright and faced him in the dim light. The horrid idea shot through her mind that it was his custom to come thus to his son's room in the night and lash him. Clenching her little hands hard, she stood like a small David between the bed and the coming Goliath.

"Get out of this," he said, with the sternness of wrath suppressed.

"I came to take him away," said Amy, trembling from head to feet. "It is my business to take care of him."

"Your business to take him from his own—mother?" which certainly was the more fitting word.

"If," answered Amy, "a man is to leave father and mother and cleave to his wife, it's the least thing the wife can do to take care of him from his father!"

Mr. Raymount stood confounded. What could the hussy mean? Was she going to pretend she was married to him? Indignation and rage began to rise afresh, but if he gave way what might he not be guilty of a second time? A rush of shame choked the words that crowded to his lips, and with the self-restraint came wholesome doubt: was it not possible he had married her? Would it not be just worthy of him to have done so and never told one of his family?

"Do you mean to tell me," he said, "that he has married you—without a word to his own father or mother?"

Then Cornelius spoke at last, rising on his elbow in bed. "Yes, father, I have married her. It is all my fault, not one bit hers. I could never have persuaded her had I not made her believe you knew all about it and had no objection."

"Why did you not let us know then?" cried the father in a voice which ill-suited the tameness of the question.

"Because I was a coward," answered Corney, speaking the truth with courage. "I knew you would not like it."

"Little *you* know of what I like or dislike!"

"You can soon prove him wrong, sir!" said Amy, clasping her hands, and looking up in his face through the growing light of the morning. "Forgive us, and take me too. I was so happy to think I was going to belong to you all! I would never have married him without your consent. It was very wrong of Corney, but I will try to make him sorry for it."

"You never will!" said Corney, again burying his head in the pillow.

Now first the full horror of what he had done broke upon Mr. Raymount. He stood for a moment appalled.

"You will let me take him away then?" said Amy, thinking he

273

hesitated to receive her.

Either from an impulse of honesty toward her, or to justify himself, he instantly returned, "Do you know that his money is stolen?"

"If he stole it," she replied, "he will never steal again."

"He will never get another chance. He cannot get a situation."

"I will work for both. It will certainly be me instead of him, and that's no difference; he belongs to me as much as I do to him. If he had only kept nothing from me, nothing of this would have happened. Do come, Corney, while I am able to walk. I feel as if I were going to die."

"And this is the woman I was such a savage to last night!" said Mr. Raymount to himself. "Forgive me, Amy!" he cried, stretching out his arms to her. "I have behaved like a brute! But you must forgive me for Christ's sake."

Amy came to his arms, clinging to him as he held her fast. The strong man was now the weaker; the father and not the new daughter wept.

She drew back her head. "Come, Corney," she cried. "Out of your bed and down on your knees to your own blessed father and confess your sins. Tell him you're sorry for them, and you'll never do them again."

Corney obeyed, for she had reached his conscience as well as his heart. He got out of bed, went down on his knees, and though he did not speak, was presently weeping like a child. It was a strange group in the gray of the morning—a new morning for them, the girl in the arms of the elderly man, and the youth kneeling at their feet, both men weeping and the girl radiant.

Gerald Raymount soon backed away, closed the door on the pair, and hastened to his wife to tell her all.

"Then surely will the forgiveness of God and his father take away Corney's disgrace!" said the mother.

Amy was falling into a severe illness even as the strain was passing from her. Corney in his turn became nurse, and improved from his own anxiety, her sweetness, and the sympathy of everyone—his father included. She began to recover rapidly, and was soon ready to take her place in the house.

Chapter 60

MARK'S MESSAGE

Little Mark did not get better, and it soon became very clear to the major that the boy would leave them before long. The rest said the summer would certainly restore him, but the major expected him to die in the first of the warm weather. The child himself believed he was going soon, and he was patient, resting upon entire satisfaction with what God pleased.

"Isn't it nice, Majic," he said more than once, in differing forms, "that I have nothing to do with anything—that there is no preparation, no examination wanted for dying? It's all done for you! You have just to be lifted and taken—and that's so nice! I don't know what it will feel like, but when God is with you, you don't mind anything."

Another time he said, "I was trying, while you were resting, to tell Saffy a dream I had, but she said, 'It's all nonsense, you know, Mark! It's only a dream!' What do you think, Majie?"

"Was it a dream, Mark?" asked the major.

"Yes, it was a dream, but is a dream nothing at all? If it is a good dream, it must be God's. For you know every good as well as every perfect gift is from the Father of lights. He made the thing that dreams and the things that set it dreaming, so He must be the Master of the dreams! The Father of lights!" he repeated. "What a beautiful name! The Father of all the bright things in the world. Hester's eyes, and your teeth, Majie! And all the shines of the fire on the things in the room! And the sun and the faraway stars that I shall know more about by and by! And all the glad things that come and go in my mind, as I lie here and you are sitting quiet in your chair, Majie! Oh, I will love Him, and be afraid of nothing. I know He is in it all, and the dark is only the box He keeps his bright things in!

"Oh, He is such a good Father of lights! Do you know, Majie, I used to think He came and talked to me in the window seat when I was a child. What if He really did, and I should be going to be made sure that He did—up there, where Jesus went when He went back to His Papa. Oh, how happy Jesus must have been when He got back to His Papa!"

Here he began to cough, and could not talk more, but the major did not blame himself that he had not found the heart to stop him. The child, when moved to talk, must be happier talking; and what if he died a few minutes sooner for it—was born anew rather? For the child's and the soldier's souls had indeed grown near to each other.

Mark not only was a new influence on the major, but had stirred up and brought alive in him a thousand influences and memories besides—words of his mother, a certain Sunday evening with her, her last blessing on his careless head, the verse of a well-known hymn she repeated as she was dying, old scraps of things she had taught him. In dying, Mark gave life to these and many other things. The major had never properly been a child, but now lived his childness over again with Mark, in a better fashion.

"I have had such a curious, such a beautiful dream, Majie!" Mark said, waking in the middle of one night.

"What was it, Markie?" asked the major.

"I should like Corney to hear it," returned Mark.

"I will call him, and you can tell us together."

"Oh, I don't think it would do to wake Corney up! He would not like that! He must hear it sometime—but at the right time, else he would laugh at it, and I could not bear that. You know Corney always laughs, without thinking first whether the thing was made for laughing at!"

By this time Corney had been to see Mark often. He spoke kindly to the boy now, but always as a little goose, and Mark did not like the things he wanted to say "to go in at Corney's ears to be blown away by Corney's nose!" For Corney had a foolish and scornful way of laughing through his nose, and Mark would not expose to that what he loved.

"But I'll tell you what, Majie," Mark went on. "I'll tell you the dream, and then if I should go away without having told him, you must tell it to Corney. I don't think he will laugh then. Do you promise to tell him, Majie?"

"I will," answered the major, drawing himself up with a military salute, and ready to obey.

"I was somewhere," Mark began, "I don't know where, and it don't matter where, for Jesus was there too. And Jesus gave such a beautiful little laugh when He saw me! And He said, 'Ah, little one, now you see Me! I have been getting your eyes open as fast as I could all the time! We're in our Father's house together now. But Markie, where's your brother, Corney?' And I said, 'Jesus, I'm very sorry, but I don't know. I know that I'm my brother's keeper, but I can't tell where he is.' Then Jesus smiled again, and said, 'Never mind, then. I didn't ask you because I didn't know Myself. But we must have Corney here—only we can't get him till he sets himself to be good! You must tell Corney, only not just yet, that I want him. Tell him that he and I have one Father, and I couldn't bear to have him out in the cold, with all the horrid creatures that won't be good! Tell him I love him so much that I will be very sharp with him if he doesn't make haste and come home. Our Father is *so* good, and it is dreadful to Me that Corney won't mind Him. He is so patient with him, Markie!' 'I know that, Jesus,' I said. 'I know that He could easily take him to pieces again because he doesn't go well, but He would much rather make him go right.'

"After that, Jesus looked at me, and then said just, 'Our Father, Markie!' and I could not see Him anymore. But it did not seem to matter the least tiny bit. There was a stone near me, and I sat down upon it, feeling as if I could sit there without moving till all eternity, so happy was I, and it was because Jesus' Father was touching me everywhere; my head felt as if He were counting the hairs of it. And He was not only close to me, but far away, and all between. Near and far there was the Father! It was God everywhere, and there was no nowhere anywhere, and my heart was nothing, knew nothing but Him, and I felt I could sit there forever, because I was right in the very middle of God's heart, and was anxious about nothing and nobody."

Here he paused.

"He had a sleeping draught last night!" said the major to

277

himself. "But the sleeping draught was God's, and perhaps God may have had it given to him just that He might talk with him! Some people may be better to talk to when they are asleep, and others when they are awake!"

"And then, after a while," the boy resumed, "I seemed to see a black speck somewhere in the all-blessed. And I could not understand it, and I did not like it, and this one black speck made me at last, in spite of my happiness, almost miserable. 'Only,' I said to myself, 'whatever the black speck may be, God will rub it white when He is ready!' For He couldn't go on forever with a black speck going about in His heart! And when I said this, I knew the black speck was Corney, and I gave a cry. But with that the black speck began to grow thinner till I could see it no more, and the same instant Corney stood beside me with a smile on his face, and the tears running down his cheeks. I stretched out my arms to him, and he caught me up in his, and then it was all right. I was Corney's keeper, and Corney was my keeper, and God was all of us' keeper. And then I woke, Majie.

"Now what am I to do, Majie? You see I couldn't bear to have that dream laughed at. Yet I must tell it to Corney because there is a message in it for him! I do not think that He wanted me to tell Corney the minute I woke, and He will let me know when the time is come. But if I found I was dying, I would try and tell Corney, whether he laughed at it or not, rather than go without having done it. But if Corney knew I was going, I don't think he would laugh."

"I don't think he would," returned the major, looking at the child with his soul in his eyes. "Corney is a better boy than he used to be. You will be able to speak to him by and by, I fancy."

The days went on. Every new day Mark said, "Now, Majie, I do think today I shall tell Corney my dream and the message I have for him!" But the day grew old and passed, and the dream was not told. The next day and the next passed, and he seemed to the major not likely ever to have the strength to tell Corney.

The whole household began to feel Mark's room to be a little piece cut out of the new paradise and set glowing in the heart of the old house of Yrndale. The family often sought the spot where the treasure of the house lay, his sweet face reflecting already the light of the sunless kingdom. When several were in the room, he would lie looking from one to another like a miser contemplating his riches—and well he might, for such riches neither moth nor rust corrupt, and they are the treasures of heaven also.

One evening most of the family were in the room, save Mr. Raymount and Corney; a vague sense had diffused itself that the end was not far off, and an unconfessed instinct had gathered them.

"Majie," Mark said, "I want to tell Corney."

The major, on his way to Corney, told the father the end was nigh. With sorely self-accusing heart, for the vision of the boy on the stone in the middle of the moor haunted him, he repaired to the anteroom of heaven.

Mark kept looking for Corney's coming, his eyes turning every other moment to the door. When his father entered, he stretched out his arms to him. The strong man bending over him could not repress a sob. The boy pushed him gently away far enough to see his face, and looked at him as if he could not quite believe his eyes.

"Father," he said—though he had never called him *father* before—"you must be glad, not sorry. I am going to your Father and my Father—to our great Father."

Then seeing Corney come in, he stretched his arms toward him past his father, crying, "Corney! Corney!" Corney bent over him, but the outstretched arms did not close upon him; they fell.

With his last strength he signed to the major. "Majie," he whispered with an expression into the meaning of which the major never finished inquiring, "tell Corney!"

Then he went.

It was the grief at the grave of Lazarus that made our Lord weep, not his death. One with eyes opening into both worlds could hardly weep over any law of the Father of Lights! It was the impossibility of getting them comforted over this thing death, which looked to Him so different from what they thought it, that made the Fearless One weep and give them in Lazarus a foretaste of His own resurrection.

The major alone did not weep. He stood with his arms folded, like a sentry relieved, and waiting the next order. Even Corney's eyes filled with tears, and he murmured, "Poor Markie!" It should have been, "Poor Corney!" He stooped and kissed the insensate face, then drew back and gazed with the rest on the little pilgrim-cloak the small prophet had dropped as he rose to his immortality.

Saffy, who had been seated gazing into the fire, and had no idea of what had taken place, called out in a strange voice, "Markie! Markie!"

Hester turned to her, and saw her following something with her eyes along the wall from the bed to the curtained window. She gazed there for a moment; then her eyes fell, and she sprang to her feet and ran to the bed, crying again, "Markie! Markie!" Hester lifted her, and held her to kiss the sweet white face. Content, she went back to her stool by the fire, and sat staring at the curtained window like one gazing into regions unknown.

That same night the major took Corney to his room, and recalling every individual expression of the little prophet-dreamer, executed, not without tears, the commission entrusted to him.

Corney did not laugh, but listened with a grave, sad face, and when the major ceased, his eyes were full of tears. "I shall not forget Markie's dream," he said. Thus all things came to help the youth who had begun to mend his ways.

And shall we think the boy found God not equal to his dream of Him? He made our dreaming—shall it surpass in its making His mighty self?

Chapter 61

A BIRTHDAY GIFT

When Mark's little cloak was put in the earth, the house felt cold for a while—as if the bit of Paradise had gone out. Mark's room was like a temple forsaken of its divinity. But it was not to be drifted up with the sands of forgetfulness! The major petitioned that it might continue to be called Mark's, but should be considered the major's; he would like to put some of his things in it, and occupy it when he came. Everyone was pleased with the idea. They no longer would feel so painfully that Mark was not there when his dear Majie occupied the room.

To the major, it would be chamber and chapel and monument, but should not be a tomb save as was upon the fourth day the sepulcher in the garden! He would fill it with live memories of the risen child. Very different was his purpose from that sickly haunting of the grave in which some loving hearts indulge. We are bound to be hopeful, and not wrong our greathearted Father.

Mark's books and picture remained undisturbed. The major dusted them with his own hands, and read every day in Mark's Bible. The major's sword, which he had placed unsheathed upon the wall for the firelight to play upon and Mark to admire, he now left there, shining still. In Mark's bed the major slept, and to Mark's chamber he went always to shut the door. In solitude there he learned a thousand things his busy life had prepared him for learning. The Master had come to him in the child, and fulfilled a phase of the promise that whosoever receives a child in the name of Jesus receives Jesus and His Father.

Through ministering to the child, he had come to know the child's elder Brother and Master. It was the presence of the Master in the child that had opened his heart to Him, and he had thus entertained more than an angel.

Time passed, and under the holy influences of duty and love and hope, the family's flowers began to cover their furrows of grief. Everything began to go well at Yrndale—thanks to the stormy and sorrowful weather that had so troubled its spiritual atmosphere, and killed so many evil worms in its moral soil!

Corney soon began to show a practical interest in Yrndale— first in its look, its order and tidiness, and then in its yield, beginning to develop a faculty for looking after property. Next he took to measuring the land. Here the major could give him no end of help, and having thus formed a point of common interest, they began to be drawn a little together, and to conceive a mild liking for each other's company. Corney saw by degrees that the major knew much more than he, and the major discovered that Corney did have some brains.

Hester informed her parents of the dissolution of her engagement to Lord Gartley. The mother was troubled, for it is the girl that suffers evil judgment in such a case, and she knew how the tongue of the world would wag. But those who despise the ways of the world need not fret that low minds attribute to them the things of which low minds are capable. The world and its judgments will pass; the tongue is a fire, but there is a stronger fire than the tongue. Her father and the major cared little for public opinion. The world is a fine thing to save, but a wretch to worship. Neither did the father care much for Lord Gartley, though he had liked him.

Hester herself was annoyed to find how soon the idea of his lordship came to be a thing of her past, a thing to trouble her no more. At his natural distance from her, she could not fail to see what a small creature she had chosen as her companion and help. But she was able to look on the whole blunder with calmness, and a thankfulness that grew as the sting of her fault lost its burning and brought humility.

There was nothing left her now, she said to herself, but the best of all—a maiden life devoted to the work of her Master. She would no more risk losing her power to help the poor Lord's creatures, downtrodden by devils, rich people, and their own miserable weaknesses and vices. Marriage to Gartley would have brought her continuous disappointment and the mockery of a false unity; even remaining constant to duty, she must have lost the health and the spirits necessary to fulfill it. In constant opposition to her husband, spending the best part of her strength in resistance before it could reach the place where it ought to be applied entire, with strife consciously destroying her love and keeping her in a hopeless unrest, how could any light have shone from her upon those whose darkness made her miserable? Now she would hold herself free! What a blessed thing to be her own mistress and the free slave of the Lord!

Her spirits soon returned more buoyant than before. Her health was better. She had been suffering from oppression—already in no small measure yoked, and right unequally. Only a few weeks passed, and she looked a yet grander woman than before. The humility that comes with the discovery of error had made her yet more dignified—true dignity comes only of humility. Pride is the ruin of dignity, for it is a worshiping of self, and that involves a continuous sinking. Humility, the worship of the ideal—Christ Jesus—is the only lifter-up of the head.

Everybody felt her more lovable than before. Her mother began to feel an enchantment of peace in her presence. Her father sought her company more than ever, and not only talked to her about Corney, but talked about his own wrong feelings toward him, and how he had been punished for them by what they wrought in him. He had begun, he told her, to learn many things he had supposed he knew; he had only thought and written and talked about them!

Even Corney perceived a change in her. Scarce a shadow of that "superiority" remained which used to irritate him so much, making him rebel against whatever she said. She became more and more Amy's ideal of womanhood, and by degrees Amy taught her husband to read more justly his beautiful sister. She pointed out to him how few would have tried to protect and deliver him as she had done; how few would have so generously taken herself, a poor uneducated girl, to a sister's heart. So altogether, the family was bidding fair to be a family forevermore.

Hester's birthday was at hand. The major went up to London to bring her a present, determined to make the occasion a cheerful one. He wrote back to his cousin Helen asking if he might bring a friend with him. His host and hostess would not know him, but Hester did; he was a young doctor, and his name was Christopher. He had met him among Hester's friends, and was much taken with him.

Hester said she would be most happy to see Dr. Christopher, and told her parents something of his history. Mr. Raymount had known his grandfather a little in the way of business, and was the more interested in him.

Miss Dasomma came to spend a few days with Hester and help celebrate her birthday. She was struck with improvement in Hester where she would have been loath to allot it either necessary or possible.

Hester's birthday was the sweetest of summer days, and she looked a perfect summer-born woman. She dressed herself in white, but not so much for her own birthday as for Mark's entry into the heavenly kingdom.

After breakfast all except the mother went out. Hester was little inclined to talk, and the major was in a thoughtful mood. Miss Dasomma and Mr. Raymount alone conversed. When the rest reached a spot where Mr. Raymount had led them for the sake of the view, Hester had fallen a little behind, and Christopher walked back to meet her.

"You are thinking of your brother," he said in a tone that made her feel grateful.

"Yes," she answered.

"I knew by your eyes," he returned. "I wish I could talk to you about him. The right way of getting used to death is to go nearer the dead. Suppose you tell me something about him! Such children are prophets to whose word we have to listen."

He went on like this, drawing her from sadness with gentle speech about children and death, and the look and reality of things. They wandered about the moor for a little while before joining the rest.

Mr. Raymount was much pleased with Christopher, and even Corney found a strength in him that offered protection.

The day went on in the simplest, pleasantest fashion. After lunch, Hester opened her piano, and asked Miss Dasomma to sit down and play "upon *us*," she said. And in truth she did, for what the hammers were to the strings, the sounds she drew from the strings were to the human chords stretched expectant before her. Vibrating souls responded in the music that is unheard. A rosy conscious silence pervaded the summer afternoon and the ancient drawing room.

Mr. Raymount sat in a great soft chair with a book in his hand, listening more than reading, while his wife lay on a couch and soon passed into dreams of pleasant sounds. Hester sat on a stool beside her mother and held her sleeping hand. Corney and "Mrs. Corney," as for love of Mark she liked to be called, sat on a sofa side by side. Saffy played with a white kitten; neither attended to the music, which may yet have been doing something for both. The major stood tall behind Miss Dasomma, with his arms folded across his chest.

Christopher sat on a low window seat in an oriel, where the balmiest of perfumed airs freely entered. Between him and all the rest hung the heavy folds of a curtain, which every now and then swelled out like the sail of a barge. The tears rolled down his face, for the music seemed such as he had only dreamed of before. It was the music of climes where sorrow is but the memory of that which had been turned into joy. He thought no one saw him, and no one would have seen him but for the traitor wind blowing the curtain and revealing him to Hester. It was to her the revelation of a heart, and she saw with reverence.

Yes, she thought, Lord Gartley could sing, he could play, he understood the technicalities of music. But while Christopher could neither sing well nor play, there was in him a whole sea of musical delight to be set in motion.

After an early dinner, the major proposed Hester's health, and made a little speech in her honor and praise. Nor did his praise make Hester feel awkward, for praise which is the odor of love neither fevers nor sickens.

"And now, cousin Hester," concluded the major, "you know that I love you like a child of my own! It is a good thing you are not, for if you were then you would not be half so good, or so beautiful, or so wise, or so accomplished as you are! Will you oblige me by accepting this deed, which I hope will serve to make this blessed day yet a trifle more pleasant to look back upon when Mark has got his old Majie back again. It represents a sort of nut, itself too bulky for a railway truck. If my Hester chooses to call it an empty nut, I don't mind: the good of it to her will be in the filling of it with many kernels."

With this enigmatical speech, the major made Hester a low bow, and handed her a folded sheet of foolscap, tied with white ribbon: the title deed to the house in Addison Square. She gave a cry of joy, got up, and threw her arms round Majie's neck and kissed him.

"Aha!" said the major. "If I had been a young man now, I should not have had that! But I will not be conceited; I know what it is she means it for—the kiss collective of all the dirty men and women in her dear slums, glorified into an angel of God!"

Hester was not a young lady given to weeping, but she did here break down and cry. Her long-cherished dream come true! She had no money, but that did not trouble her; there was always a way when one was willing to begin small!

This is indeed a divine law! There shall be no success to the man who is not willing to begin small. Small is strong, for it only can grow strong. There are thousands willing to do great things for every one willing to do a small thing; but there never was any truly great thing that did not begin small.

Without opening the deed, Hester handed it to Christopher, convinced that he would understand the delight it gave her. With a look asking if he might, he opened it.

The major had known for some time that Mr. Raymount wanted to sell the house, and believed he could not rejoice Hester better than by purchasing it for her. So, just as it was, with everything in it, he handed it as his birthday gift to her.

"There is more here than you know," said Christopher, handing her back the paper. She opened it and saw something about a thousand pounds—the thousand a year the major had offered her if she would give up Lord Gartley. She gave loving and joyous thanks as a new paradise of labor with God opened before her delighted eyes.

In the evening they went for another walk. Perhaps the major had his hand in it, but somehow in the middle of a fir wood, Hester found herself alone with Christopher. The wood rose toward the moor, growing thinner as it ascended. They were climbing westward full in the face of the sunset, which was barred across the trees in gold, blue, rosy pink, and that lovely green which cannot live except in the after sunset. The fir trees and bars of sunset made a glorious gate before them.

"O Hester!" said Christopher. "If that were only the gate of heaven, and we were climbing to it now to go in and see all the dear people!"

"That would be joy!" responded Hester.

"Come then—let us imagine it awhile. There is no harm in dreaming."

"Sometimes when Mark would tell me one of his dreams, I could not help thinking how much reality there was in it than in most so-called realities."

Then came a silence before Christopher began again. "Suppose one claiming to be a prophet appeared, saying that in the life to come we were to go on living just such a life as here, with the one difference that we should be no longer deluded with the idea of something better; that all our energies would then be, and ought now to be, spent in making the best of what we had—without any foolish indulgence in hope or aspiration. What would you say to that?"

"I would say," answered Hester, "that he must have had his revelation either from a demon, or from his own heart. It could not be from God because it makes the idea of God an impossibility; it must come from a demon or from himself, and in neither case is worth paying attention to. The essential delight of this world seems to me to lie in the expectation of a better."

They emerged from the wood. The bare moor spread on all sides before them, and lo, the sunset was countless miles away! Hills, fields, rivers, mountains, lay between! Christopher stopped, turned, and looked at Hester.

"Is this the reality?" he said. "We catch sight of the gate of heaven, and set out for it. It comes nearer and nearer. All at once something they call a reality of life comes between, and the shining gate is millions of miles away! Then cry some of its pilgrims, 'Alas, we are fools! There is no such thing as the gate of heaven! Let us eat and drink and do what good we can, for tomorrow we die!' But is there no gate because we find none on the edge of the wood where it seemed to lie? There it is, before us yet, though a long way farther back. What has space or time to do with being? Can distance destroy fact? What if one day the chain of gravity were to break, and from the edge of the pinewood we flew farther toward the bars of gold and rose and green! And what if even then we found them recede as we

287

advanced, until heart was gone out of us, and we could follow no longer, but, sitting down on some wayside cloud, fell a-thinking! Should we not say we are justly punished, and our punishment was to follow the vain thing we took for heaven's gate? Heaven's gate is too grand a goal to be reached on foot or wing. High above us, it yet opens inside us; and when it opens, down comes the gate of amber and rose, and we step through both at once!"

He was silent. They were on the top of the ridge, where a little beyond stood the dusky group of their companions. And the world lay beneath them.

"Who would live in London who might live here?" asked the major.

"No one," answered Hester and Christopher together.

The major turned and looked at them almost in alarm.

"But I *may not*," said Hester. "God chooses that I live in London."

Said Christopher, "Christ would surely have liked better to go on living in His Father's house than go to where so many did not know either Him or His Father! But He could not go on enjoying His heaven while those many lived only a death in life. He must go and start them for home! Who, seeing what Christ sees and feeling as Christ feels, would rest in the enjoyment of beauty while so many are unable to desire it? We are not real human beings until we are of the same mind with Christ. There are many who would save the pathetic and interesting and let the ugly and provoking take care of themselves! Not so Christ, nor those who have learned of Him! I would take as many with me through the gate as I might, for it would be sorrow to go in alone!"

Every man who, according to the means he has, great or small, does the work given him to do, stands by the side of the Saviour, and is a fellow worker with Him. The one who is weighed and found wanting is the one whose tongue and life do not match—who says "Lord! Lord!" and does not do the thing the Lord says.

In this spirit Hester labored and Christopher labored. And if one was the heart and the other the head, the major was the right hand. But what they did and how they did it would require a book, and no small one, to itself.